August Wilson's Pittsburgh Cycle

August Wilson's Pittsburgh Cycle

Critical Perspectives on the Plays

Edited by
SANDRA G. SHANNON

McFarland & Company, Inc., Publishers
Jefferson, North Carolina

LIBRARY OF CONGRESS CATALOGUING-IN-PUBLICATION DATA [new form]
Names: Shannon, Sandra Garrett, 1952– editor.
Title: August Wilson's Pittsburgh cycle : critical perspectives on the plays / edited by Sandra G. Shannon.
Description: Jefferson, North Carolina : McFarland & Company, Inc., Publishers, 2016 | Includes bibliographical references and index.
Identifiers: LCCN 2015038585| ISBN 9780786478002 (softcover : acid free paper) | ISBN 9781476622996 (ebook)
Subjects: LCSH: Wilson, August—Criticism and interpretation. | Historical drama, American—History and criticism. | African Americans in literature.
Classification: LCC PS3573.I45677 Z575 2016 | DDC 812/.54—dc23
LC record available at http://lccn.loc.gov/2015038585

BRITISH LIBRARY CATALOGUING DATA ARE AVAILABLE

ISBN (print) 978-0-7864-7800-2
ISBN (ebook) 978-1-4766-2299-6

© 2016 Sandra G. Shannon. All rights reserved

No part of this book may be reproduced or transmitted in any form or by any means, electronic or mechanical, including photocopying or recording, or by any information storage and retrieval system, without permission in writing from the publisher.

Front cover images: Playwright August Wilson, 1987; *Fences* performance, with Charles Brown, James Earl Jones and Mary Alice (Stage, 46th St. Theatre, New York, 1987-88) © Photofest

Printed in the United States of America

McFarland & Company, Inc., Publishers
 Box 611, Jefferson, North Carolina 28640
  www.mcfarlandpub.com

Acknowledgments

The work that went into editing *August Wilson's Pittsburgh Cycle*—or any volume of essays—is much like an intricate dance whose mastery not only involves keeping all participants in step but also requires multiple unseen maneuvers on the part of the editor to make the finished product appear as graceful and as seamless as possible. With each new and equally demanding ensemble that I choreograph as either editor or co-editor comes an even greater appreciation for the synchronized efforts of each individual member. In essence, then, I owe a debt of gratitude to the individual authors whose names are listed on the Table of Contents that follows. I acknowledge them here for accepting my initial invitation to be a part of this collection and for seeing this dance to fruition.

Table of Contents

Acknowledgments	v
Introduction	1
"The emancipated century": Remapping History, Reclaiming Memory in August Wilson's Dramatic Landscapes of the 20th Century—JOYCE HOPE SCOTT	15
"A big bend there, a tree by the shore": Situated Identity in *The Janitor*—JACQUELINE ZEFF	39
Two Trains Running: Bridging Diana Taylor's "rift" and Narrating Manning Marable's "living history"—SARAH SADDLER *and* PAUL BRYANT-JACKSON	49
World War II History/history: Essential Contexts in *Seven Guitars*—ELLEN BONDS	60
The Use of Stereotype and Archetype in *Ma Rainey's Black Bottom*—MICHAEL DOWNING	76
Gem of the Ocean's Fugitive Movements —ISAIAH MATTHEW WOODEN	88
Reclaiming the Mother: Women, Documents and the Condition of the Mother in *Gem of the Ocean* and *Ma Rainey's Black Bottom*—JESSLYN COLLINS-FROHLICH	101
A Century Lacking Progress: The Fractured Community in *Gem of the Ocean* and *King Hedley II* —CHRISTOPHER B. BELL	117
"He gonna give me my ham": The Use of Food as a Symbol for Social Justice—PSYCHE WILLIAMS-FORSON	128

Resurrecting "phantom limb[s] of the dismembered slave
and god": Unveiling the Africanisms in *Gem of the Ocean*
—Artisia Green   142

Epiphany and the "drama of souls"—Owen Seda   164

Conjuring Africa in August Wilson's Plays
—Connie Rapoo   175

Re-Evaluating the Legacy of the Ten-Play Cycle
—Susan C.W. Abbotson   187

About the Contributors   203
Index   205

Introduction

> I believe in the American theatre. I believe in its power to inform about the human condition, I believe in its power to heal, "to hold the mirror as 'twere up to nature," to the truths we uncover, the truths we wrestle from uncertain and sometimes unyielding realities. All of art is a search for ways of being, of living life more fully.
> —August Wilson, *The Ground on Which I Stand*, 1996

For August Wilson, writing plays was an intensely personal affair. While it afforded him the means by which to celebrate the "unique particulars" of black life, this medium also offered him a road map for negotiating the tricky contours of his own life. Beyond the lingering and well documented influences of a distant white father, a stalwart black mother, a motley mix of paternal surrogates, and a passionate black cultural nationalist agenda, August Wilson was driven by a lesser known deep-rooted existential quest to get at the truth of his own existence. Toward this end, his playwriting became a way for him to make sense of the world around him and to determine his place within it in the face of "uncertain and sometimes unyielding realities" (*The Ground* 46).

At some indistinguishable point on his way toward maturing and becoming a "serious playwright," Wilson felt compelled to distance himself—both emotionally and culturally—from his German immigrant father. Yet while he relegated Frederick Kittel to the background of his life, he filled that void by becoming even more impassioned about the cultural and racial heritage of his African American mother and his maternal grandmother—a woman who reportedly trekked from North Carolina to Pennsylvania to trade backbreaking labor in the tobacco fields for a better life in Pittsburgh's thriving steel mill industry. This decision to identify with his African American mother and grandmother's cultural heritage apparently moved young Wilson—blessed early on with a poet's sensibility—to discover a symbolic correlation between their examples of endurance and racial pride and his incessant quest for the truth of his being.

Emboldened by this connection, Wilson began to understand that his own existentialist yearnings were also part of a larger odyssey for all Africans in America; that is, in coming to terms with his blackness—especially as he bore the imprint of both African and European racial and cultural ties—Wilson would soon realize that the narrative of his singular life ran parallel to that of the black masses in America. The results of this major epiphany moved him to create art out of the depths of his own uneasy experience, negotiating and translating the world from his precarious position as an African in America and, more specifically, from his perspective as a black male. More than once he likened this constant state of negotiation to wrestling with demons. In one of his most cited observations about his playwriting process that can be traced to a 1988 interview with journalist Bill Moyers, he notes,

> You discover that you're walking down this landscape of the self, and you have to be willing to confront whatever it is that you discover there. The idea is to emerge at the end of the landscape with something larger than what you had when you went in—something that is part of the illumination of truth. If you're willing to wrestle with your demons, you will find that your spirit gets larger. And when your spirit gets larger, your demons get smaller. For me, this is the process of art. The process of writing the plays is a very liberating thing [178].

For August Wilson, completing his ten-play century cycle, which he likened to his "400-year-old autobiography" (Palmer 47), was tantamount to constructing his own private landscape where he not only wrestled with the demons that plagued his life, but also channeled the hardships of African American people. Reminiscent of psychologist and theorist Carl Jung's archetype of the wounded healer, Wilson sought to heal himself while prescribing remedies in the form of plays to treat what he believed ailed his people.[1]

From Wilson's active imagination came a succession of characters fashioned in his own likeness and tortured by similar demons that so menaced their creator. While his portrayal of tragic figures such as Herald Loomis in *Joe Turner's Come and Gone*, Levee in *Ma Rainey's Black Bottom*, Troy in *Fences*, and King in *King Hedley II* strike universal chords of familiarity, in some measure each is faced with the same demons that plagued him. Study carefully any of these social outcasts and misunderstood case studies at the center of these plays to find clues into the playwright's own conflicted universe. Uprooted, restless, tormented, and driven, characters such as Citizen Barlow, Herald Loomis, Levee, Troy Maxson, King Hedley II, and Harmond Wilks go to great lengths to settle a score, right a wrong, get what is their due, or come to terms with self. Also portrayed in several of Wilson's best known plays are enigmatic, shaman-like characters who mirror Wilson in the emotional baggage that they carry that frequently manifests in the form of physical or emotional scars that bespeak of unspeakable pasts. The earth mother and community healer Aunt Ester Tyler (*Gem of the Ocean*), the voodoo wise man Bynum Walker (*Joe Turner's Come and Gone*) and the cutter waitress Risa (*Two Trains Running*), for example, possess the dual propensity to uncover and wrestle with their personal truths so that others may not suffer a similar fate.

Much of Wilson's work in the role of artist turned cultural healer was in teaching and arguing the rightful place of Africa at the core of African American identity. As he attempted to cope with an estranged father, choose between warring cultural allegiances, and formulate an Africanist aesthetic, he faced a state of constant psychological turmoil. Author and critic Paul Carter Harrison explains what might stoke this type of tempestuous inner battle in Wilson in a seminal essay entitled "August Wilson's Blues Poetics." Here, Harrison asserts that "marginalization prompted African Americans to probe the recesses of ancestral memory for recognizable African values, linguistic techniques, and aesthetic constructions that could be cultivated as a source of ethnic reaffirmation" (292). Harrison further argues that "the revival of a collective, African memory had a chastening effect on contemporary black artists, urging them away from a posture of cultural ambivalence to achieve a vigorous, uncompromised expression of ethnic ethos in the creative process" (298). Africa, then, became the refuge for Wilson as it did for many artists having to contend with still relevant tensions caused by what Langston Hughes referred to as "the racial mountain."[2]

Ironically, it is the tension Wilson experienced in efforts to negotiate the gap between his father's European roots and his mother's ties to Africa that, arguably, inspired his greatest work. In an essay titled "Audience and Africanism in August Wilson's Dramaturgy," I observed, "For August Wilson, discovering, claiming, and foregrounding his own African identity fuels both a personal and professional odyssey" (152). Proof of this can be seen in his assortment of male characters who mirror the playwright's struggles to define and to hold fast to his Africanness while his cultural sensibilities were bombarded by the omnipresence of western white hegemony. In his role as culture bearer, Wilson offers up a defensive message—

though, as theatre critics attest, for much of the African American audience, it was unrelatable: "My idea is that somewhere, sometime in the course of the play, the audience will discover these are African people. They're black Americans, they speak English, but their worldview is African" (Powers 53).

Perhaps more so than the other plays, *Joe Turner's Come and Gone, Fences,* and *King Hedley II* approximate several of the internal struggles that August Wilson uncovered and wrestled with during his personal, political, and artistic life. These include, for example, his deep-seated angst about the alienation, victimization, and devaluation of the African American male by white America, his frustrations about a growing chasm among contemporary African Americans who resist claiming Africa as their cultural center, and his persistent quest to find a surrogate father. The traumatic kidnapping of the nomadic Herald Loomis, his seven-year enslavement, and his subsequent release profoundly alienates him from his community, a site that Alan Nadel regards as "central to Wilson's understanding of the human, of the historical, and more specifically, of the African American condition" (4). Once freed and in the process of putting himself back together again, this outcast of a husband, father, church deacon, and member of his community must now face a dissolved marriage, a displaced child, and, his Christian religion that, in his estimation, has failed him miserably. The virtual shutout of black garbage man Troy Maxson from major league baseball renders him devalued and essentially invisible to this predominantly white-controlled institution. Still, he manages to reject the label "victim" and wield a significant amount of agency (though arguably misguided) in both his personal and work-related choices.

A good deal of Wilson's own imprint can be found in the potentially explosive King Hedley II, who is haunted by demons not of his own making; undisclosed circumstances of his birth have predetermined his fate. Reminiscent of the prototypical Aristotelian tragic figure, King's attempt to avenge the murder of a mistaken father goes awry when he learns much too late that his mission is misguided. He is also obsessively driven to settle a lingering score against a local man who called him "chump" and who permanently disfigured his face. While under the ubiquitous influence of vigilante street justice that rules in the drug infested environment of the play's 1985 setting, King's own ultimate demise appears certain. When read as manifestations of the artist's inner turmoil, each of these scenarios highlights demons similar to those that wreaked havoc on Wilson, who was no stranger to a house divided, who was accustomed to the totalitarian rule of a domineering father, who was perhaps unwittingly cognizant of a deep-seated desire to replace him, and who opted out of an educational system that, for all intents and purposes, rejected him.

In his various roles as medium, storyteller, culture bearer or as an African-in-America, August Wilson can best be described as an autoethnographer. That is, he placed himself squarely within his ten-play narrative as both subject and object. His stories about separation, migrations, and reunions at once reflect the plight of thousands of African Americans subjected to the lingering traumatic splintering effects of slavery and mass migration and their ongoing quests to reconnect. While Wilson's individual narratives of black life in Pittsburgh and Chicago may suffice as microcosms of black life in America, the mirror may also be turned inward to reflect the playwright's own fragmented life exacerbated by a complete disconnect with his biological father, by his flight from a racist Pittsburgh's school system, and by his discovery or "reunion" with the blues, Africa, Amiri Baraka, and by his newfound regard for the vernacular of fellow Pittsburgh natives. Like many of his characters who are cut off from their source, he wrestled with his past and—in search of its truths—set out to reassemble himself out of the disparate parts and gradually found solace in affirming his black cultural connections.

That Wilson grounds his plays in the naturalism provided by actual street names, specific addresses, familiar neighborhoods, and boyhood acquaintances made in Pittsburgh's Hill District puts him in the company of fellow Pittsburgh native and African American writer John Wideman, whose fiction also draws heavily upon this same urban milieu. As Tracie Guzzio observes in *All Stories Are True: History, Myth, and Trauma in the Works of John Wideman*:

> The genre allows the writer to form a gap or clear a space within the narratives of the dominant culture to tell an alternate history. The audience of the autoethnographic text is not just the mainstream; the autoethnographic text also reminds the community from which it originates that their culture exists concurrently with the dominant one. Thus, the discourses of autobiography and the ethnography, both stories, occur simultaneously. The effect is balance and equality—all stories are true [104–105].

More than recouping and telling a lost history, the autoethnographic impulse of August Wilson's creative process is concerned with reassembling or reconnecting fragments of a culture still suffering the effects of diasporic splintering occasioned by slavery and mass migration North. Francois Lionnet argues that the genre "establishes connections among the children of the diaspora, and remembers the scattered body of folk material so that siblings can again touch each other" (119).

That Wilson and Wideman draw from similar wells of African American cultural experience in Pittsburgh (Homewood and the Hill District) underscores the freedom of expression each had to create and speak from the perspective of the universal "I." In "Performing Absence: The Staged Personal Narrative as Testimony," for example, Linda Park-Fuller reasons that the writer who assumes such a symbiotic role in their autobiographical discourse "often speaks about acts of transgression. In doing so, the telling of the story itself becomes a transgressive act—a revealing of what has been kept hidden, a speaking of what has been silenced—an act of reverse discourse that struggles with the preconceptions born in the air of dominant politics" (26). Tami Spry sees in autoethnographic writing a vehicle that has allowed her to become an "active agent with narrative authority over many hegemonizing dominant cultural myths that restricted my social freedom and personal development" (711).

Wilson's role as autoethnographer seemed to crystallize as early as 1984, when he admitted to interviewer Kim Powers, "I write from the center, the core, of myself. You've got that landscape and you've got to enter it, walk down that road and whatever happens, happens. And that's the best you're capable of coming to. The characters do it, and in them, I confront myself" (53). Later, in 1987, on the heels of the back-to-back successes of *Ma Rainey's Black Bottom* and *Fences*, he told a New York *Newsday* reporter that he was engaged in writing "a 400-year-old autobiography, which is the black experience" (Palmer 47). Cast in the form of ten plays, Wilson's "autobiography" is an attempt to make sense of his life while capturing the lingering psychological toll that the Middle Passage and slavery, the perilous migration North, and several watershed historical moments, such as the Civil Rights, Black Power, and Black Arts movements have taken on his people. As Heewon Chang notes in his article "Autoethnography as Method: Raising Cultural Consciousness of Self and Others," like ethnography, "autoethnography pursues the ultimate goal of cultural understanding."

In turning to writing plays as a way to uncover and wrestle with perplexing truths "from uncertain and sometimes unyielding realities" (*The Ground* 46) of his existence as an African, as an African American, and as an African American male in America, Wilson combines his role as autoethnographer of the black experience with that of the archetypal wounded healer. That is, he found in his suffering, wandering, reconnecting, and remembering what Jungian psychology follower Paul Levy refers to as "a transformative and healing effect" prompted by "a personalized reflection or instantiation of the collective suffering that pervades the entire field of consciousness" in "the footprint and signature of the collective wound in which we all share and participate" ("The Wounded Healer"). Perhaps unwittingly, then, Wilson grew to understand also that his over twenty-five years of playwriting provided a way to "re-contextualize our personal conflicts, problems and wounds as part of a wider transpersonal pattern enfolded throughout the global field of human experience" ("The Wounded Healer"). What is least known about August Wilson among those who experience his Pittsburgh Cycle is how writing these plays that connected his angst with that of the larger African American community gave meaning to and, arguably, may have extended his own life.

Four of the thirteen essays that follow grapple with various aspects of what Harry Justin Elam notes in his book *The Past as Present in the Drama of August Wilson* as "a new experience of history"—an experience that Wilson captures, not as an historian, but as one who "uses history" and regards it as "an important part of [his] work" (Shannon, *Dramatic Vision* 202). The premise of this first study to assess the holistic impact of Wilson's entire ten-play project is that the playwright creates "a new experience of history, a new contestatory and contingent engagement with the past that puts into question the historical categorization of race as it interrogates the meaning of blackness" (Elam xiii). While Wilson disqualified himself as an historian, in keeping with his role as wounded healer, he concedes in the preface of *Seven Guitars* that he "tried to extract some measure of truth from their lives as they [Africans-in-America] struggle to remain whole in the face of so many things that threaten to pull them asunder. I am not a historian" ("A Note from the Playwright").

Joyce Hope Scott begins this collection with an essay on Wilson's use of history, "'The emancipated century': Remapping History, Reclaiming Memory in August Wilson's Dramatic Landscapes of the 20th Century," in which she retraces the cartography of Wilson's dramatic geographies, specifically in *Joe Turner's Come and Gone* and *The Piano Lesson*. In the process she reveals a picture of "progress for African Americans in the 20th century." Jacqueline Zeff argues the advantages of "lived history" and of bearing witness for the youthful audience in one of Wilson's lesser known early plays in "'A big bend there, a tree by the shore': Situated Identity in *The Janitor*." In a 1999 interview for *The Paris Review*, August Wilson describes what drew him to the dramatic form: "I was, and remain, fascinated by the idea of an audience as a community of people who gather willingly to bear witness." To be sure, she maintains that, in his full-length plays, Wilson frequently offers both male witness testimony and witness communities on stage, but the assertion of that testimony as a way to create and reveal male agency is never more clearly dramatized than in his one-act play *The Janitor*.

Sarah Saddler and Paul Bryant-Jackson, in "*Two Trains Running*: Bridging Diana Taylor's 'rift' and Narrating Manning Marable's 'living history,'" places Marable and Taylor's theoretical paradigms in dialogue to examine how August Wilson dramaturgically constructs Marable's vision of an African American "living history" through the intersection of material archive and embodied repertoire. According to Sadler and Bryant-Jackson, Marable challenges the erasure of black heritage within the American archive in order to advocate for a "living history" that exposes the racialized growth of global apartheid. They argue further that Wilson's oeuvre for the theatre draws extensively from a West African oral tradition: stories, memories, and history. These three impulses converge in *Two Trains Running* and throughout the Century Project.

Ellen Bonds' "World War II History/history: Essential Contexts in *Seven Guitars*" shows Wilson turning to history to teach the example of the wounded healer through allusions to the historic boxing bout between famed boxer Joe Louis—more informally known as the Brown Bomber—and Billy Conn. According to Bond, the political history surrounding World War II, for African Americans, can be read, in part, as a history of broken promises. Joe Louis both personifies a litany of broken promises while he also provides the cultural context for the play and extends the metaphor of promises made and broken. The injustices that the wounded healer Joe Louis experienced personally before, during, and after World War II parallel the injustices that the cast of seven characters in this play suffer. While the example of Joe Louis prevails in *Seven Guitars*, his presence is evoked onstage in the form of a radio broadcast of the 1941 fight with Billy Conn.

Michael Downing finds paradoxical meaning in what he sees as Wilson's tendency to "flip" and diffuse negative stereotypes used to describe African Americans. In "The Use of Stereotype and Archetype in *Ma Rainey's Black Bottom*," he demonstrates how the playwright's role as cultural mythmaker extends to elevating the commonplace to the holy and to portraying an initial pejorative, racist stereotype from one that evokes criticism, suspicion, and scorn to an archetypal one that evokes empathy, understanding, and compassion, thus promoting the characters and situations to mythical status.

Isaiah Matthew Wooden's "*Gem of the Ocean*'s Fugitive Moments" both exposes and explores the blurred lines that he argues exists between law and justice in one of Wilson's last written plays in the Pittsburgh Cycle. Readers will find in this play (written in the early 2000s) and in Wooden's analysis interesting parallels with today's rash of high profile clashes between law enforcement and the African American community. He argues,

> Wilson's decoupling of the oft-consolidated notions of law and justice in *Gem of the Ocean* opens critical space to investigate a history that sees the law consistently reconfigured and reorganized to criminalize the black: that is, a history that pits blackness against the law, a history that archives the necessary alignment of blackness with the fugitivity of justice. More significantly, the disentanglement of law from justice in *Gem of the Ocean* invites a serious consideration of the question: Why is justice so fugitive, particularly for the black?

In "Reclaiming the Mother: Women, Documents and the Condition of the Mother in *Gem of the Ocean* and *Ma Rainey's Black Bottom*," Jesslyn Collins-Frohlich identifies an alternative view of written documents that have historically objectified human beings. She maintains that for Aunt Ester and Ma Rainey, the key to successfully navigating matriarchal/patriarchal and oral/written dichotomies is their ability to use documents to question the ways official histories use gender and the written word to reduce people to property and property holders. She argues that Aunt Ester and Ma Rainey create a counterinsurgent logic for approaching documents that reclaims the once repressive idea of the "condition of the mother" and shapes it into a vital tool for maintaining communities and ensuring cultural continuity that also offers a means of resistance.

Christopher B. Bell holds up for scrutiny in "A Century Lacking Progress: The Fractured Community in *Gem of the Ocean* and *King Hedley II*" the popularly accepted notion that African American communities should serve as healing oases. He demonstrates that the same community that Wilson regards as essential to cultural health among African Americans has, by all accounts, reneged on its obligations and has failed. Bell's essay examines *Gem of the Ocean*, the first play in August Wilson's Pittsburgh Cycle, and its penultimate one, *King Hedley II*, arguing that Wilson depicts a community largely responsible for its own dissolution, a theme that, according to Bell, has received little attention in Wilson studies.

Psyche Williams-Forson convincingly argues in "'He gonna give me my ham': The Use of Food as a Symbol for Social Justice" that food can also function as a liberating device. From the ham in *Two Trains Running* to the Coca-Cola in *Ma Rainey's Black Bottom*, the watermelon and pork chops in *The Piano Lesson*, the biscuits in *Joe Turner's Come and Gone*, and the myriad foods in *Seven Guitars*, her essay considers some of the ways that Wilson uses "anthropologist's eyes" to incorporate food into his plays. Examining food enables readers and viewers to gain deeper insight into the dynamics of African American culture and into the ways that food serves as a symbol of social justice and cultural survival and continuity. She bolsters her argument by alluding to two of Wilson's own admissions about the culturally empowering function of food: "Anthropologists, they want to know what you eat, they want to know why you eat what you eat, they want to know your social manners, how your community is organized, how you court, whatever it is" (xi). "I try to approach people with an anthropologist's eyes. That's why I make constant references to food. If you study culture, you want to know what people eat, what their social organization is."

Artisia Green, Owen Seda and Connie Rapoo offer intriguing essays that underscore the importance of African ritual and ancestry as conduits to truths with which Wilson and all Africans in American wrestle. Green argues in "Resurrecting 'phantom limb[s] of the dismembered slave and god': Unveiling the Africanisms in *Gem of the Ocean*" that beneath *Gem of the Ocean*'s Judeo-Christian tropes and pseudo-American patriotism is a Yoruban cosmology situated within the characters and the architecture of the text. Her essay seeks to illuminate the play's spiritual potency by first discussing the characterizations informed by Òrìṣà archetypes while simultaneously noting significant objects and spaces, followed by comments on the temporal coordination of the architecture of the play. As such, Green's essay arguably rivals—and perhaps exceeds—earlier scholarship on African retentions in Wilson's work by Amadou Bissiri in "Aspects of Africanness in August Wilson's Drama: Reading *The Piano Lesson* through Wole Soyinka's Drama" (1996) and by Sandra Richards in "Yoruba Gods on the American Stage: August Wilson's *Joe Turner's Come and Gone*" (1999) in terms of her thoroughness at teasing out the Africanist underpinnings in one of Wilson's last written plays.

In "Epiphany and the 'drama of souls,'" Owen Seda argues that by foregrounding the provenance and efficacy of ancestry and ancestor worship in the lives and destinies of his characters, Wilson uses the "drama of souls" to expose and offer Africans in America solutions to the challenge of marginality and racial otherness in epiphanic and significant ways. Similarly, Rapoo, in "Conjuring Africa in African American Plays," analyzes the staging of ritual observances in August Wilson's *Joe Turner's Come and Gone* and *Gem of the Ocean*. She considers these plays as theatrical offerings that re-memorialize the African historical, cultural, and spiritual past and argues that African ritual observances and enactments of spiritual commitment in these plays reinforce the characters' acts of self-determination and sense of collective identification.

Susan C.W. Abbotson rounds out this collection of new critical essays on August Wilson with salient observations about the playwright's legacy, especially in light of his now-completed cycle. She points to additional possibilities for the study of Wilson's work in "Re-Evaluating the Legacy of the Ten-Play Cycle" where she pries open new spaces for inquiry by asking, "Should August Wilson be judged as an old-fashioned realist, whose work only has significance to the black community, or might his plays be discussed in light of their more universal uncertainties of modern existence?" She suggests that by approaching Wilson's plays through a critical lens foregrounded by the positive humanism of postmodern critics such as Alan Wilde, John McGowan, and Linda Hutcheon, we can draw out an underlying moral pattern that weaves through Wilson's cycle. She offers a paradigm shift that is timely, innovative, and wide in its implications. This expanded lens can yield new critical perspectives upon Wilson's plays based upon a humanistic, and ultimately, optimistic outlook.

Since Wilson's death and with the cycle complete, critical perspectives have broadened to encompass the arc of his ten-decade opus, as have the frequency of theatrical productions, such as the Kennedy Center's 2008 presentation of the full cycle, ranging from full productions to staged readings. New vistas have also been made possible by the 2013 reading and recording series of all ten of Wilson's plays in his celebrated chronicle of African American life in the 20th century. Sponsored by New York's Jerome L. Greene Performance Space from August 26 through September 28, 2013, a host of cast members who have appeared in one or more of Wilson's plays along with longtime collaborators performed live dramatic readings of Wilson's plays, all of which were recorded to be preserved for future generations. Just as important, Wilson scholarship and overall interest in his work stand to benefit exponentially with the 2015 release of the American Masters documentary *August Wilson: The Ground on Which I Stand*, coupled with a well-funded and concerted campaign to make Wilson's plays more accessible in the classroom.

Notes

1. The archetype of the wounded healer is a term created by psychologist Carl Jung. The idea states that an analyst is compelled to treat patients because the analyst himself is "wounded." The idea, believed to have origins in Greek mythology, is a particularly appropriate analogue for describing Wilson's playwriting quest—a quest that goes beyond the satisfaction of fulfilling a mission to write ten plays. Wounded

healer reveals that it is only by being willing to face, consciously experience and go through our wound do we achieve enlightenment. For more on Carl Jung's concept of the "wounded healer," see Claire Dunn's *Carl Jung: The Wounded Healer of the Soul* (New York: Parabola, 2000).

2. "The Negro Artist and the Racial Mountain" (1926) was a short essay written by poet Langston Hughes for *The Nation* magazine. In it Hughes said that black artists in America should stop copying whites, that they will never create anything great that way. Instead they should be proud of who they are, proud to be black, and draw from black culture. It became the manifesto of the Harlem Renaissance.

WORKS CITED

Chang, Heewon. "Autoethnography as Method: Raising Cultural Consciousness of Self and Others." Web. 19 March 2015. http://www.academia.edu/2116956/Autoethnography_as_method.

Elam, Harry Justin. *The Past as Present in the Drama of August Wilson*. Ann Arbor: University of Michigan Press, 2004.

Guzzio, Tracie Church. *All Stories Are True: History, Myth, and Trauma in the Works of John Wideman*. Ebook in Margaret Walker Alexander Series in African American Studies. Jackson: University Press of Mississippi, 2011. 104–105. Web. 19 March 2015. http://catalog.wrlc.org/cgi-bin/Pwebrecon.cgi?BBID=12939450.

Harrison, Paul Carter. "August Wilson's Blues Poetics." *August Wilson: Three Plays*. Pittsburgh: Pittsburgh University Press, 1984. Print.

Levy, Paul. "The Wounded Healer, Part I in *Awaken in the Dream*." Web. 5 February 2015. http://www.awakeninthedream.com/wordpress/the-wounded-healer-part-1/.

Lionnet, Francois. *Autobiographical Voices: Race, Gender, and Self-Portraiture*. Ithaca: Cornell University Press, 1989. Print.

Moyers, Bill. "August Wilson: Playwright." In *A World of Ideas*. New York: Doubleday, 1989. Print.

Nadel, Alan. Introduction. *August Wilson: Completing the Twentieth-Century Cycle*. Ed. Alan Nadel. Iowa City: Iowa University Press, 2010. 1–13. Print.

Palmer, Don. "He Gives Voice to Nameless Masses." New York *Newsday*, 20 April 1987, 47. Print.

Park-Fuller, Linda. "Performing Absence: The Staged Personal Narrative as Testimony." *Text and Performance Quarterly* 20.1 (2000): 20–42.

Powers, Kin. "An Interview with August Wilson." *Theater* 16 (Fall-Winter 1984): 50–55.

Roberts, Brian Henry. "Can You Tell Me How to Get to the Crossroads? A Cultural Analysis of Community Rituals in Five Major Plays by August Wilson." *Dissertation Abstracts International* (UMI No. AAT 3066017). Retrieved October 26, 2006, from Digital Dissertations Database, 2002, xi. Print.

Savran, David. "Interview with August Wilson." *In Their Own Words*. New York: Theatre Communications Group, 1988. Print.

Shannon, Sandra. "Audience and Africanisms in August Wilson's Dramaturgy."

African American Performance and Theatre History: A Critical Reader. Eds. Harry J. Elam and David Krasner. Oxford: Oxford University Press, 2001. Print.
____. The Dramatic Vision of August Wilson. Washington, D.C.: Howard University Press, 2013.
Spry, Tammy. "Performing Autoethnography: An Embodied Methodological Praxis." *Qualitative Inquiry* 7.6 (2001): 706–732. Print.
Wilson, August. *The Ground on Which I Stand.* Dramatic Context Series. New York: Theatre Communications Group, 1996. Print.
____. *Seven Guitars.* New York: Dutton, 1996. Print.

"The emancipated century": Remapping History, Reclaiming Memory in August Wilson's Dramatic Landscapes of the 20th Century

Joyce Hope Scott

Postmodern U.S. historiographers consider it their duty to enlighten the American public about our collective past; however, their approaches also have often resulted in a particularly narrow spatialization, constricting our understanding of specific periods, places, events and people. Yet the reality of our experience as a nation requires enlightenment in a broader and more multifaceted manner to understand the array of themes that represent our comprehensive American experience. Ray Raphael's landmark text, *A People's History of the American Revolution: How Common People Shaped the Fight for Independence*, represents a departure from traditional historiography and challenges our understanding of this specific period of history by featuring the experiences and roles of those who were previously voiceless, the common people—the free and the enslaved. To this end, Raphael re-invokes W.E.B. DuBois' contribution to the competing narratives of history relative to the period of Reconstruction in his seminal work, *Black Reconstruction in America 1860–1880* (1935).

DuBois deconstructs mainstream historians' omissions and negative portrayals of the role of African Americans during the post–Civil War period. He particularly observes the impact of historians' prejudicial predisposition toward blacks in this tendency with his final chapter entitled "The Propaganda of History." DuBois especially focuses on the influence of racism on the political agenda of historiography and revises accounts of the failure of resettlement efforts as due to administrative mismanagement rather than the ignorance of black elected officials and greedy Northern carpetbaggers. DuBois's observation is, indeed, echoed by John Ernest who points out that at various stages of U.S. history, black people were consistently confronted with reformulations of "the palimpsest of race." This "palimpsest of race" and the politics of historical commemoration is what playwright August Wilson's ten-play cycle captures in foregrounding various moments in the decades following the Civil War, the "emancipated century" for African Americans. In the plays, "testimonies to his participation in an ongoing tradition of African American expressivity" (Wall), Wilson remaps the history of the black experience of the 20th century on the powerful canvas of the theatre, through the poetry, imagination, everyday language, rhythm, and song of African Americans of the Great Migration, capturing the tragedy, the triumph and the resiliency of everyday people who fled the violent South and wound up in cities like Pittsburgh.

Wilson's plays are transformative historical revisions that serve to impact the collective African American and national memory. In this fashion, he seeks to enrich our understanding of this specific cultural phenomenon from our collective past—emancipation—through a broadening of its often narrowly-confined temporal and spatial dimensions. The stage becomes the site for public communal memory. It claims the physical space to reconstruct cultural memory, "a crucial aspect of authentic [reparative] historiography" (Newby-Alexander). With the plays, Wilson appropriates the tradition of revisionist history of DuBois and Raphael by imposing his own creative maps of the black experience on the American stage. Reparative history is concerned with critical cultural experiences and representations located in particular histories and groups and the impact of their legacies on contemporary society. His theatricality is interrogative like DuBois' *Black Reconstruction* and Raphael's *A People's History of the American Revolution* in that it raises the question of how we construct representations of the African American past and what it means to turn to history for revision and redress in the present.

Retracing the cartography of Wilson's dramatic geographies, specifically in *Joe Turner's Come and Gone* (1988) and *The Piano Lesson* (1990), I suggest, interrogates the notion that the event of emancipation and migration at the dawn of the 20th century equated to progress for African Americans and that, in fact, embracing memory and mythos to assess this progress is a necessary process which requires returning to the past as consistently as it requires embracing the future. August Wilson's drama series, created to commemorate the experiences of African Americans in the decades following Reconstruction, underscores the role imaginative, artistic representations have in reconstructing contested pasts. The cartography of his renderings of the period consists of a theatrical map of the psychological and spatial geographies of the lives of men and women uprooted from tradition with identities fractured by a conflicting sense of self.

This cartography—a careful array of cultural referents of early 20th century urban black America: boardinghouses, folktales, storytellers, refugees all from Jim Crow violence and the convict-lease system, transient relationships, and blues music—permits Wilson to sketch the contours of an historical cultural pattern of the Great Black Migration that framed the lives of many African American migrants. *Joe Turner* and *The Piano Lesson* re-historicize this period and challenge standard historical studies of the Great Migration and the commonly-accepted idea of the impetus behind the movement of hundreds of thousands of African Americans from the rural South to the urban areas of the North and the Midwest. Scholars have typically theorized that this movement was forced by the ever-present reality of lynching and other white terrorist acts. While Wilson's plays have these realities as an unspoken subtext, he also proclaims the power of black agency and self-initiated acts as major factors motivating the migration of blacks northward to what they thought was the modern Promised Land. In his study of the event, David M. Katzman concludes that

> migration has been one of the defining characteristics of black life in the United States since the forced migration of African slaves to the New World.... The Great Migration was a grass-roots, leaderless movement. All the migrants—male laborers, women domestics, families—made individual decisions to move. Nonetheless, the deterioration of the quality of life of southern blacks in the two decades prior to World War I, coupled with a labor shortage in the industrial North, stimulated the migration. In the South, the rise of Jim Crow, the disfranchisement of black voters, and the spread of lynchings and other mob violence against blacks provided strong impetus for individuals and families to move [114].

As DuBois and Raphael retrieved marginalized narratives of their respective historical events, Wilson's staging of blacks' experience of Northern resettlement re-appropriates orature, the rich body of folk material that is found in the liminal spaces of communal memory and that forms the context of black life in the 20th century. Wilson's representations of African American culture's collective creations allow us to contrast his retrieval of these forms with the way that the discourse of social scientific research may view them, as static elements, unverifiable by the methods of logos. Toni Morrison addresses these outlaw cultural forms in her essay "Rootedness: The Ancestor as Foundation":

> We were very practical people, very down-to-earth, even shrewd people. But within that practicality we also accepted what I suppose could be called superstition and magic, which is another way of knowing things. But to blend those two worlds together at the same time was enhancing, not limiting. And some of those things were "discredited knowledge" that black people had; discredited only because black people were discredited therefore what they knew was "discredited" [1].

Mikhail Bakhtin claims that "every age re-accentuates in its own way the works of its most immediate past" (421). *Joe Turner's Come and Gone* is a powerful engagement with the meaning of emancipation and the role of cultural traditions in the reconstructed black community of the early 20th century North.

Migration, Blues and the Road

Oh they tell me Joe Turner's in this town
They tell me
Well they tell me Joe Turner's in this town
He's a man I hate, I don't want him hangin' around
He's a man I hate, don't want him hangin' around
If you don't arrest him, I'm gonna shoot him down
["Joe Turner Blues," Mississippi John Hurt].

Set in 1911, August Wilson's *Joe Turner's Come and Gone* re-invokes the historical moment of migration as well as the conditions of life for Southern blacks arriving in big cities like Pittsburgh in the 1900s, only 44 years after the institution of the infamous Black Codes—which would later lead to Jim Crow segregationist laws. The play is not just a presentation of geographic movement but rather a cartography, mapping out "a profoundly human terrain" (Maxwell). This terrain consists of "oppositional locations" (Maxwell) that form a narratology of African Americans' experience of emancipation: Seth Holly's boarding house and the collection of orphans and strays who wander in for lodging and refuge from the uncertainty of Northern life and the vicious Jim Crow vagrancy laws of the South; Holly's garden, a location in which Bynum Walker has respatialized ancient African spiritual rituals; and the road, which, for these early 20th century blacks, can be a mystical place, where Bynum Walker met his "shiny man" and where blues singer Robert Johnson met the Devil and sold his soul (Compagna). These sites of memory unfold an unofficial history of the instability of black lives at the end of the 19th century.

Wilson captures the sense of determination in these people, in spite of loss and confusion in the wake of freedom: "From the deep and the near South the sons and daughters of freed African slaves wander into the city. Isolated, cut off from memory, having forgotten the names of the gods and only guessing at their faces, they arrive dazed and stunned, their hearts kicking in their chest with a song worth singing" ("Setting," *Joe Turner's Come and Gone*). The profound dispossession is conveyed through his characters:

> BYNUM: [to Herald Loomis] Where you coming from, Mister ... I didn't get your name.
> LOOMIS: Name's Herald Loomis. This my daughter, Zonia.
> BYNUM: Where you coming from?
> LOOMIS: Come from all over. Whicheverway the road take us that's the way we go [Act 1, Scene 2].

The infamous man-catcher, Joe Turney, referenced by the name Joe Turner in the play, has wreaked havoc upon black families by his abrupt capture and imprisonment of black men.[1] This unrepresented irony of the history of emancipation for blacks is embodied in Wilson's character Herald Loomis, who comes with his daughter to Seth Holly's boarding house seeking his wife. One of the men impressed into bondage by Joe Turner, he explains that Turner rounded up as many as forty people and kept them as long as seven years. Wilson infuses this tragic historical event as a dominant motif of the historical experience of African American life after the Civil War. His collection of migratory blacks are all, in a sense, orphans, lost from their families and their histories. The impact of Joe Turner and the vicious post-slavery system of capitalist exploitation appears to have affected them all. Wilson re-presents the individual pain and desperation that accompanied Northern migration.

The staging of these "cartographies of struggle" (Ballantyne) is achieved through the disparate stories of the lodgers. All have been "cut off from memory," and "having forgotten the names of the gods and only guessing at their faces, they arrive dazed and stunned, their hearts kicking in their chest with a song worth singing" (*Joe Turner's Come and Gone*). Wilson's theatrical revision of history unfolds a story of the many roads that blacks have walked and routes they have traveled on their way out of the South, yet these have not led them to the growth and progress promised by the thriving steel mills and booming housing industries of Pittsburgh and other American cities.

One historical site of memory that served to ease the pain of this disappointment was the spiritual healer, in this case Bynum Walker. His presence in Seth Holly's boarding house functions to reconnect the people and "rebind" them to their African cultural legacy.

The Great Migration is characterized as the largest and most significant movement of African Americans from the South in search of better conditions in the North and West. Southern Jim Crow laws plus train transport and jobs in industry were compelling forces fueling this extraordinary internal migration in American history. In time, the Great Migration replaced slavery and emancipation as the monumental cultural memory for black artists. In Wilson's theatrical revisioning, the migration fundamentally altered the African American experience, fracturing families and transforming traditional culture but creating also a renaissance in the arts and culture of African Americans. Numerous historians look at the Great Migration from the perspective of macro-causes like shifts in the American economy and community structure from rural to urban, noting that blacks were propelled by these forces like whites (Allison). In contrast, others maintain that the impetus of the people themselves to migrate has to be considered, that history is not the work of impersonal economic forces, but rather the result of the agency of the people (Allison).

Joe Turner's Come and Gone is an exposé of this cultural phenomenon employing theatre as a device for the reordering and repairing of a fragmented history and culture by underscoring the crucial role of ancestral roots for a truthful account of black history. Bynum Walker becomes the force of this reordering by advocating Africa and African spirituality as the force to reconnect black people and "rebind" them in cultural cohesion. Bynum's prescription for healing is that they find their song, just as the mystical "shiny man" has helped him find his song, the dispossessed and alienated people of the rooming house must find their own and re-establish an African American vision of cultural cohesion. Bynum's healing solution is for the people to find their song; as the "shiny man" on the road has helped him find his. Through his sacrificial rituals with pigeons each morning to nearly-forgotten African gods, his ability to mystically join people together, and his belief that the song (the creative source) of each person's life is a spiritual expression that establishes his or her identity and connectedness, Bynum is a re-configuration of the traditional African Babalawos and Bokonons of IFA and Vodoun. Wilson reclaims this traditional icon of African spirituality as a marker of black resilience against cultural erasure as well as the ritual of juba, which lingers in the memory of all the members of the little community.[2] In his respatialization of the social geography of emancipated blacks, Wilson's assertion of the centrality of these Africanisms dismantles claims of cultural amnesia as a result of the trauma of slavery and Jim Crow laws.

Misunderstanding Bynum's reference, Herald Loomis is reluctant to engage in any act of binding:

> "Everywhere I go people wanna bind me up, Joe Turner wanna bind me up! Reverend Tolliver wanna bind me up.... Well Joe Turner's come and Gone and Herald Loomis ain't for no binding" [Act 2, Scene 4].

Yet Wilson deconstructs the negative association of binding with historical enslavement through Bynum who suggests that the term here really refers to reconnection to memory and true black identity as he recounts his spiritual encounter on the road with the "shiny man":

> "I turned around to look at this fellow and he had this light coming out of him. He shining like new money with that light ... I wandered around there looking for that road ... and I looked over and seen my daddy standing there.... Told me he was gonna show me how to find my song.... I stayed in that place a while and my daddy taught me the meaning of this thing I had seen and showed me how to find my song" [Act 1, Scene 1].

The implication here is that contrary to the mainstream's insistence on the centrality of education or schooling as the major solution to problems that African Americans encounter in the society, it is the memory of ancestral knowledge that will ultimately heal the splintered soul of black America and form the bridge that links the past to the present and the future. "Memory time lasts longer" than any tangible experience, Bynum affirms (Act I, Scene 4), and the archival site of that time is African American music. "Song," Wilson suggests, "is the central metaphor" (Haagensen) that functions to locate the characters in historical time as well as identify the prescriptive solution to their loss of identity and purpose. Bynum Walker tells Herald Loomis that Joe Turner wanted to steal his song (symbolically his historical memory, his knowledge and sense of self or agency), and that is why he imprisoned Loomis:

> "What he wanted was your song. He wanted to have that song to be his. He thought by catching you he could learn that song.... Now he's got you bound up to where you can't sing your own song. Couldn't sing it them seven years 'cause you was afraid he would snatch it from under you. But you still got it. You just forgot how to sing it" [Act I, Scene 2].

Commenting on August Wilson's embrace of Africanity in his theory of art, Paul Carter Harrison affirms that in that philosophy, "it becomes imperative to alter perceptions of self by jettisoning the aesthetic models of western tradition that have forged ... [negative] ... perceptions of blackness" (1) and to replace them with "the 'spiritual temperament' of the ancestors whose songs, dances, and art were a manifest act of 'the creator from whom life flowed'" (1). Captured in the history of black emancipation in the 20th century is the complexity of the struggle to affirm blackness, African roots, and cultural continuity and cohesion. Wilson continues the retrieval of this unacknowledged legacy begun by DuBois and others, insisting that the untold story is bound up in the unofficial knowledge located in the vast black oral tradition. Respatializing this site of memory on the stage provides a forum for a more inclusive reassessment of 20th century black history which unpacks those cultural creations.

Bridging Dimensions: The Living and the Dead

Revisionist historians often engage the question of how the past is constructed as a discourse. August Wilson centers his plays on the same concern in the domain of performance as a way of reordering historical narratives that present a counter-discursive account which authenticates communal memory as cultural currency in the artistic rendering of experience. *The Piano Lesson* implies that theatre, indeed, can be the domain for re-inscribing orality and memory, a dimension through which historical accounts can be retrieved. In essence, it is "a dimension of a community's mode of remembering, an exercise, literally and metaphorically, of *re*-membering, of [materializing and] putting back together aspects of ... common life so as to make visible what has been obscured, what has been excluded, what has been forgotten" (Scott). In *The Piano Lesson*, Wilson "[assembles] and re-[assembles] ... the sources that make memory possible" (Scott) for the Charles family. These "keep alive the events and figures, the sensibilities and mentalities, the knowledges and rationalities that have been part of shaping and reshaping [theirs and the community's] traditions" (Scott). Such forms for Wilson become crucial to a theatrical revision of the historical experience of African Americans of the Great Migration. He accomplishes this with a device that bridges the distance between the past and the present, the living and the dead.

While *The Piano Lesson* was inspired by Romare Bearden's painting of the same name, the title of Wilson's drama refers to a family heirloom, an upright piano onto which their enslaved grandfather carved images of the family and its history. Thus, he simultaneously creates a "reactive/constructive engagement with the representation of blacks and the representation of [20th century] history by the dominant culture.... In this sense, the transmission of history becomes a binding ritual through which his characters obtain an empowering self-knowledge" (Morales 106). The Charles family of Pittsburgh, Great Migration refugees from the South like the people of Seth Holly's boarding house, carries the weight of painful histories which incapacitate them emotionally and spiritually. Also like Seth Holly's boarders, they want to escape memory of the architects of that pain. Yet if the authentic history is to be recaptured, those archival memories and the pain they engender must be confronted.

French historian Pierre Nora addresses the problem of the struggle between historiography and memory in his seminal work, *Between Memory and History: Les Lieux de Mémoire* [sites of memory]. *Lieux de mémoire*, he claims, "are fundamentally remains, the ultimate embodiments of a memorial consciousness that has barely survived a historical age that calls out for memory because it has abandoned it" (11). Nora continues:

> The defense by certain minorities, of a privileged memory that has retreated to jealously protected enclaves ... intensely illuminates the truth of *lieux de mémoire*—that without commemorative vigilance, [official] history would soon sweep them away. We buttress out identities upon such bastions, but if what they defended were not threatened, there would be no need to build them.... If history did not besiege memory, deforming and transforming it, penetrating and petrifying it, there would be no *lieux de mémoire* [11].

In essence, Wilson's reclamation of a family heirloom and artifact of material culture, as well as the music and song of the post-Reconstruction era, argues for such creations as sites of memory that must be interrogated for a more authentic historiography of African Americans of the 20th century. The importance of the heirloom in *The Piano Lesson* locates it among Pierre Nora's representations of "memorial consciousness" (11). The piano functions not only as a family artifact but also as an archive of slavery's brutal inhumanity and as black resistance to the discursive silences of official history.

August Wilson, who focused on a family artifact in *The Piano Lesson* as the main site of memory, reflects Nora's observations about history and its "transforming and deforming" impact on communal memory of the marginalized. Prior to Wilson's appropriation of the piano as a dramatic device, a major champion of cultural creations as vital to revisionist historiography, was W.E.B. DuBois, who re-historicized the black experience during the period of the New Negro Renaissance and the Great Migration by capturing African American song, painting, literature, and other artistic creations. Through the NAACP's *Crisis Magazine*, DuBois archived "artifacts of black print culture practices," unveiling "artistic and photographic images of untold stories" (Benjamin). For DuBois, these artifacts from material culture and their embedded stories revealed a legacy that deconstructed historical discourse portraying "the Negro problem" as fundamentally due to African Americans' inability to measure up to their white counterparts. What is revealed through these unofficial visual narratives is African American agency and resilience and the complexity and multifaceted nature of the black experience of emancipation and migration.

The play turns on the trope of memory and storytelling replete with ghostly spectres of slavery and Jim Crow, revealing both the remorse and determination of a post-Reconstruction black family. This is foregrounded by both Wining Boy and Doaker Charles. Wining Boy is a roving, traveling man, a piano player and gambler. His story about an encounter with the "Ghosts of the Yellow Dog" at the crossroads refocuses the conversation on those ancestors as another site of memory that lends strength and renewal in the telling of it. Wining Boy declares that after the engagement with these forces, he received a gift of good luck lasting three years. With Wining Boys' celebratory gesture, Wilson foregrounds the role of ritual in enabling access to memory or "re-memory," a term Toni Morrison uses in *Beloved*, which "functions to re-collect, re-assemble, and re-organize [memories] into a meaningful sequential whole through ... the process of narrativization" (Henderson 62–86). While necessary, this reclamation of the ancestral past is painful. Despite the importance of the piano as an archive of family memory and history, Berniece makes her ambiguity toward it clear when she speaks about her relationship to it:

> "When my mama died I shut the top on that piano and I ain't never opened it since. I was only playing it for her. When my daddy died seem like all her life went into that piano. She used to have me playing on it ... had Miss Eula come in and teach me ... say when I played it she could hear my daddy talking to her. I used to think them pictures came alive and walked through the house. Sometime late at night I could hear my mama talking to them. I said that wasn't gonna happen to me. I don't play that piano cause I don't want to wake them spirits" [Act II, Scene 2].

Even though she distances herself from the powerful memories of the piano's past, it is, nevertheless, connected to both Sutter's ghost and the

"Ghosts of the Yellow Dog" and she functions as the medium through which the ancestors communicate with the living.

Parchman Farm and the convict-lease system is another site of memory of historical significance re-invoked by Wilson in *The Piano Lesson* as it was in *Joe Turner's Come and Gone*. Doaker and the other men re-experience it and construct a new narrative about it at the same time through the a cappella/communal rendering of "Berta, Berta." Parchman Farm, located in Sunflower County, Mississippi, is referenced immediately in the opening scene of the play. When Doaker first sees Boy Willie and Lymon at his door, he is surprised, exclaiming, "Boy Willie, what you doing here? I thought you was still in Sunflower County, Mississippi" (Act 1, Scene 1). Here, Wilson directly invokes this institution and the lingering horrors that black men and women experienced as a result of its destructive power. The song "Berta, Berta" is a narratival exposé itself through which the suffering creators capture in plaintive lyrics the history of that prison farm. Wilson suggests that relocation cannot, and perhaps must not, obliterate such a memory. In his seminal study *Worse Than Slavery: Parchman Farm and the Ordeal of Jim Crow Justice*, David M. Oshinsky points out that among the variety of blues creations that came from those who spent time at Parchman Farm is the famous song "Midnight Special," based on the train that left Jackson every Saturday night to carry wives and lovers to visit inmates at the prison. "Berta, Berta" seems to be a direct reference to this practice. The forlorn prisoner, perhaps despairing of his chances to ever be with his lover, tells her,

> O Lord Berta Berta O Lord gal well
> Go 'head marry don't you wait on me oh-ah
> Go 'head marry don't you wait on me well now.

William Banks Taylor explains in his text *Down on Parchman Farm: The Great Prison in the Mississippi Delta* the availability of (and even facilitation of) sex for black men from prostitutes who were housed near the warden's quarters at Parchman Farm. Girls like "Berta" should marry a railroad man, like Doaker Charles, a man whose job allowed him to have clean hands, who could ensure that "everyday [would be like] Sunday," because she could count on having money in her hand. Wilson's men, like hundreds of others of the period, have all had experiences with such an institution, and while the early references to it are mentioned in a jovial fashion, the actual singing of the song functions as a restorative ritual that re-situates them momentarily among their fellow sufferers of the convict-lease system. The glass clinking and foot stomping function to replicate the sound of chains on the tramping feet of the prisoners. This scene actually re-imagines the brutalization that is only suggested by the characters in *Joe Turner's Come and Gone*.

The men's common experience of Parchman Farm is one that serves as a historical link through the generations as Doaker, Wining Boy, Boy Willie, and Lymon have all had an encounter with that infamous institution. Parchman Farm, along with a racist legal system, continues the ghost of slavery in their lives. In particular, Lymon's anecdote of fleeing Stovall after his arrest and sale into bondage can only evoke the memory of the runaway slave and the slave patrols whose job it was to hunt him down. Thus, for Lymon, the North holds a vision of optimism and promise of a better future. As John D. Baskerville observes,

> The optimism that overwhelmed many of the new migrants was part of a more pervasive and growing attitude that was engulfing many in black America at this time. African Americans everywhere during the early decades of the twentieth century anticipated great changes in their lives—economically, socially, and culturally. Inspired by leaders, such as Booker T. Washington, who were convinced that the road to black advancement could be achieved through hard work, thrift, and a resolute will, a number of African Americans were convinced that freedom and equality was right around the corner ["African American Migration"].

Oshinsky exposes the prominence of the convict-lease of the South to the memory of those who moved North during the Great Migration and points out that

> as it developed in Mississippi [the Charles family's home state] convict leasing successfully replaced racial bondage with a system of racial castes while at the same time fueling the economic development of the late 19th century "New South." The mortality rate was high, and the system encompassed all ages. The state penal code made no distinction between juvenile and adult offenders, so that by 1880 "at least one convict in four was an adolescent" [46–47].

He continues, explaining that "the movement to end convict leasing in Mississippi resulted in the creation of Parchman Farm…. Using race-baiting and fears of black lawlessness and criminality to gain power, Governor James K. Vardaman was convinced that a prison farm, like an efficient slave plantation, was necessary to provide young African Americans with the 'proper discipline, strong work habits, and respect for white authority'" (110). Wilson's reconstituted and re-imagined history of the period focuses on the Charles men and their friends' participation in this system, like thousands of other Southern black men. Representatives of three generations of dispossessed freedmen relocated in 1930s Pittsburgh, the Charles family affords Wilson an opportunity to re-memorialize one of the powerful historical facts that confronted the black migrant.

Rachel F. Van Cleave discusses the issue of property, restitution, and ownership rights invoked in the play to the story of those who were enslaved. She points out that

> *The Piano Lesson* teaches us to understand the magnitude of the tragedy beyond the loss of tangible property: the loss of history and community and the potential loss of identity. The failure to recognize and address these concerns in a meaningful way risks generating, or perhaps perpetuating, the type of alienation and desperation that slavery and ... [Reconstruction] ... policies wreaked on the African American community [101].

Van Cleave notes further that "[the play] runs a broad gamut: definitions of ownership, fungible value versus personal value, history as property, property as identity, and most obviously, the tragedy of treating people as property" (101). While Sutter's ancestor meant the piano to represent an exchange of property, a token of his love for his wife, Miss Ophelia, Papa Boy Willie's carving of the family's history on it represents an artistic act of transgression and resistance to legalistic annihilation. Since his family was traded for the piano, they and the musical instrument both were pieces of property. With the Charles family history of theft of the piano, Wilson stages the historical reality of black resilience and subversion in the face of usurpation of their personhood by an oppressive institution.

Doaker explains to Lymon how the piano came to be in his house so many years later in the 1930s. The story illustrates the inhumanity of a system that could trade people for a gift, an accessory, and then ask the one who lost his family in the trade to reconfigure his lost loved ones as an artifact of memory in a white woman's narrative. This is an ultimate show of power and control. While Papa Boy Willie has been denied the opportunity to write this history because of laws prohibiting education to the enslaved, he, nevertheless, has the artistic skill and determination to memorialize them on the very instrument that symbolized their loss. The piano as an object of pleasure and of historical suffering functions in a similar fashion to the quilts that enslaved women created as gifts and accessories for white slave-owners but at the same time served as radical discourses of subversion, escape, and rebellion (Tobin and Dobard).

Also connected to these memories of Parchman is Wining Boy's folk philosophy of the lack of legal protection for African Americans by noting the difference between the white and black man, a difference that lies in the white man's ability to use and control the law: "Now, I'll tell you the difference between the colored man and the white man. The colored man can't fix nothing with the law" (Act 1, Scene 2). His stark observation here transcends the specific moment as it embodies a vast legacy of American injustice, beginning with federal and state laws redefining captive Africans as property. Harry Elam suggests, "It is a moment of embodied performance within performance, within and yet beyond the limitations of theatrical time.... The scene symbolizes the personal hardships and collective social memory of unfulfilled dreams and compensatory separations that blacks suffered under forced enslavement" (27). It is a dramatic moment when Wilson recaptures the fact of ongoing denial of full citizenship that confronted black people even with emancipation.

The play is a performance of African Americans' historical responses to these exigencies. John D. Baskerville characterizes the landscape of the Charleses' world in Pittsburgh as an exposé of blacks' tendency to withdraw into themselves and their community, which functions as a counter-hegemonic process that better facilitates the community's needs. *The Piano Lesson* re-appropriates this revitalization process and what it meant, suggesting that it represented the revival of central cultural beliefs and values that sustained the African American community since the period of enslavement. Such internal markers of black agency are not captured in mainstream historiography, but for Wilson, as his characters reveal, they embody the very foundation for remapping a vibrant subjectivity which sustained the new black migrant community of the North.

African as Site of Memory

Again, as in *Joe Turner*, Wilson's theatrical geography in *The Piano Lesson* shows that blacks were obliged to negotiate the cartographies of memory of traditional African spiritual beliefs, alongside a hostile geographical terrain, to liberate themselves from the shackles of pain and suffering of their ancestral past and to plot a future course in urban America. The ghost of Sutter in the play is a descendant of Robert Sutter who owned the Charles family during slavery. The "Ghosts of the Yellow Dog" are believed to be the spirits of Boy Charles and the other black men burned to death in a boxcar set on fire by white men searching for the piano. Here, they are portrayed as the living dead, or *Tchamba Adé* ancestors whose deaths have not be properly mourned and ritualized.[3] This notion of transcendence and life force beyond death is part of the legacy of Africa and located among the cultural practices and beliefs of early 20th century

African Americans. In *The Piano Lesson*, the legacy affords a powerful counter-claim for African connectedness that disrupts discourse purporting the contrary.

It is a vision that echoes Du Bois' double consciousness and the liminal spaces occupied by blacks for most of the century of their emancipation, yet as Carpentier, Galeano, and Harris suggest, such visions bring all of the characters to a crossroads (domain of the Yoruba god Legba), a place of transformation and transition. In appropriating ghosts of the Charles and Sutter families, Wilson—like Toni Morrison and other African American writers—embraces the importance of African and African American cosmology and folk traditions to black people's identity and concept of self in the early days of the 20th century. To classic historiography, this is often seen as superfluous, nonscientific knowledge, unimportant to the "facts" of the black experience, as typically rendered in mainstream history. W.E.B. DuBois is among the first to reclaim this tradition as vital to capturing a full account of African Americans' world view in his classic *Souls of Black Folk* where each chapter is announced with tracks from one of the black spirituals.

In his study *Postmodernist Fiction*, Brian McHale refers to postmodernist writing as a "confrontation between worlds, through transgressions of ontological levels or boundaries, or through vacillation between different kinds and degrees of 'reality'" (232). From this perspective, then, Wilson's ghosts become important cartographic dimensions of the "ontological borders" of black reality. Susana Vega-Gonzalez refers to this characteristic as a kind of remapping of the "dualistic vision of reality [that is the either/or], typical of the Western culture, [which] gives way to a symbiotic hybridity that puts into question traditional binary opposites such as science/spirituality, natural/supernatural, good/evil, life/death, past/present" (173). In this way, Wilson reclaims and re-animates the marginalized ancestral voices of the African American past, silenced by the oppressive power of the Euro-American narrative of nation, asserting their centrality to his reparative representations of black history. Vega-Gonzalez goes on to suggest that such a "harmonious dialogue between realities" equates to a "counter culture of the imagination ... allowing writers to rebuild historical realities and cultural values that have been systematically oppressed" (173).

This creative act is what Toni Morrison has referred to as "literary archeology" ("Site" 112). "The aim in such an effort is to reconstruct those historical omissions and rescue them by means of memory and imagination" (Vega-Gonzalez 173). Wilson re-appropriates African American vernacular culture on the stage as the vehicle that allows for the resurrection of suppressed histories of the black experience in the 20th century using symbols from this marginalized culture. Again, following in a trend set by DuBois, who framed the text of his revisionist narrative *Souls of Black Folk* with such presentations, August Wilson's piano, with its subversive carvings of the Charles family ancestors, reclaims enslaved Africans' resistance and, like Henry Louis Gates' signifying monkey, offers a key for retracing the routes and maps for decoding the Charles family's (and their community's) legacy of historical resistance. Thus, it is reparative history.

Saunders Redding supports the idea of revisionist historiography in his essay "The Problems of the Negro Writer." Redding maintains that African Americans "preserved their race pride and dignity by dealing with the folk tradition" (57). Similarly, cultural anthropologist Geneva Smitherman claims that "the oral tradition has served as a fundamental vehicle for "gettin' ovuh." That tradition, she argues, "preserves the African American heritage and reflects the collective spirit of the race through song, story, folk sayings, [and beliefs] and rich verbal interplay among everyday people. [For] ... [l]essons and precepts about life and survivals are handed down from generation to generation" (73). Literary artist and anthropologist Zora Neale Hurston as well acknowledged the centrality of African American folklore (and thus the vernacular tradition) as crucial to accurate historical accounts of the African American experience by referring to it as "the boiled-down juice of human living" (qtd. in Hemenway 157).

With the intrusion of the ghost of Sutter as both a literal manifestation and a symbol of the past that both Berniece and Boy Willie, in their different ways, are trying to ignore, Wilson sanctions this cultural referent as a reconnective memory, as way of knowing for African Americans of the Great Migration period. In fact, it can be argued that, as it is a site of memory from the black folk tradition, the ghost affirms that "cultural memory girds the individual in the continuity of life ... [that it is] a conduit for personal and collective memory" (Lassane). At the beginning of the play, as Boy Willie and Doaker talk about Sutter's death, it is clear that their vernacular beliefs are grounded in the historical memory of the community and in conflict with those of Berniece:

> BOY WILLIE: We fixing to have a party. Doaker, where your bottle? Me and Lymon celebrating. The Ghosts of the Yellow Dog got Sutter.
> BERNIECE: Say what?
> BOY WILLIE: Ask Lymon, they found him the next morning. Say he drowned in his well.

Everybody say the Ghosts of the Yellow Dog pushed him.
BERNIECE: I don't want to hear that nonsense. Somebody down there pushing them people in their wells [Act I, Scene 1].

Boy Willie and the other men believe that the "Ghosts of the Yellow Dog" killed Sutter, "like everybody else," Boy Willie says. The African American residents of Sunflower County, Mississippi, attribute these mysterious deaths to those murdered ancestors killed by a white mob. Milton M. Gordon, among other sociologists, has referred to this manifestation as "the sense of peoplehood" (24) or a "shared belief cultivated by a common consciousness resulting in the construction of 'controversial' facts for which there is no simple explanation" (24). Wilson re-appropriates these supernatural forces as integral to evidence of historical accounts of what happened to blacks during the Jim Crow period. Ghosts, or hants, are etched in black memory in the American experience, and black writers like Toni Morrison and Paule Marshall have employed them in narrative respatializations of the black experience in the U.S. "The Ghosts of the Yellow Dog" are, in any event, a phenomenon which concerns the ancestors which, in the tradition of many black Americans of the early 20th century, are crucial to personal and familial grounding.

Innocent Onyewuenyi explains that ancestors are crucial because they are the foundational anchor of traditional African religion and spirituality. He notes further that the essence or nature of anything is conceived by the African as (cosmic) "force," or *Ashé*:

> In line with the hierarchy of forces, the dead ancestors assume an enhanced vital superiority of intelligence and will over the living ... and because of the ontological relationship existing among members of the clan, they interact with the living.... Due to their preoccupation with immortality and deathlessness, the ancestors are concerned with the increase of their and their descendants' vital force for the well-being and continuity of the clan [1].

Henry Louis Gates, Jr., observes in *The Signifying Monkey: A Theory African American Literary Criticism,*

> There can be little doubt that certain fundamental terms for order that the black enslaved brought with them from Africa and maintained through the Mnemonic devices peculiar to oral literature continued to function both as meaningful units of New World belief systems and as traces of their origins ... this topos functions as a sign of the disrupted wholeness of an African system of meaning and belief that black slaves recreated from memory, preserved by oral narration, improvised upon in ritual ... and willed to their own subsequent generations, as hermetically sealed and encoded charts of cultural descent [4–5].

August Wilson retrieves the cosmic figuration of the ghost for its historical centrality to the notion of ancestral timelessness or "hauntology" (Francois) inherent in the black experience and respatializes it in the theatrical cartography of both *Joe Turner's Come and Gone* and *The Piano Lesson*. Not only is this African and African American cosmological fixture underscored, but it is also portrayed as crucial to the attainment of agency and self-affirmation for the brother and sister. In *Joe Turner's Come and Gone*, as well, Bynum Walker's concluding ritual re-invokes the importance of such cosmic manifestations historically as the one re-enacted in the final scene of *The Piano Lesson*. In essence, Berniece, Boy Willie, and the other characters are placed in contestatorial dialogue with African mystical traditions.

That the theatrical geography of Wilson's reparative history of the black experience reclaims a metaphysical, performative dimension that embraces the African American vernacular is evident as the characters must witness the spirits of the Charles ancestors in cosmic contention with those of the Sutter family for the salvation of their progeny, Boy Willie. In re-historicizing blacks' acquisition of agency and subjectivity via such vernacular devices, Wilson renounces the superior claims of eurocentric logos and re-positions black communal knowledge as of irrefutable importance for personal and communal transformation. An ideological account of what happens to Berniece and others in the liminal space of Doaker's home in the scene of Boy Willie's regeneration is articulated by Carpentier, Galeano and Harris in their discussion of a hermeneutical framework for interpreting African spirituality: "This Africa-informed Omni-American attentiveness to a re-grounding ritual practice moves [the characters] to repossession of mind and body and multiple sources of soul (or self)" (9). While Wilson's characters' northerly movements have caused a spiritual dislocation, the respatializing that takes place in this moment has a transformative impact. Wilson underscores the importance of the vernacular as a site of memory in his revisionist theatrical rendering of blacks' experience of emancipation. Berniece must embrace the ancestral knowledge that she used to play the piano for her mother as a child so that she can recognize her role as the spiritual servant of family and communal ritual in the moment when her brother is in a seeming life and death battle with Sutter's ghost. In the final struggle between Boy Willie and Sutter's ghost, Berniece mystically speaks from memory of African rites and addresses the ancestral spirits on the piano; in animating its power or *Ashé*, she accepts responsibility as the guardian of the sacred historical text and the link to the ancestral world:

> I want you to help me
> I want you to help me
> Mama Berniece
> I want you to help me
> Mama Esther
> I want you to help me
> Papa Boy Charles
> I want you to help me
> Mama Ola
> I want you to help me [Act II, Scene 5].

Wilson proclaims the vitality of this dimension of black life and insists on its uniqueness in recapturing the authentic, multidimensional story of black emancipation.

In *Joe Turner's Come and Gone* and *The Piano Lesson*, Wilson's dramatic cartography not only re-situates blacks in 20th century American history, but also produces a counter-discursive testimony and, indeed, engages in a contentious dialogue with other historical discourses about what post-slavery entailed for black people. Wilson's dynamic re-inscriptions allow re-readings of the century of emancipation that unveil the power of cultural traditions hidden in the recesses of black communal history and are vital to the reparation of historical knowledge of the U.S. and of the African American construction of self and community. Theatre, as Addison Gayle has suggested, can be characterized as "ritualized history" (269) since drama affords an occasion for psychic participation on the part of the observer. This being the case, Wilson succeeds in making the audience more cognizant of their responsibility for historical realities that have shaped their lives, as well as of their capability to change those realities which are oppressive and destructive to the society and its people.

August Wilson's *Joe Turner's Come and Gone* and *The Piano Lesson* are dramas that facilitate remappings of the emancipated century in performativities that re-possess the uncelebrated knowledge of African Americans at the margins of American historiography to engage in a reparative account of black urban life in the 20th century. Wilson's appropriation of storytelling and other vernacular devices embraced by black people to archive their experiences reframe emancipation as theatre and becomes a geographic space to re-narrativize the black experience. This use of performance to re-invent history serves not only to excavate a hidden black past, but also to produce a counter-discursive testimony of the African American experience that revises hegemonic historiography of the 20th century. In particular, within the mythic spatiality of the stage, Wilson's recuperations of cultural deposits in African American memory reveal a story of black agency even under conditions of uncertain freedom and citizenship.

Notes

1. According to Leon F. Litwack, Joe Turney embodied the convict leasing system: "By the 1890s, the distribution of black prisoners, most of them arrested on minor charges, and their use (and abuse) as convict laborers had become a way of life in the New South—a source of immense profits for the states and employers, and a source of extraordinary suffering for black men who were all too often worked to death" (270–271). Litwack goes on to point out that

> most of the prisoners had been rounded up for minor infractions, often when police raided a craps game set up by an informer; after a perfunctory court appearance, the blacks were removed, usually the same day, and turned over to Turney. He was reputed to have handcuffed eighty prisoners to forty links of chain. When a man turned up missing that night in the community, the word quickly spread, "They tell me Joe Turner's come and gone" [270].

2. Juba is an African American dance of West African origin created on the slave plantation. According to scholars, enslaved Africans performed the dance during meetings and gatherings and it had its origins in the *djouba* or *gioube* dances of Africa. Juba is not only performed by blacks of the American South, but also by African peoples of Dutch Guiana, Haiti, and other nations of the Caribbean. The dance involved moving in a counterclockwise circular motion accompanied by a foot shuffling, hand clapping, and slapping of the body to approximate the beat of the drum, which was outlawed with the Slave Laws of the 1740s as whites feared slave rebellions. The Africans created substitutes for the drum including "bone-clapping, jawboning, hand-clapping, and percussive footwork" (*World eBook Library*, 30 June 2015). Juba was danced by a circle of men performing a variety of steps, "the juba, the long dog scratch, the pigeon wing" in harmony with call and response rhythms of the other dancers (*Encyclopedia Britannica*, 25 June 2015).

3. According to Togbé Kaley Akpoli, grand hounon of the goddess Mami Wata in the Republic of Bénin, the *Tchamba* are a kind of corporation or assembly of the dead called the *Adé*, which signifies those who did not die a normal death. They died, for example, by accident, by shipwreck at sea or in pirogues, by hanging, war or poison, or by burning in the case of Boy Charles and the other "Ghosts of the Yellow Dog." He indicates that the *Adé* are always present in invisible nature with the Vodou, and because of their abrupt departures, they are restless and usually violent, as they seek restitution and atonement from the living. While I am not suggesting that August Wilson was aware of this specific notion of *Adé* ancestors, the idea that ancestors can be belligerent and dangerous is a common one accepted by both Africans on the continent and African descendants in the diaspora. Their collectivé, according to Kaley Akpoli, is under *Mama Tchamba*, the divine Vodou goddess who has been prominent in her manifestations since the beginning of the

African world (personal interview with Togbé Kaley Akpoli, in Porto-Novo, Republic of Bénin, 11 January 2004).

Àwòtunde Yáò Fáseyan adds the following explanation:

> Because of the Ancestral memories of these people that formed Gorovodu they created, as a central point of the tradition, special rights that honored enslaved Afrikans collectively referred to as *Tchamba* (a Hausa word that means "slave"). It is reported that when the spirits "mount" a Gorovodu devotee the language that is communicated could be one of a number of languages that were exchanged due to the tragedies of slavery, and the cultural amalgamations that followed afterwards. The presence of the *Tchamba* rites is proof that these Afrikans realized the importance of a reconciliation and continual atonement with those Ancestors that had been wronged through the slave tragedy of the Maafa whether it had been done by their Ancestors or not [Àwótunde Yáò Fáseyan, "Traditional African Religion," 17 September 2007, http://newafrikan vodun.com/navthesis.html].

A more recent study has been done on the *Tchamba Adé* ancestors of Yeveh/ Gorovodu spirituality by Judy Rosenthal who argues,

> Yeveh/Gorovodu [*Tchamba Adé*] law says that it is time to respect and commemorate ... this history, these complex [ancestral] relationships, with a new and different longing and a refined concept of sacred debt, [and obligation] thus pushing out ghosts (unwelcome guests) of morbid guilt and rancor, who have long worn out their welcome ... the identities of the ghos-ti, the strangers, hosts, ancestral and foreign guests, with whom Americans have reciprocal duties are ... [the divine *Tchamba* slaves].... Everybody owes the slave spirits— their own descendants and the descendants of the masters and even [those of the Americas] who have no history in common with enslaved Africans, for we all now live on the grounds of their labors and their cultures" [156].

Works Cited

Allison, Robert. "Great Migration: What Caused the Great Migrations?" *History in Dispute. Vol. E: American Social and Political Movements, 1900–1945: Pursuits of Progress.* Detroit: St. James Press, 2000. Print.

Bakhtin, Mikhail. *The Dialogic Imagination.* Austin: University of Texas Press, 1982. Print.

Ballantyne, Darcy. "Respatializing Black Women's Geographies." *Topia. Diasporic Pasts and Futures: Transnational Cultural Studies in Canada.* 17 (Spring 2007). Web. 22 June 2015. http://topia.journals.yorku.ca/index.php/topia/issue/view/ 560/showToc.

Baskerville, John D. "African American Migration." Web. 30 June 2015. http://www. uni.edu/historyofblackhawkcounty/peopimmigrants/African-AmericanMig/ HeadingNorth.htm.

"Behind the Marker." *Explore PA History.* Web. 27 August 2013. http://explorepa history.com/hmarker.php?markerId=1-A-2B.

Blackmon, Douglass A. *Slavery by Another Name: The Re-Enslavement of Black Americans from the Civil War to World War II*. New York: Anchor, 2009. Print.

Carpentier, Alejo, Eduardo Galeano, and Wilson Harris. "Voodoo Hermeneutics/the Crossroads Sublime: Soul Musics, Mindful Body, and Creole Consciousness." Web. 27 March 2014. http://www.thefreelibrary.com/Voodoo+hermeneutics%2Fthe+crossroads+sublime%3A+soul+musics,+mindful...-a0123414397.

Compagna, Adam. "The Devil in Robert Johnson: The Progression of the Delta Blues to Rock and Roll." Web. 27 March 2014.

Davis, Francis. *The History of the Blues: The Roots, the Music, and the People*. Cambridge, MA: Da Capo, 2003. Print.

DuBois, W.E. Burghardt. *Black Reconstruction in America 1860–1880*. New York: Free Press, 1998. Print.

———. *The Souls of Black Folk*. New York: Dover Thrift, 1994. Print.

Elam, Harry Justin, Jr. *The Past as Present in the Drama of August Wilson*. Ann Arbor: University of Michigan Press, 2006. Print.

Ernest, John. *Chaotic Justice: Rethinking African American Literary History*. Chapel Hill: University of North Carolina Press, 2009. Print.

Fishman, Joan. "Romare Bearden, August Wilson, and the Traditions of African Performance." *May All Your Fences Have Gates: Essays on the Drama of August Wilson*. Edited by Alan Nadel. Iowa City: University of Iowa Press, 1994. Print.

The 14th Amendment. Cornell University Law School. Web. 20 August 2013. http://www.law.cornell.edu/constitution/amendmentxiv.

Francois, Irline. "History, Memory and Forgetting: Danticat and Lahens' Haunting Narratologies." Paper presented at the International CAAR Conference. 25 June 2015. Hope University, Liverpool, UK.

Gates, Henry Louis, Jr. *The Signifying Monkey: A Theory of African American Literary Criticism*. New York: Oxford University Press, 1989. Print.

Gayle, Addison. *The Black Aesthetic*. Garden City, NY: Doubleday, 1971. Print.

Gordon, Milton M. *Assimilation in American Life: The Role of Race, Religion and National Origins*. New York: Oxford University Press, 1964. Print.

Haagensen, Erik. "Joe Turner's Come and Gone." *Backstage*. Web. 3 July 2015. http://www.backstage.com/review/ny-theater/broadway/joe-turners-come-and-gone/.

Harrison, Paul Carter. "Praise/Word." In *Black Theatre: Ritual Performance in the African Diaspora*, edited by Paul Carter Harrison, Victor Leo Walker II, and Gus Edwards. Philadelphia: Temple University Press, 2002. Print.

Hemenway, Robert. E. *Zora Neale Hurston: A Literary Biography*. Urbana: University of Illinois Press, 1980. Print.

Henderson, Mae G. "Toni Morrison's Beloved: Re-Membering the Body as Historical Text." In *Comparative American Identities: Race, Sex, and Nationality in the Modern Text*, edited by Hortense J. Spillers. New York: Routledge, 1991. Print.

Katzman, David M. "Black Migration." In *Reader's Companion to American History*, edited by Eric Garraty and John A. Foner. New York: Houghton Mifflin, 1991. Print.

Lassane, Patricia Williams. "'We Carry These Memories Inside of We': The Preservation of Gullah Traditions and Sensibilities in Historic Charlestown." Paper presented at the International CAAR Conference. 25 June 2015. Hope University, Liverpool, UK.

Litwack, Leon F. *Trouble in Mind: Black Southerners in the Age of Jim Crow*. New York: Vintage, 1999. Print.

Maxwell, Justin. "Cartography Lessons with Caridad Svich." Theatre Communications Group. Web. 21 June 2015. https://www.tcg.org/publications/at/julyaugust09/cartography.cfm.

McHale, Brian. P*ostmodernist Fiction*. New York: Routledge, 1987. Print.

Morales, Michael. "Ghosts in the Piano: August Wilson and the Representation of Black American History." In *May All Your Fences Have Gates*, edited by Alan Nadel. Iowa City: University of Iowa Press, 1994. Print.

Morrison, Toni. "Rootedness: The Ancestor as Foundation." In *Black Women Writers*, edited by Marie Evans. New York: Anchor Doubleday, 1984. Print.

———. "The Site of Memory." In *Inventing the Truth: The Art and Craft of Memoir*, 2d ed., edited by William Zinsser. Boston: Houghton Mifflin, 1995. Print.

Newby-Alexander, Cassandra. "Remembrances, Commemorations, and the Spirit Voice: Sacred Spaces in Hampton Roads." Paper presented at the International CAAR Conference. 25 June 2015. Hope University, Liverpool, UK.

Onyewuenyi, Innocent. "Reincarnation: An Impossible Concept in the Framework of African Ontology." *ATR Special Topics*. Web. 20 January 2011. http://www.afrikaworld.net/afrel/atr-reincarnation.htm.

Oshinsky, David M. *"Worse Than Slavery": Parchman Farm and the Ordeal of Jim Crow Justice*. New York: Free Press, 1996. Print.

Pearson, Barry Lee, and Bill McCulloch. *Robert Johnson: Lost and Found*. Urbana: University of Illinois Press, 2003. Print.

Raphael, Ray. *A People's History of the American Revolution: How Common People Shaped the Fight for Independence*. New York: Harper Perennial, 2002. Print.

Redding, Saunders. "The Problems of the Negro Writer." *The Massachusetts Review* 6, no. 1 (Autumn 1964–Winter 1965): 57–70. Web. 30 June 2015. http://www.jstor.org/stable/25087221.

Rocha, Mark William. "August Wilson and the Four B's Influences." In *August Wilson: A Casebook*, edited by Marilyn Elkins. New York: Garland, 1994. Print.

Rosenthal, Judy. *Possession, Ecstasy, and the Law in Ewe Voodoo*. Charlottesville: University of Virginia Press, 1998. Print.

Scott, David. "Introduction: On the Archaeologies of Black Memory." *Anthurium: A Caribbean Studies Journal* 6, no. I (2008). Web. 29 June 2015. http://scholarlyrepository.miami.edu/anthurium/vol6/iss1/2.

Smitherman, Geneva. *Talkin' and Testifyin'*. Boston: Houghton Mifflin, 1977. Print.

"Southern Black Codes of 1865–66." *Constitutional Rights Foundation*. Web. 20 August 2013. http://www.crf-usa.org/brown-v-board-50th-anniversary/southern-black-codes.html.

Taylor, William Banks. *Down on Parchman Farm: The Great Prison in the Mississippi Delta*. Columbus: Ohio State University Press, 1999. Print.

Tobin, Jacqueline L., and Raymond G. Dobard. *Hidden in Plain View: A Secret Story of Quilts and the Underground Railroad*. New York: Anchor, 2000. Print.

Van Cleave, Rachael A. "Property Lessons in August Wilson's *The Piano Lesson* and the Wake of Hurricane Katrina." *Digital Commons: The Legal Scholarship Repository.* Golden Gate University School of Law. Web. 30 June 2015.

Wall, Cheryl A. *Zora Neale Hurston: Folklore, Memoirs, and Other Writings.* New York: Library of America, 1995. Print.

Wilson, August. *Joe Turner's Come and Gone.* New York: Plume, 1988. Print.

———. *The Piano Lesson.* New York: Plume, 1990. Print.

"A big bend there, a tree by the shore"[1]: Situated Identity in *The Janitor*

Jacqueline Zeff

In a 1999 interview for *The Paris Review*, August Wilson describes what drew him to the dramatic form: "I think it was the ability of the theater to communicate ideas and extol virtues. And also I was, and remain, fascinated by the idea of an audience as a community of people who gather willingly to bear witness" (2). When asked how his own testimony of and for the African American community had grown during the 1980s, Wilson acknowledges the challenge in his own evolution as a playwright:

> As you get older there are some things that you can see more clearly than you could five years ago and certainly more clearly than you could twenty years ago ... I can see myself as a young man, when we were trying to alter the relationship of black Americans to the society in which we lived. One of the ways of doing that, of course, was to get some power, and also to alter our shared expectations of ourselves. But one of the things I realized as I was writing *Two Trains Running* was that we had isolated ourselves from the Sterlings of the world. We isolated ourselves from that energy. Somehow by trying to speak for the people we got way out in front of the people and left the people behind; we forgot to follow them where they were going [Pettengill 166].

To be sure, in his full-length plays Wilson frequently offers witness testimony and witness communities on stage, but the assertion of that testimony as a way to create and reveal male agency is never more clearly dramatized than in his one-act play—for monologue it is not—*The Janitor*. As Wilson told Sandra Shannon in their 1991 interview, he was asked to write a four-minute play as part of a fundraiser for New Dramatists, a non-profit workshop for playwrights in New York City which Wilson joined in 1983. Such a constraint proved a productive challenge as Wilson explains:

This was kind of difficult. How do you write a four-minute play? ... So I came up with the idea of a janitor who is someone this society ignores and someone who may have some valuable information, someone who has a vital contribution to make, and yet you have relegated him to a position where they sweep the floor.... And I look at how the Israelis are just absolutely delighted in the fact that they have close to a million Soviet Jews that are coming into the country, and they are looking forward to what those Soviet Jews have to contribute. This is a lot of intellectual power and intellectual potential that is coming into their country, and they're going to use that. And we're sitting here with thirty-five million blacks who have a lot of untapped potential. So there's the idea of not taking advantage of your potential. So I thought I'd show this guy here who is sweeping up the floor, and there's this microphone, and he just goes up and starts talking into the microphone [Shannon 128–129].

It is interesting that Wilson compares the experience of African Americans to that of Soviet Jews, for this is not the first—nor last—time that Wilson finds metaphors and models from the Jewish historical experience. Perhaps in part because Wilson's childhood neighborhood in Pittsburgh was "mostly a mixture of Syrians, Jews, and blacks" (Livingston 41)—but also because Wilson found in the biblical and contemporary Jewish experience a narrative that resonates with his understanding of black history as a "400-year autobiography" (Livingston 60) with its attendant assault on African American culture, language, and space. In his 1988 interview with Bill Moyers, Wilson explores his definition of "African sensibilities" by comparison to the Passover Seder where the narrative of Jewish slavery and redemption is relived every year. Wilson recalls his firsthand experience of the Seder:

A friend of mine invited me to Passover once, and I was struck by the very first words. It starts off, "We were slaves in the land of Egypt." That's the first thing. "Next year in Jerusalem" comes at the end. But they were constantly reminding themselves of what their historical situation had been. I find it criminal that after hundreds of years in bondage, we do not celebrate our Emancipation Proclamation, that we do not have a thing like the Passover, where we sit down and remind ourselves that we are African people, that we were slaves.... Part of the problem is that we don't know who we are, and we're not willing to recognize the value of claiming that, even if there's a stigma attached to it [Moyers 74–75].

Wilson suggests to Moyers that the Juneteenth celebration "should be celebrated like the Jewish Passover wherever blacks find themselves" (Moyers 75). Of course, for Wilson, redemption comes not from miracles performed by an attentive deity: "you're never saved by any outside force. It all comes from within you" (Rosen 195). Even one's connection to the divine is defined from within. Wilson observes in a 1990 interview with Vera Sheppard, "Toledo in *Ma Rainey* says: 'We forgot the names of the gods.' But I have a very simple viewpoint toward that—when you look in the mirror, you should see your God. If you don't then you have somebody else's God" (110).

These lifelong concerns that infiltrate Wilson's interviews and plays explain in part his signature devotion to listening to his characters speak and lead him to create "long speeches that are an unconscious rebellion against the notion that blacks do not have anything important to say" (Sheppard 104). Mr. Collins reflects that viewpoint at the end of *The Janitor* when he urges Sam to "quit wasting time and get this floor swept. There's going to be a big important meeting here this afternoon." But of course Sam has said it all, as Wilson observes: "They're going to get all of these people at this conference to talk about youth—a conference on youth. And all of these people with academic backgrounds and status are not going to say as much in all of their days of seminars and conferences as this man has said there in five minutes. And that was my idea in the play" (Shannon 129).

Wilson's attention to his characters' language is not the only dramatic emphasis in *The Janitor*. In his *Paris Review* interview, after identifying the major influences on his *style*—"*my four Bs*—the blues, then Borges, Baraka, and Bearden"—Wilson explains that his dramatic *form* derives from classical western conventions:

> While I certainly recognize that there are other forms, other approaches to theater, African ritual theater and Japanese Kabuki theater, the theater that I know and embrace is essentially a European art form—the age old dramaturgy handed down by the Greeks and rooted in Aristotle's *Poetics* [5].

Of the six elements of drama considered by Aristotle—plot, character, thought, diction, music and spectacle—it is this last element that prevails and permeates the other aspects of Wilson's play. Spectacle refers to all visual aspects of a production—costumes, props, scenery, lighting. And while years after his *Paris Review* interview Wilson anticipates a truly American theater form that transcends the *Poetics* (Shannon and Williams 242) he manipulates Aristotelian structures to great effect. Aristotle might have considered spectacle the last and least of the elements of a play, according to drama critic Hubert Heffner, but

> when a play is staged through visual and tonal means, spectacle becomes a major part of its presentation. Hence we may say that music and spectacle

become the means of joining the art of dramatic composition to the art of stage presentation [350].

Wilson's readers witness a marvelous affirmation of Heffner's observation and a significant transformation in spectacle from the concept to the script of *The Janitor*. In his description of the emergence of an idea for his contribution to the fundraiser for New Dramatists (cited earlier) Wilson imagines "there's this microphone, and he just goes up and starts talking into the microphone." But the actual stage directions to the play are *"He gets an idea, stops, and approaches the lectern. He clears his throat and begins to speak."* The microphone is not mentioned nor even suggested by any action such as testing or tapping the microphone to determine whether it is on and working. Sam speaks unaided, under his own linguistic power, to what he imagines as a ballroom filled with people. A powerful example of what Wilson calls "loud action" (Livingston 55).

By linking Sam's teachings to a conference on "youth" Wilson invites us to consider what social and cultural factors contribute to the autonomy and integrity of the young learner, especially young black "fellows." By applying what education researchers have described as "situated identity" we may gain a fuller appreciation for Sam's rich imagery, narrative, and sense of self-worth as he testifies from his own lived experience to an audience yet to come. For, as Wilson explains, "I try to position my characters so they're pointed to the future" (Savran 30).

In his article "Identity, Agency, and Culture: Black Achievement and Educational Attainment," Peter C. Murrell, Jr., challenges the popular and in his view simplistic underpinnings of "an achievement gap" mindset in educational research and reform. According to Murrell, the conventionally held position that the underperformance of African American students, especially males, derives from their *"disidentification"* with educational goals and schooling in general (90):

> a stock explanation of black academic underachievement is some version of the notion that African American students *disidentify* with schooling. Operating with this assumption, some authors seem to lay blame for lower academic performance with the individual students and the choices they make that lead to their diminished academic attainment.... Others seem to locate the blame in the bleak prospects of opportunity in the broader social, historical, and political context and the subsequent nihilism felt by young African Americans that diminishes their effort in school [90].

Instead, Murrell offers a deeper interpretation of achievement or underachievement for African American learners that integrates the psychosocial development model formulated by Erik Erikson with what Murrell describes as "situated identity" for African American student learners:

> Situated identity, in simple terms, means that our sense of self, or identity, is not a static, unitary entity but is better thought of as being fluid and situationally expressed. In contrast to the psychological formulation of racial identity as a stable, staged entity, this framework posits racial identity formation as a process reflective of, and situated in social and political-historical struggles.... Situated-mediated identity theory enlarges on the psychobiosocial notion of Erikson's theory by focusing on identity as it is socially mediated and determined by our intentional action—identity is mediated by culture as well as one's own agency.... In the situated-mediated framework, identity is our agency in activity—who we are is constituted by what we choose to do and how we choose to invest that doing [Murrell 98–99].

Or, as Sam explains, "but what you are now ain't what you gonna become." For Murrell—and, I would argue, for Wilson's theater—"an identity is a work in process, but can be mediated in predictable and positive ways if the social context of others is constructed and assembled in ways supported to development" (100). Sam's speech is such a constructed context for his young listeners and offers them a very positive message: that the uncertainties and challenges and even the mistakes they will make do not condemn their futures, which are theirs to control. It is revealing that the sign hanging across the ballroom says it will be a conference *"on* Youth" suggesting an audience of caregivers, teachers or other professionals whereas Sam imagines a conference where he speaks *to* youth.

Murrell outlines three processes of social development essential to an authentic situated identity: an *intrapersonal* identity, an *interpersonal* identity, and a *transpersonal* identity. In *The Janitor* we can see Wilson's remarkably full bodied vision of these processes.

The *intrapersonal identity* development process is that of ego-identity theorized by Erik Erikson. According to Erikson's theory, the adolescent must answer the question, "Who am I?" which can only be found when earlier conflicts in childhood are resolved and one feels independent, competent and in control of one's life. As Justin T. Sokol notes in his article "Identity Development through the Lifetime: An Examination of Eriksonian Theory,"

> When the individual is able to assess their [sic] personal attributes and match these with outlets for expression available in the environment, Erikson would say an identity has been formed.... It is personal coherence or self-sameness through evolving time, social change, and altered role requirements [142].

Sam begins his speech by asserting his sense of self and competence to address the topic of the day: "I's fifty-six years old and I knows something about youth. The first thing I knows ... is that youth is sweet before flight ... and its odor is rife with speculation and its resilience ... that's its bounce back ... is remarkable." While readers are often tempted to interpret the ellipses, for example, when Sam reads the banner aloud, as signs of his lack of literacy or confidence, I would argue that they underscore thoughtful pauses that reveal his determination to be precise and communicate clearly. He in fact explains the terms he is using—a sign of confidence and awareness of his audience. And Wilson's own stage direction notes, "*He chooses his ideas carefully*."

The *interpersonal* identity development process is that of interactional positioning or "footing" as theorized by Erving Goffman. In his examination of face-to-face interactions, Goffman posits that speech should be seen not as a linguistic but as a social or dramaturgical act whereby a speaker positions himself or herself through verbal and nonverbal signals suited to the *context* or situation. For Goffman the world really is a stage. In *The Presentation of Self in Everyday Life* Goffman describes an individual's interaction with others in theatrical terms as *front stage* when the person adjusts his or her behavior to the expectations of an audience—employer, community, social group—or *back stage* when the person is truly oneself and rejects the roles operating when in front of others. Ironically, then, *The Janitor* occurs front stage only for the last line of the play: "Yessuh, Mr. Collins. Yessuh." Back stage, Sam explains himself by referring to one of the all-time situational experts, Iago: "One of them fellows in that Shakespeare stuff said, 'I am not what I am.' See. He wasn't like Popeye'"—i.e., fixed in aspect, tone, and preference for spinach. Sam advocates and reassures his young audience, "You are just what you have been ... whatever you are now. But what you are now ain't what you gonna become ... even though it is with you now ... it's inside you now this instant." Sam confesses that he has sometimes lost his footing, "See ... just like you forgot who I am. I forgot what happened first," but what is clear here is the transactional, interactive nature of the verbal event.

The *transpersonal* identity development process, developed by Murrell, offers a way for youth to gain the "*agency* to improvise their own expressions of self in dynamic interaction with others who may attempt to ascribe unwanted and ego-degrading projections to the individual" (Murrell 97). Improvisation—and interrogation—are the components of agency that permeate Sam's witness testimony and advice. Sam's rich amalgamation of biblical/philosophical/literary metaphors is not the ramblings of an old man but rather underscores his ability to improvise, to capture the fragments of truth and insight that are uniquely his and to offer them to his audience—the river whose name he forgot, our hands in the soup, the music he plays "just so," the down payment on his troubles, Gabriel's horn. He acknowledges those forces that would degrade his understanding of the self, "and like everybody else I have tried to fool them with my dancing ... and guess at their faces." The most compelling of these metaphors is what Sam names "wrestling with Jacob's angel."

According to the biblical narrative, Jacob and his entire household are on their way back to his homeland and to a meeting with his estranged brother Esau. Fearful of Esau's enduring envy and bitterness toward him, Jacob receives the news that Esau approaches with 400 men. Fearful for his family Jacob "divides the people with him, and the flocks, and herds and camels, into two camps, thinking, 'If Esau comes to the one camp and attacks it, the other camp may yet escape'" (Gen. 32: 8–9). These fears lead Jacob to send ahead a caravan of presents for his brother, in hopes they will abate Esau's presumably dire intentions. After sending his family and all his remaining possessions ahead, Jacob sleeps alone. It is in this state of heightened anxiety he must wrestle with an angel all night. When the angel cannot prevail against him he wrenches Jacob's hip at its socket (Gen. 32: 26). Then the angel asks Jacob to release him but Jacob refuses to let go without receiving a blessing, and interrogates the angel about his own name. It is through this act that Jacob receives a new name, Israel—the name of a community—for "you have striven with beings divine and human and have prevailed" (Gen. 32: 29). Jacob is forever wounded by this "wrestling" as manifested by his strained hip. The Bible is unusually clear in connecting this wrestling to Jewish dietary rules: "That is why the children of Israel to this day do not eat the thigh muscle that is in the socket of the hip, since Israel's hip socket was wrenched in the thigh muscle" (Gen. 32: 33). Jacob's story echoes many of the characters in Wilson's plays who are wrestling with contrary fears and dreams, wounded, and ultimately re-named with a new sense of community. Sam comes to this biblical story after proclaiming "we are all victims of ourselves." A most fitting analysis of Jacob's night in the desert. Sam teaches, "You bargaining for your future. See. And what you need to bargain with is that sweetness of youth. So ... to the youth of the United States I says ... don't spend that sweetness too fast! 'Cause you gonna need it. See. I's fifty-six years old and I done found that out."

Situated identity is not only useful in appreciating the complex authenticity of *The Janitor* but may help Wilson's readers unpack and defend his description of Black Nationalism. For Wilson, Black Nationalism has three components: "self-determination, self-respect, and self-defense" (Livingston 57). Wilson's components correspond in fundamental ways to Murrell's paradigm. For Murrell, the situated identity framework offers new insights into how racial identity operates: "The important main idea here is that African Americans do not walk around with 'being black' in their heads, but rather the sense of racial identity of 'being a black person' is evoked by experience in a situational event" (99). To illustrate, Murrell offers his own growing up a black male during the civil rights movement of the 1960s:

> I noted (and still notice) whenever I enter an unfamiliar social setting, whether or not there is another black person in the scene. This is an example of the type of instance that will invoke the sensibility of being African American—that "activates" if you will, my racial identity. It is the particular social frame combined with my personal history of being black that combine to evoke an awareness of being black. Not only does the situativity of a setting evoke the awareness, but it also evokes particular strategies of coping and self-representation (called positioning) regarding how I want to construe myself as a black man in this milieu. The situativity of social identity, and awareness of racial identity, are underscored by the fact that most of the time, in the absence of a race-relevant situational context, I do not walk around with "being black" in my head. Yet any particular moment and situation can evoke a historically shaped, experientially unique racial identity. And this is not to say that positioning requires an explicit awareness of the race-dynamics in a cultural scene [99].

Murrell illuminates racial identity as a situated response that potentially permeates Wilson's own evolution of his conception of Black Nationalism and specifically his positioning as "being black" in the cultural scene that is American theater. And of course, for Wilson, positioning may not have required but surely manifested "an explicit awareness of the race dynamics" of American drama enterprises.

In his critique of Wilson's call for a black theater in support of Black Nationalism embodied in his famous—or "infamous," as Dana A. Williams asserts—speech "The Ground on Which I Stand," John Valery White challenges Wilson's reliance on the "frame" of a Black Power/Black Arts aesthetic. For White, Wilson's argument leaves him devoid of historical or social context and reveals Wilson's dependence on an aesthetic whose "subjectivism preferences the notions of blackness of those who speak loudest and most forcefully" (72). According to White, the social noise created by a political discourse that relies so heavily on symbol, image, and art at the expense of organization, mobilization, and democratic accountability earns Wilson's muddled critique of the problems of the black theater an uncritical celebration that ultimately does a disservice to the cause of rectifying the problems with which he is concerned [72].

And while his critique raises important logical and substantive challenges to Wilson's ideological stance, White's "at least five separate issues demanding quite different responses" in essence are answered in an important way in *The Janitor*. White's five stated issues include

> (1) the funding of black theater, (2) the production of black playwrights' works, (3) the dearth of meaningful opportunities for black directors, actors, performers, and others to work in the theater, (4) the limitations on black artists' self-actualization as artists, given the limited opportunities to express their particular reconciliation of personal and social implications of blackness, and (5) the making of a (or many) black aesthetic(s) [74].

Wilson's advocacy for "self-determination" or altering "the relationship of yourself to the society you live in" (Livingston 58) appears to encompass White's focus on play production and black aesthetics (or definition); "self-respect" includes the self-actualization of an artist's vision; and "self-defense" attends to the economic issues of funding and opportunity to work. Indeed, all five of White's challenges are, subtly, answered by Wilson in the actions and intentions of Sam. Sam solves his funding and production issues by occupying—in actual and political terms—the established theatrical space of the hotel ballroom. His self-promotion from janitor to writer/performer provides him with an opportunity to reconcile his personal experience within historical and social settings; and his call not to "spend that sweetness [of youth] too fast" declares Wilson's belief in the beauty of African American life, even in the days of slavery. For Sam—as for Wilson—"Black America is a tremendous triumph" (Dezell 256).

If indeed identity is "situated," then one must approach life as Wilson describes his janitor: *"He is a man who approached life honestly, with both eyes open."* In fact, Sam's speech-making process resonates with Wilson's description of his own artistic process. When asked by Kim Powers in 1984 if he writes from the audience's total perspective or from the viewpoint of each character Wilson admits that the "characters actually do what they want to do" and the process can be terrifying:

> You're either wrestling with the devil or Jacob's angel, the whole purpose being that when you walk through that landscape you arrive at something larger than you had when you started. And this larger something should be illuminating and as close to the truth as you can understand [Powers 10].

When Sam goes back to sweeping as the lights go down, we know that Wilson's dramatic purpose has been achieved—and in only four minutes.

NOTE

1. The first part of my title comes from Wilson's concluding remarks in *The Paris Review* interview. See Works Cited for full citation.

WORKS CITED

Bryer, Jackson R., and Mary C. Hartig, eds. *Conversations with August Wilson*. Jackson: University of Mississippi Press, 2006. Print.

Dezell, Maureen. "A 10-Play Odyssey Continues with *Gem of the Ocean*." Bryer and Hartig 253–256.

Ditton, Jason, ed. *The View from Goffman*. New York: St. Martin's Press, 1960. Print.

Goffman, Erving. *The Presentation of Self in Everyday Life*. New York: Doubleday, 1956. Print.

Heffner, Hubert. *The Nature of Drama*. Boston: Houghton Mifflin, 1959. Print.

Livingston, Dinah. "Cool August: Mr. Wilson's Red-Hot Blues." Bryer and Hartig 38–60.

Moyers, Bill. "August Wilson: Playwright." Bryer and Hartig 61–80.

Murrell, Peter C., Jr. "Identity, Agency, and Culture: Black Achievement and Educational Attainment." *The SAGE Handbook of African American Education*. Ed. Linda C. Tillman. Thousand Oaks, CA: SAGE, 2009. 88–106. *SAGE Knowledge*. Web. 14 May 2014.

Palmer, Don. "Interview with August Wilson: 'He gives voice to Nameless Masses.'" The New York *Newsday*. 20 April 1987. 47. Print.

Powers, Kim. "An Interview with August Wilson." Bryer and Hartig 3–11.

Rosen, Carol. "August Wilson: Bard of the Blues." Bryer and Hartig 188–203.

Savran, David. "August Wilson." Bryer and Hartig 19–37.

Shannon, Sandra G. "August Wilson Explains His Dramatic Vision: An Interview." Bryer and Hartig 118–154.

____, and Dana A. Williams. "A Conversation with August Wilson." Bryer and Hartig 241–252.

Sheppard, Vera. "August Wilson: An Interview." Bryer and Hartig 101–117.

Tanakh: The Holy Scriptures. Philadelphia: Jewish Publication Society, 1985. Print.

White, John Valery. "Just 'Cause (Or Just Cause): On August Wilson's Case for a Black Theater." *August Wilson and Black Aesthetics*. Eds. Dana A. Williams and Sandra G. Shannon. New York: Macmillan, 2004. 63–77. Print.

Wilson, August. "The Art of Theater No. 14." *The Paris Review* (Winter 1999). Web. 24 Dec. 2013.

____. "The Janitor." *Literature and Its Writers: An Introduction*. Eds. Ann Charters and Samuel Charters. Boston: Bedford, 1997. 1901–1902. Print.

Two Trains Running: Bridging Diana Taylor's "rift" and Narrating Manning Marable's "living history"

Sarah Saddler *and* Paul Bryant-Jackson

> "The darkest aspects of American history have often been hidden from plain view because of the power of the past—or at least the power of the popularly perceived past—to shape the realities of our daily lives."
> —Manning Marable, *Living Black History*

> "The rift, I submit, does not lie between the written and spoken word, but between the archive of supposedly enduring materials ... and the so-called ephemeral repertoire of embodied practice/knowledge."
> —Diana Taylor, *The Archive and the Repertoire*

> "I'm definitely a part of the story. It's my story ... I claim the right to tell it in any way I choose because it's in essence my autobiography."
> —August Wilson, *Two Trains Running*

Following Dr. Manning Marable's death in 2011, the *New York Times* remembered the noted historian and activist as "one of the most forceful and outspoken scholars of African American history and race relations in the United States" (Grimes). Marable's book *Living Black History: How Reimaging the African American Past Can Remake America's Racial Future* (2006) challenges the erasure of African American history within the American archive in order to advocate for a "living history" that exposes the racialized growth of global apartheid. Three years prior to the publication of Marable's text, performance studies scholar Diana Taylor published *The Archive and the Repertoire: Performing Cultural Memory in the Americas* (2003), which addressed how repertoires of embodied practices work in tandem with archival textuality to create and sustain cultural memory. Furthermore Wilson's oeuvre for the theatre draws extensively from a West African oral tradition: stories, memories, and history. These three impulses braid throughout *Two Trains Running* and the Century Project. This essay places Marable and Taylor's theoretical paradigms in dialogue to examine how playwright August Wilson dramaturgically constructs Marable's vision of an African American "living history" through the intersection of material archive and embodied repertoire.[1] The authors have chosen *Two Trains Running* amongst Wilson's century cycle as our point of departure to interrogate how Wilson works to reconstruct and illumine a living African American history through the voices of Marable and Taylor. *Two Trains Running* is Wilson's homage to the racialized politicality of the 1960s, arguably a very pivotal decade in regard to African American history in the 20th century.

Manning Marable begins *Living Black History* by describing his historical inspirations: the death of Civil Rights leader Medgar Evers and the writings of intellectual C.L.R. James. Marable laments Evers' having been gunned down outside of his home in Jackson, Mississippi, in 1963. Marable commends NAACP chairman Evers' tactics to mobilize thousands of black citizens to fight for equal rights throughout the Civil Rights Movement. Marable argues that Evers' legacy has been almost erased from the American political consciousness/text. This has happened through the destruction of archival remains that documented his actions. Marable presents this as evidence that "too often the study of history is an exercise in nostalgia or political myth-making rather than an honest interaction with the raw materials of the past" (xiv). He contextualizes this argument through citing the case of Marxist intellectual C.L.R. James. James's writings on postcolonialism and race are now inaccessible through a series of unfortunate events that occurred after the sudden death of his research assistant. For Marable, such incidents make evident how the intellectual remains of the "great black forerunners" are destroyed for two central reasons: either the institutions harboring such historical documentation neglect to maintain them properly, or the American public chooses to remember only the ideologically pertinent facts of our ancestors.[2] Marable uses the example of Martin Luther King, Jr., to prove this last point. "The Kings' goal is to 'freeze' Martin on the steps of the Lincoln Memorial" (xvii). The authors argue that Marable's project is to uncover a framework by which scholars can historicize and dramaturgically realize a fragmented African American history. Marable suggests that a more nuanced understanding of the dangers of the archive, as well as historiographic attentiveness to the multidisciplinary tools of the repertoire, allows for the illumination of a "living" history (xx).

Living Black History poses new questions concerning the nature of the archive and reframes how the history of racial oppression within the United States is conceived and made operational. Marable's living history methodology is multidisciplinary. He further argues that the methodology must be accompanied by "the tools of oral history, photography, film, ethnography, and multimedia digital technology" (xx). This multiple-prong manipulation of historiographical tools views the archive and repertoire as fluid categories that are constantly in flux and made manifest within the representational practices of everyday life. In total this manipulation creates a living history and begins a civic project that has a firm historiographic agenda and seeks to revitalize scholarly conversations surrounding race within local and national contexts.

Marable labels the previous centuries as periods of "structural racism" that have created a particular politics of seeing in which "the darkest aspects of American history have often been hidden from plain view" (3). Drawing upon elements of critical race theory, a living history approach prompts new forms of visibility. These forms make evident how state-sponsored, institutional racisms affect the everyday lives of citizens of color, in this case, specifically African Americans. This critical approach is based upon Marable's belief that the casting of white citizens as the nation's "primary actors" has created a hegemonic national history that renders all citizens complicit in the erasure of histories of oppression (20). The historian suggests that in order to begin scripting this living history, we must first construct "the authentic history of black people." This authenticity features African American performers and sheds light on an African American perspective.

It is important to note that while this essay focuses on August Wilson, Suzan-Lori Parks' published writings and her play *The America Play* (1994) address similar concerns and label the erasure the "Black Whole of History." The issue is broad and the question of authenticity remains open for debate. Nonetheless and most importantly, Marable also makes clear that he came to realize the necessity of "a multidisciplinary approach, in which archival investigation at traditional institutions might play only a secondary role" (20). This multidisciplinary approach thus finds its origins in historiographical practices and seeks to challenge a master American narrative that legitimizes the oppression of African Americans across all strata of society.

Many scholars in Performance Studies have utilized Marable's interdisciplinary and historiographical approach in composing history. Diana Taylor, in her much-cited book *The Archive and the Repertoire: Performing Cultural Memory in the Americas*, is one such scholar. Taylor urges her readers to consider everyday events that occur in the public sphere as performances in that they rehearse concepts such as "civil obedience, resistance, citizenship, gender, ethnicity, and sexual identity" (7). The peaceful protests of the Civil Rights Movement, the death of Medgar Evers, the assassination of Martin Luther King, Jr., all have performative qualities in that they hold the power to effect and inspire social change. Such a definition of the term "performance" inspires Taylor to consider other definitions of the word, as well as raise some questions about the overall nature of how we as scholars analyze performance events. She asks, "Is performance always and only about embodiment? Or does it call into question the very contours of the body, challenging traditional notions of embodiment?" (4).

In *The Archive and the Repertoire*, Taylor argues that embodied memory, in the form of non-archival material such as photographs, dance, song, etc., have the power to transmit knowledge in innumerable ways. Like Marable, she also expresses concern regarding the valorization and academic anxiety surrounding the material of the archive. Her project calls for a turn away from the written archive in favor of understanding the influence of our performative repertoire. She writes, "nonverbal practices—such as dance, ritual, and cooking, to name a few—that long served to preserve a sense of communal identity and memory, were not considered valid forms of knowledge" (18). In fact, some performances of the past were prohibited altogether, invoking Marable's argument that certain racial memories have been "hidden from plain view" (3). Taylor elaborates,

> The rift, I submit, does not lie between the written and spoken word, but between the archive of supposedly enduring materials (i.e., texts, documents, buildings, bones) and the so-called ephemeral repertoire of embodied practice/knowledge (i.e., spoken language, dance, sports, ritual).

Certain things, Taylor recognizes, have both an "archival and an embodied dimension" (22). Furthermore the rift between oral societies and those rooted in "paper" cannot be minimized or discounted. In all social practices or events, the archive and the repertoire must work alongside each other—simultaneously constructing the past, present, and future of that practice. Taylor cites the historical feats of Christopher Columbus, genocidal concerns notwithstanding, and Neil Armstrong as instances of this transaction. From here, she again reminds us, "the tendency has been to banish the repertoire to the past" (21). Taylor argues that this banishment has "contributed to the maintenance of a repressive social order," and uses certain examples to prove her point that traditionally viewed relationships between the archive and repertoire "often proved antagonistic in the struggle for cultural survival or supremacy" (22). Most interesting for this analysis is that one such example Taylor recognizes here is the lynching of African Americans throughout history. Taylor like many scholars argues that lynchings took the form of performances staged in order to display state power.[3]

The Archive and the Repertoire has retained its seminal status within the field of performance studies as a marker of a paradigm shift that challenges traditional notions of performance's ephemerality.[4] In particular, Taylor proposes a re-thinking of the methodologies by which scholars understand the creation and formation of cultural memory through notions of embodiment. She writes, "Instead of privileging texts and narratives, we could also look to scenarios and meaning-making paradigms that structure social environments, behaviors, and potential outcomes" (28). The *Oxford English Dictionary* defines scenario as "the sketch or outline of the plot of a play." Drawing on and departing from the work of anthropologist Victor Turner, the scenario is an important conceptual tool when reframing the relationship between the archive and repertoire, because it "frames and activates social dramas" (28). The scenario lends its focus not only to written text, but also to embodied behaviors that also serve to e/affect the outcome of that social drama, and thus "history" itself. Taylor's book is the (ironically archivable) exercise into this mode of analysis.

In *Living Black History*, Marable's historiographic-approach toward reclaiming the African American past follows along a similar path as Taylor's performance studies-based analysis of the archive and repertoire. Marable's interdisciplinary/historiographical approach could be read as a call toward the capitalization of the repertoire being enacted as response to the absence of a complete/published African American archive. While it can be said that the historian Marable's methodological focus is not as attached to specifically embodied practice in the same way that Taylor's is, his turn toward non-archived sources as a way of accessing authentic African American history works *alongside* Taylor's framework. Both propose a fresh interdisciplinary approach toward constructing a more authentic history of the convergence of the various cultures that make up our American community. Both also share resonances with Suzan Lori-Parks. The authors would also be remiss in their responsibility in omitting or not mentioning this methodology present in the work of Nobel laureate

Toni Morrison's *Beloved* (1987). *Beloved* is a performative novel that is rooted in African American enslavement, derived from an historical event and is also an imagined living history text. It is a much earlier work that negotiates similar terrains to those in the writings of Parks, Marable and Taylor. There are other "creative" works.

Marable and Taylor recognize that their separate approaches to understanding history are a departure from traditional methods of analyzing and recording the past. Their separate yet interrelated and interdisciplinary approaches toward reclaiming a cultural past have also been a large part of the work of playwright August Wilson. Theatre scholars and historians widely revere Wilson as a playwright interested in textually (and through performance) reclaiming the history of African Americans. Wilson's work takes no concern with recalibrating the African American voice of the past and future. Wilson loudly and often proclaimed throughout the writing of his Pittsburgh century-cycle plays, "I am not particularly interested in history ... you can get that from the history books." Wilson has admitted he relies less on the almost non-existent African American archive and more upon a repertoire of embodied practices, including folklore, dance, and blues music (Shannon). Wilson depends less on historical accuracy and more on the everyday lives of African Americans. Wilson uses the tools of folklore, legend, mythology, and music as powerful devices that push and indeed inform the plot of each story forward. Yet, in Wilson's work, the archive looms in the background, manifested in the presence of the historically significant events of the 20th century. A significant example of how Wilson remakes America's racial future through using a careful combination of the archive and the repertoire is in *Two Trains Running* (1990).

Two Trains takes place in 1969 and as such (re)members much of the 1960s. The '60s were a tensely liminal moment of the African American past. The moment in *Two Trains* illumines the point where the King-inspired period of the Civil Rights Movement is struggling against the recent birth and confrontation of "Black Power." Stokely Carmichael coined the term "Black Power" in 1967, two years prior to the time of *Two Trains*. In 1966, Carmichael was revered in an *Ebony* article, "Stokely Carmichael: Architect of Black Power." Carmichael exploded onto the political scene of the '60s articulating words dripping of radicalism and change. "I refuse to debate the black man's right to self-defense ... to ask anybody in Mississippi to be nonviolent is tantamount to encouraging suicide, and I don't believe in encouraging self-destruction" (Bennett 2). Carmichael's words sharply reflect the changing ideologies and mobilization of the 1960s: a drift from the nonviolent earlier 1960s crusades of the Civil Rights Movement into the starkly confrontational conflict that derived itself from Black Power. Wilson's *Two Trains Running* therefore allows itself the vantage point to look back onto the entire decade and specifically that ideological shift.

The legacy of Medgar Evers not only serves as an inspiration for Marable's *Living Black History* text, but also offers the historical framework behind the events of *Two Trains*. Nine lines into the play, the character Wolf makes first mention of the NAACP and its usefulness. Fiercely fighting using its non-bullet-proof anti-lynching shield, the realism of the NAACP's presence is keenly felt throughout the course of *Two Trains*. The '60s, as evidenced in *Two Trains*, reflect the fact that the Civil Rights Movement was a particularly traumatic moment for the NAACP. Within the same decade that *Two Trains* was written, the organization had dealt with numerous incidents including the murder of its field secretary Evers outside of his home, the assassination of Dr. King, the tumultuous integrations of several southern universities, the continued resurgence and terrorism of the Klan, the assassination of Robert F. Kennedy (seen as a friend to the Negro) and radical ideological shifts occurring within the African American community. These events could be read as a seismic repertoire of activity. (It could be argued that *Two Trains* archives the remains of the 1960s, then performs and lives it as repertoire.) Since the NAACP sought to pass legislation using governmental access, the character Wolf's comment "The NAACP got all kinds of lawyers. It don't do nobody no good" at the opening of the play also suggests a desire for more action and less civil cooperation, a popular Hill District sentiment of the late 1960s. Further and more importantly August Wilson, as young black revolutionary poet, could have also been articulating Wolf's words.

Malcolm X is an important inspiration that motivates and inspires August Wilson's *Two Trains Running*. For a period in the 1960s, Malcolm X was a spokesperson for the Nation of Islam. In his extensive biography on Malcolm X, Manning Marable quotes Malcolm speaking to a *New York Times* reporter in 1964: "There will be more violence than ever this year. The whites had better understand this while there is time." It is important to note that Malcolm X would travel to Mecca shortly after this interview and experience a major philosophical shift in his approach to the teachings and understandings of Islam. (The authors would strongly encourage readers to access Marable's biography for a more comprehensive and evolutionary picture of the African American leader.) Wilson would interject that *Two Trains* embodies a host of voices speaking and reflecting discourses around Malcolm X's earlier and more popular separationist sentiments as well as other sentiments of the 1960s. Memphis, for example, reflects a Malcolm X inspired kind of nationalist consciousness in an early speech, "These niggers talking about freedom, justice, and equality and don't know what it mean. You born free. It's up to you to maintain it." Later on in the text, however, we see Sterling eager to attend the rally commemorating the birthday of Malcolm X with Risa.

The authors spoke of Memphis earlier and would like to return briefly to him and his continued political and thus economic positionality. Memphis can also be read as a reflection of the Fair Housing Act of 1968, a significant legislative move of that decade. Memphis' main concern throughout the play is his property, the restaurant he purchased for $5500 in the Hill District of Pittsburgh. In Act One, Scene One he recalls the moment he purchased the café: "I had seen a way for me to take off my pistol. I got my deed and went right home ... took off my pistol and hung it up in the closet." For Memphis, a hard-working man looking to make his place in the world, as well as a sense of monetary satisfaction, his restaurant informs his self-worth. It is his American Dream. However, now that the city of Pittsburgh is undergoing a vast urban renewal project, Memphis' restaurant must be sold. Declaring that most property belongs to the white man anyway, Memphis is determined to earn at least $25,000 for his building. Importantly, it would be beneficial to remember that the Civil Rights Act of 1968 prohibited discrimination against the refusal to rent/sell property to anyone because of his or her racial status. The necessity for this legislation emphasizes how severe the plight of Memphis would have been at the time if the Housing Act was not present. African American property owners had to fight not only to gain the proper amount of capital that they deserved, but also had to fight against the white-dominated housing market, a market filled with biased and discriminatory practices against African Americans. Memphis does not receive the financial offer he wants at the conclusion of *Two Trains*. Nonetheless he is able to see some gain. Ironically the plight of Memphis foreshadows a central argument of Wilson's last play, *Radio Golf* (2005): gentrification.

These examples indicate how throughout the text of *Two Trains* August Wilson showcases and maintains a dependence on an existing African American archive to shape the text of his plays. Upon a second and closer examination of the text, we can also see a dependence on the repertoire of an embodied West African cosmology, manifested primarily in the characters of Hambone and Aunt Ester. In several of Wilson's plays, he scripts characters that possess spiritual qualities, and an innate knowledge of a West African-inspired universe. Hambone is such an example. Hambone is able to utter one sentence. It is derived from an experience he suffered earlier in his life. The audience hears "I want my ham" numerous times throughout the performance of *Two Trains*. The only deviation from this line that Hambone utters serves as a sort of mystical message to the audience. We hear "United we stand, divided we fall," and "black is beautiful." August Wilson scripts a character who takes charge of what could be the most important lines uttered in *Two Trains*. These are phrases that beautifully capture the struggle of the African American community during this historical period of change. What remains interesting is that Hambone was unable to say, "Malcolm lives," even when Sterling screams at him to utter the sentence. Perhaps this small bit of dialogue was something interjected by Wilson in order to inform the audience that Malcolm X was not, at that time, alive and fighting but should not be forgotten.

Aunt Ester is another character who plays not only a central role within *Two Trains*, but also within the body of work consisting of Wilson's century cycle. Characters flock to Aunt Ester, who is three hundred and forty-nine years old at the time of the play, for her spiritual wisdom and her keen sense of looking into the afterlife. For example, West goes searching for Aunt Ester to inquire into whether or not his dead wife is in heaven. He never receives answers, because he refuses to enact the task that Aunt Ester submits to him. Aunt Ester tells him to go and deposit $20 into the river. Opting for financial satisfaction over knowing whether his wife sleeps in heaven or hell, pragmatism over spirituality, West loses faith in his belief that Aunt Ester is a spiritual being. Belief in the presence of others who possess divine knowledge also manifests itself in the character of Prophet Samuel. People on the hill also flock to him for religious insight. While the other characters, namely Risa, Wolf, and Memphis, remain skeptical of Samuel's actions, his presence suggests Wilson's interjection of spirituality as an important component during this decade and hence into his plays.

Alongside the possibility of the existence of a spiritual dimension, death too plays a leading role throughout the text of *Two Trains*. The overtones of mortality, as well as the funeral ritual, "remain" in the foreground from the opening to the closing of the play. At the start of the action, the audience first hears about the recent death of Prophet Samuel and the upcoming funeral. The last two words they hear from the play centers on arrangements for Hambone's casket. The act of dying and the afterlife is something Wilson also embodies primarily in the characters of Hambone and Aunt Ester. This is seen in Aunt Ester's relationship with those that have died, and the unexpected death of Hambone himself. The combination of the political realities of the 1960s and the spiritual dimensions that exist within African American life illustrates how Wilson has scripted a play that intertwines both the archive of history from the 1960s as well as the embodiment of an African spiritual realm within *Two Trains*.

Two Trains Running is a "living history" text. Recalling Manning Marable, it reflects the everyday lives of African Americans in order to tell a story not available in conventional history books and offers a complex American narrative. It bridges the rift that Diana Taylor has identified between the archive and repertoire by using a methodology that begins to tell an imagined and authentic history of the African American experience. This authentic living history is achieved through its interdisciplinary reliance on the conflicts that arose in the midst of the 1960s political scene. These are imagined at the personal/political level as well within a global and spiritual realm crafted in Wilson's own knowledge of West African spirituality. *Two Trains Running* is indeed August Wilson's story. The play exists as a complex performed and historiographic account of the Hill District, Pittsburgh, Pennsylvania, U.S.A., 1969, and thereby narrates and samples collective African American experiences.

NOTES

1. The authors recognize that Taylor's definitions of "archive" and "repertoire" have been hotly debated because of her claims to materiality—namely, that the archive solely consists of materials (not bodies or temporalities, it is only materials), and that the repertoire is only embodied (which further discounts the idea of bodies as texts, etc.). We are aware that scholars of choreography as well other scholars draw different distinctions.

2. Due to legal complications stemming from the treatment of James' intellectual property post-mortem, those interested in perusing his archive are barred from access; his writings remain boxed up in Columbia University's Butler Library (Marable xvi).

3. A theoretical study of lynching within the context of performance and power is part of the center of the work of scholar Harvey Young's work. Publications of lynching plays are also an element in the works of Perkins and Stevens.

4. This is not to argue that Taylor's work on ephemerality is the first of its kind. The conception of performance as one that "disappears" makes reference to the debate pioneered by performance studies scholar Peggy Phelan in her work *Unmarked: The Politics of Performance* (1993). Phelan argues that the ontology of theatrical practice is manifested in its disappearance, ephemerality, and loss.

WORKS CITED

Fair Housing Act of 1968 with Explanation. 1968. Print.

Grimes, William. "Manning Marable, Historian and Social Critic, Dies at 60." *New York Times*, 1 April 2011. Web. 3 Mar. 2015.

Marable, Manning. *Living Black History: How Reimaging the African American Past Can Remake America's Racial Future*. New York: Basic Civitas Books, 2006. Print.

____. *Malcolm X: A Life of Reinvention*. New York: Penguin, 2011. Print.

"Mission Statement." NAACP: National Association for the Advancement of Colored People. N.p., 2012. Web. 1 May 2012. naacp.org.

Morrison, Toni. *Beloved: A Novel*. New York: Knopf, 1987. Print.

Parks, Suzan-Lori. *The America Play, and Other Works*. New York: Theatre Communications Group, 1995. Print.

Perkins, Kathy A. *Strange Fruit: Plays on Lynching by American Women*. Bloomington: Indiana University Press, 1998. Print.

Shannon, Sandra. "August Wilson Explains His Dramatic Vision: An Interview." In *Conversations with August Wilson*, eds. Jackson R. Bryer and Mary C. Hartig. Jackson: University of Mississippi Press, 2006. 118–154. Print.

Taylor, Diana. *The Archive and the Repertoire: Performing Cultural Memory in the Americas*. London: Duke University Press, 2003. Print.

Wilson, August. *Two Trains Running*. New York: Theater Communications Group, 2008. Print.

Young, Harvey. *Embodying Black Experience: Stillness, Critical Memory, and the Black Body*. Ann Arbor: University of Michigan Press, 2010. Print.

World War II History/history: Essential Contexts in *Seven Guitars*

Ellen Bonds

> "I am not a historian."
> —Wilson, "Note" to *Seven Guitars*

In the prefatory "Note" to *Seven Guitars*, August Wilson avers that he pursued his "interest in history" by imbuing his plays with an "overall historical feel" and foregrounding his characters' "personal histories" as he fit them into the "historical context in which they live." Throughout his cycle, Wilson's interest in history centers on African American history: slavery and its aftermath from the Middle Passage to the Great Migration. And while he sets each of his plays within an historical context of a particular decade, he relies on the culture of that time more so than political events to provide historicity. In *Seven Guitars* Wilson does not recount World War II history; rather, he focuses on the characters' post–World War II struggles to overcome broken promises, social, civil, and economic injustices, and continued conflict on both an internal and communal level—to progress beyond the war and its aftermath.

Still, an understanding of the political history as well as the cultural contexts of the World War II period (late 1930s–late 1940s) helps inform our reading of *Seven Guitars*. If, as Harry J. Elam contends in his *The Past as Present in the Drama of August Wilson*, history can both "shackle" and "empower" African Americans, readers should investigate how Wilson situates his characters within World War II history, in particular African American involvement in the war effort as well as the cultural history represented (in part) by Joe Louis.[1] By considering these essential contexts, readers understand that *Seven Guitars* fulfills Wilson's often-stated purpose: to illustrate the "most important issues confronting black Americans for that decade" (qtd. in Shannon *Dramatic Vision* 3). At issue in 1940s America is the usurpation of racial progress that preceded and exceeded the World War II era and that produced rising frustrations as the consequence of false promises made by white political leaders (including, in particular, Franklin Delano Roosevelt).

Understanding Wilson's incorporation of history in his plays can be challenging because of his use of "deliberate anachronisms" or "multifarious temporalities."[2] In his "Introduction" to *August Wilson: Completing the Twentieth-Century Cycle*, Alan Nadel explains the reciprocal relationship between drama and history as Wilson represents it. Wilson's use of "multifarious temporalities" produces "multifarious perspectives [that] give the specific conflicts of the play their historic dynamics [as] these dynamics give the play's conflicts their historical specificity" (3). Sandra Shannon maintains that Wilson's manipulation of time takes audiences on a "non-linear journey" where the boundaries between "upper-case" events in History and the equally important but often disregarded personal experiences of history are blurred.[3] It is a place where the historical past meets the present. But in *Seven Guitars*, the present environment reflects a determination to move on and forget the past including the war.

A single reference to World War II appears in Scene 4 of *Seven Guitars* where Floyd says, "That's why we won the war.... They got the atomic bomb and everything" (44). Here, Wilson's use of two competing pronouns—"we" and "they"—indicates the uncertain inclusion of African Americans in the national victory. Without Floyd's comment, only the cultural references to Joe Louis and certain blues songs (e.g., "That's All Right") provide clues to the time in which the play is set. Even then, readers must consider not only the post-war year, 1948 or even the decade of the 1940s, but a time that exceeds and transcends categorization along conventional thinking of historical chronology.

Readers can determine the historical time period that informs the play by employing William James' "saddle-back" technique (looking to both the past and the future from the vantage point of the present).[4] Doing so helps reveal the "overall historical feel" of this era, one of racial oppression and African Americans' resistance to oppression, a degree of progress in terms of racial equality, but America's resistance to said progress. *Seven Guitars*, set in 1948, occupies a mid-point in the twentieth century and the mid-point in Wilson's cycle. Looking to the past, readers can note both political and cultural events that helped create the post-war environment in which the characters live. For example, riffing on the number seven from the play's title (as Tony Kushner suggests in his Foreword to *Seven Guitars*), readers can recall that seven years in the past, 1941, the United States entered World War II and Joe Louis fought Billy Conn for the first time. The World War II political history for African Americans involved the fight to overcome continuing oppression on the home front as much as the battle against the enemy overseas. The cultural history, Louis's victory over Conn, provided hope that progress in terms of racial equality could be achieved. The characters in *Seven Guitars* continue to resist injustice as they hope for a better future. Readers can consider how the fight for racial justice during World War II continued seven years into the future, 1955 (the year many consider as the start of the Civil Rights movement). Significantly, scholars have credited African Americans' fight for racial justice during World War II with serving as an origin for the Civil Rights movement of the 1950s.[5]

Even though *Seven Guitars* begins and ends in 1948, the origins of the story's conflict and the consequences of its violent resolution exceed a single year, indeed a single decade. Wilson, no doubt, recognized that the distinction between start dates and origins is important because history cannot be restricted to rigid time lines. In his "Beginning Again, Again," Alan Nadel differentiates between origins and starts, examining the ways that Wilson "[reconfigured] the before/after relationship that informed his history" (15). Since *Seven Guitars* functions as a flashback, its starting point could be Floyd's death or his pre-death. For the history that informs the play, the starting point could be even more ambiguous since the causes of World War II originated decades before 1939, even before the start of the 20th century. Moreover, in *Seven Guitars* Wilson illustrates how the effects racism that existed before and during World War II remained after 1945 (the end date of the war), indeed into the following decades.

In addition to realizing that historical origins and influences transcend decades, readers can benefit from recognizing how the overlap between and among Wilson's plays reinforces the significance of the way that Wilson structured his cycle. Once again, applying James' saddle-back perspective to 1948, ten years earlier takes us to the year after *The Piano Lesson* ends. Ten years into the future takes us to the year after *Fences* begins. As Harry Elam suggests in "*Radio Golf* in the Age of Obama," readers should consider these temporal possibilities since Wilson was interested "in the gaps and fissures in history" into which African Americans' experience (their lower case history) "have too often fallen" (195). Wilson situates his plays to fill in the gaps not only retrieving but more importantly revitalizing African American experience. In *Seven Guitars*, for example, Wilson includes essential history from the past of slavery to the present of continued discrimination and segregation, from the past of the pre–World War II period to the present post-war period which may be hard to distinguish as a new and different time.

When readers examine Wilson's inclusion of essential African American history in *Seven Guitars*, they gain perspective of the play's conflicts by considering how and in what way certain historical events transcended decades. For example, Wilson's reference to the Great Migration helps express his reservations about this key event[6]: c.f., Red Carter's comment, "There ain't nothing but niggers from Mississippi in Chicago. The Sixty-One highway ... run straight north ... [and more importantly] wore many a man out"(I: 5, 59). But significantly, for the purpose of understanding Wilson's choice of the year in which he set the play, readers need to know that the pre–World War II geographical shift in African American population continued to increase during and especially after the Second World War. "Seventy-seven percent of the African American population [were living] in the South in 1940 [but] nearly 50 percent" were living in the North by 1960 ("Postwar Prosperity"). During this second-wave emigration, blacks continued to encounter "overcrowding, discrimination, and violence" in Northern cities ("Postwar"). In her reading of *Seven Guitars*, Sandra Shannon contends that Floyd "Schoolboy" Barton's plight is an affirmation that the "transplant of [the Great Migration] did not take" ("A Transplant"). The characters in *Seven Guitars* as part of a second-wave Great Migration demonstrate that not only did the Great Migration "not take" in 1948 but also for many African American migrants, it did not live up to the widespread myth of the North's being the Promised Land.

To help illustrate the pervasive oppression African Americans experienced during the World War II period, Wilson dramatizes the quest to achieve racial progress through the metaphor of moving—not only from the South to the North, from Pittsburgh to Chicago, but also past the overwhelming presence of death that existed at the end of the war. From the opening scene where they return from Floyd's funeral to Hedley's resistance to admitting the severity of his tuberculosis to Canewell's reaction to the news that George Butler died—"Every time I look up, somebody's dying..."—their attempts not to dwell on death and to move on represent the pervasive post–World War II attitude in America. However, the ability to forget the past and progress to a better future is compromised by their position in American society—a position that has changed little despite African Americans' significant contribution to the war effort.

Although Wilson foregrounds his characters' personal histories in *Seven Guitars*, he noted the significance of World War II political history in his comments about the play's setting. For example, Wilson cited African American's participation in the war effort as the determiner of his choice of year in which to set the play. In an interview with the *Seattle Times*, Wilson maintained that he considered both a pre-war and post-war setting for *Seven Guitars* and chose 1948 because post-war African Americans were full of hope and "'I wanted to touch on that period of hopefulness'" (I-Chin Tu). But John Lahr, in his *New Yorker* piece "Black and Blues: *Seven Guitars* a New Chapter in August Wilson's Ten-Play Cycle," reads the play's characters as "poised between their greatest hope and their greatest heartbreak," quoting Wilson, "'We had just gone off and demonstrated our allegiance and willingness to fight and die for the country.... We actually believed that things would be different, and that we would be accorded first-class citizenship. We came back after the war, and that was not true'" (99–100).

Certainly, before World War II, America's political history in terms of race relations made it difficult to believe that "things" could ever be different for African Americans. The history of the United States' treatment of African Americans before World War II affects the world in which *Seven Guitars*' characters live after the war. Here, readers can note the "before/after" relationship that Nadel cites as essential for informing Wilson's plays. For example, in the years leading up to World War II, African Americans continued to fight racist perceptions and discrimination on the home front. This pervasive discrimination emanated from the top. In one notable event, President Roosevelt refused to support an anti-lynching bill in 1935, a bill that had been sorely needed for decades. However, since the Dyer Bill's defeat by Senate filibuster in 1922, no anti-lynching legislation had been introduced to Congress. Walter White initiated a new proposal—the Costigan-Wagner Bill—but as in 1922 it was defeated. Essentially, Roosevelt capitulated to the southern seniority in Congress to ensure their cooperation on future legislation (Goodwin 163). Some New Deal programs did expand to become more inclusive by 1939, but any progress in racial justice was incremental and met with pragmatic concessions and outright resistance.[7] Overall, the country-wide racism that existed during the Great Depression persisted as the United States geared up for the war.

A study of the history of African Americans' determination to participate in the war effort before and during World War II helps inform the motivation of *Seven Guitars'* characters who remain both determined to strive for a better life and frustrated by continued racial discrimination in post–World War II America. This injustice existed in 1940 as patriotic fervor and calls for national unity were increasing (Goodwin 165). However, once again African Americans were excluded from participating in supporting their country, both in the defense industry and the military. Plants across the country issued statements that blatantly rejected black workers. For example, Vultee Air in California dictated, "'It is not the policy of this company to employ other than of the Caucasian race'" (qtd. in Goodwin 247). A Catch-22 existed that prohibited blacks from being hired to work unless they were union members; however, the union accepted white members only. Still, African American leaders resisted. For example, throughout early 1941, A. Philip Randolph and Milton Webster planned a march on Washington to "[win] Democracy for the Negro [by] Winning the War for Democracy" (see figure 1). Wilson may have been alluding to the history of Randolph and Webster's advocacy and the general "willingness [of African Americans] to fight and die for their country" in his comments to Lahr in the *New Yorker* piece. Previously, Wilson had commented on his characters' motivations in his "Sailing the Streams of Black Culture." In this 2000 *New York Times* essay, Wilson wrote that the characters in his plays act heroically because they "still place their faith in America's willingness to live up to the meaning of her creed so not to make a mockery of her ideals" despite America's history of racial injustice.

In *Seven Guitars*, Wilson depicts his characters' heroics in personal terms as they strive to overcome broken promises and injustice. As Floyd's betrayal of Vera occurred in a time before the action of the play takes place, so did the betrayal of African Americans by America's political leaders in the time before World War II. And, as the past is in the present affecting Floyd's attempts to move forward with his life, so do the events in pre–World War II history provide a lesson in how difficult it was for African Americans to realize progress post World War II. Throughout the late 1930s to the early 1940s, Roosevelt remained resistant to desegregation, and despite Eleanor's advocacy promised her only to "quietly" work with manufacturers and contractors to increase African Americans in their labor force (249). Consequently, A. Philip Randolph realized that more assertive action was needed. In a confrontational meeting June 18, 1941, Randolph demanded that Roosevelt issue an executive order mandating that African Americans be permitted to work at defense industry plants. At first, Roosevelt resisted, but Randolph stood firm compelling

FDR to sign Executive Order 8802 on June 25, 1941. The order promised "to provide for the full and equitable participation of all workers in the defense industries, without discrimination because of race, creed, color, or national origin." However, it would be a promise not kept. In May 1943, the federal government needed to repeat the ban on "contractors from discriminating on the basis of race" (*Chronology* "Part II"). Then on June 20, 1943, a riot erupted in Detroit, the result of continued discrimination and resentment "despite the existence of Executive Order 8802" ("Part II"). *Seven Guitars'* theme of promises made and broken originates, in part, from this history as well as from the history of the United States military's policies toward African Americans throughout the World War II period when African Americans fought not only the enemy overseas but also the perception in America that they were the enemy (see Appendix).

Wilson locates the tension in *Seven Guitars* within the dynamic between hope for progress in racial equality and the frustration at its slow pace. Recalling Kushner's suggestion in his Foreword to *Seven Guitars* to consider the time seven years previous to 1948, readers note that seven years earlier on June 25, 1941, FDR promised African Americans their due civil rights with Executive Order 8802 and the Fair Employment Practices Commission. He had previously promised A. Philip Randolph some civil rights action in return for Randolph's promise not to conduct a protest march on Washington. But it was not until July 26, 1948, that Harry S Truman helped to uphold that promise with his Executive Order 9981.[8] The World War II political history for African Americans can be read in part as a history of broken promises. Any civil rights progress that may have been achieved during the war was limited. For every promising sign of progress, a reciprocal resistance against change occurred.

Wilson dramatizes the political history that included the promise of progress and the resulting frustration from that broken promise through the characters' personal histories and their relationships with their environment and with each other. The theme of broken promises and continued injustice appears from the opening scene of the play where Canewell and Red Carter bicker to get their piece of the pie as Vera proclaims to Canewell, "There's plenty to go around." She is speaking literally about sweet-potato pie, but her statement read in the abstract conveys the belief that everyone will receive his/her just due. Louise's concern that "I don't know how long it be before I eat again" counters Vera's optimism as the reality of post-war opportunities for blacks countered the hope they may have had (8). Here, Wilson illustrates that the post-war posterity is not assured for all Americans, especially African Americans.

Competing with any sense of hope that the characters may have is their awareness of continuing injustice. In Scene 2, Floyd illustrates the relationship between civil and economic injustice when he contends to Vera that his arrest and subsequent 90 days in the workhouse resulted from false accusations and petty charges: "[The judge] gave me ninety days for worthlessness. Say Rockefeller worth a million dollars and you ain't worth two cents." In Scene 3, Canewell argues with Floyd against returning to Chicago because "they arrested me for nothing," and Floyd responds, "You don't have to be in Chicago for them to arrest you for nothing. They arrested me in Pittsburgh. I ain't done nothing but walk down the street" (25–26). Later, Floyd revises his account of his arrest: "'I done nothing. What you arresting me for?' He say, 'I'm arresting you in advance. You gonna do something'" (I: 4, 42). Red Carter contributes his story of being arrested for "having too much money," and Floyd rejoins, "They got you coming and going." Later, he lists the overall lack of fairness: "I had seven ways to go. They cut that down to six. I say, Let me try one of them six. They cut it down to five. Every time I push ... they pull" (2: 3, 78). With the characters' accounts of civil and economic injustice on an individual as well as communal level, Wilson illustrates the ongoing battle for justice that African Americans continued to fight after the war ended, thus employing the "historic [dynamic that gives the play's conflict its] "'historical specificity'" (Nadel 3).

Similarly, Wilson creates the reciprocal relationship between the dynamics of history and the conflicts of the play with the dynamics of Floyd's relationships with Vera and Canewell. These personal relationships involve conflict resulting from a pattern of promises made and broken, reflecting the pattern of betrayal evident in the political history of the World War II period. Significantly, once the play flashes back to Floyd's return, readers can note at least a dozen lines that repeat the promise of a better future in the first three scenes alone. Floyd promises Vera twice in succession, "I'll never jump back on you" (13); "The sky's the limit" (15); "It's different now" (16); "If you try me one more time, you never carry no regrets" (17). He promises Canewell "it's gonna be different this time" (25) and that "Mr. T.L. Hall gonna give us the money. It ain't gonna be like before" (26). Most importantly, he promises himself "I'm gonna play like that one day" and that Mr. T.L Hall would "fix it" so that he could (15). However, as Floyd promises Vera, "I'll never jump back on you," she reminds him that he broke that promise; "you done had more than enough chances" (13). The theme of broken promises continues—Canewell feels excluded from the success Floyd promised; Floyd waits and hopes for another chance for a successful musical recording career; Louise promises Hedley "You don't have to die.... We ain't living back when your grandmother was living" (23, 30). But by the play's conclusion, readers understand that all of these promises will be broken just as many of the political promises were during World War II.

Wilson deepens the historical context of *Seven Guitars* with his inclusion of Joe Louis, whose story provides an essential piece of the play's cultural history as it sustains the theme of promises made and broken. As many commentators attest, before, during, and even after World War II, Louis was *the* individual who represented hope and pride to the African American community. According to Chris Mead, Louis's biographer, "few events were bigger than a Joe Louis Fight" (qtd. in *Joe Louis: America's Hero Betrayed*). Maya Angelou recalls that whenever Louis fought it was "'our day'" and that the entire community came together to listen to the fight and to celebrate the victory (qtd. in *Joe Louis*). Wilson imbues his play with this "overall historical feel" in Act One, scenes 4 and 5 when the characters look forward to the Joe Louis fight and then celebrate Louis's victory.

But the promise that Louis represented for African Americans before, during, and after World War II was usurped by those in power (in both boxing and the military), who exploited Louis for their own benefit. The basic details of Louis's life are fairly well-known. His parents were sharecroppers from Alabama; when his family moved to Detroit in 1926, Louis became a participant in the Great Migration. He began to achieve some boxing success in the mid-1930s, but his two matches against Max Schmeling represented the events for which he became most famous and for which he remains best remembered. Schmeling, a German endorsed by Adolf Hitler, beat Louis in their first fight in 1936 and according to the *New York Post* "broke the hearts of the Negroes of the world." When Louis defeated Schmeling in a 1938 rematch, he recovered his reputation not just as a superior black athlete but as the American hero who defeated the representation of fascism and achieved both an athletic triumph and an ideological victory.

Louis' famous 1938 victory over Schmeling helps inform Wilson's dramatization of the fight in *Seven Guitars* a decade later when Louis remains a hero to the characters. However, Louis's 1948 contest against Jersey Joe Walcott did not provide the historical significance that Wilson desired. As Tony Kushner explains in his Foreword, Wilson changes the details of the 1948, to feature the Louis-Conn fight that had occurred seven years earlier in 1941 because a scene of Louis "in his prime, fighting against a white opponent, suited [his] purposes better than [Louis's fight against Jersey Joe Walcott, another black boxer]" (xvii).

By including this "deliberate anachronism" from Joe Louis's professional history 1938–1948, Wilson provides an essential context for the conflicts that the characters fight between and within themselves, conflicts originating from the persistence of racism in America. For example, from Louis's early success up to and during World War II, his race remained front and center in people's image of him. Jimmy Carter recalls that even for the Schmeling fight, some whites in the South were against Louis (*Joe Louis ... Betrayed*). Chris Mead attests that every nickname assigned to Louis included mention of his skin color: the Brown Bomber, the Black Menace, the Tan Tornado, Black Lightning, Sepia Shocker, Dark Dynamiter, Chocolate Soldier, and Dark Destroyer (*Joe Louis ... Betrayed*). As a result, his managers exerted influence to prevent any associations with the previous black boxing champion, Jack Johnson.[9] For example, Louis was prohibited from being photographed with a white woman and was to conform to behavior that in no way could be construed as threatening to allay white fears.[10]

Louis's managers strove to manipulate his image in a way to gain white acceptance not only of the general public but also, perhaps more importantly, of the professional boxing syndicate. As a result, they insured their own financial success. During World War II, they arranged for Louis to fight in Madison Square Garden on January 9, 1942, at the Navy Relief Society benefit (Sklaroff 958). Louis's $47,000 donation to the victims of the attack on Pearl Harbor was one of his managers' plans to bolster his reputation. So, too, was his induction into the Army (Capeci Jr. and Wilkerson).

Once Louis was in the Army, the U.S. Military began to manipulate him for their own benefit—to boost morale and to try to prove that they were treating African Americans fairly. Louis fought during World War II, but not in combat. During four months in 1943, he "boxed before thousands of soldiers.... Visited G.I.'s in hospitals," gave lectures, traveled 30,000 miles, fought nearly 200 bouts, and entertained over 2,000,000 troops (Capeci Jr. and Wilkerson, 16).

Despite the U.S. Army's attempts to use Louis for their own purposes, he served African American causes during the war. He cooperated with the National Urban League to raise funds; his "Joe Louis Day" aided black disabled veterans (Capeci Jr. and Wilkerson 15). In a Detroit speech, he contended that "[if given defense jobs] and an even break in the Army, [blacks], would show the world how to win this war" (17). He, along with

Sugar Ray Robinson, ignored a "Whites Only" sign at Camp Sibert, Alabama (resulting in their arrest). He listened to black soldiers' complaints and attempted to intercede for them. Jackie Robinson credited Louis with providing intervention that succeeded in Robinson's admission into OCS (*Chronology* "Part II"). Although Louis's participation in World War II may not have changed the military's overall treatment of blacks, "'he slapped Jim Crow in the face'" (qtd. in Capeci Jr. and Wilkerson 17–18). Consequently, Joe Louis became more than just a boxing hero for African Americans during World War II.

Seven Guitars' characters fight to remain hopeful as they refuse to accept the inequities of racial justice in post–World War II America. Their optimistic attitude parallels Louis's confident assertions during the war that African Americans could contribute to the war effort. As Louis famously said, "'Many things [are] wrong with America, but Hitler won't fix them'" and that Americans would win the war "'because we're on God's side'" (qtd. in Capeci Jr. and Wilkerson 13) [see figure 3]. However, their disappointment over the persistence of racial discrimination corresponds to Louis's post-war experience when the IRS, who dismissed his service to his country and counted the attendees at the boxing exhibitions into their calculations of his income, began to harass him for back taxes. As a result, Louis was compelled to continue fighting even after he wanted to retire. Eventually, he accepted some humiliating jobs—as a greeter in Las Vegas and, worse, appearing in staged wrestling matches.

As readers consider Wilson's inclusion of Joe Louis in *Seven Guitars*, it is not just Joe Louis the boxing hero, Joe Louis the racial hero, or even Joe Louis the war hero, that they must keep in mind; it is all of these from pre- during and post–World War II that inform the play. Louis's victory over Schmeling in 1938 represented the turning point to Joe Louis hero for black and white America. The Conn fight and Louis's participation in World War II, then, represent other significant historical touchstones. However, it is the injustice Louis experienced personally, particularly post World War II, that parallels the post war injustice the characters suffer. Moreover, the characters' response in the play, their anticipation leading up to the fight, their celebration after Louis's victory, and their devolution into an argument parallel African American experience from the 1930s to the 1940s.

Living with the persistent racism of post–World War II America, the play's characters appear disappointed—with themselves, each other, their overall position in post-war society—but Louis's fight gives them a sense of hope and their coming together to listen to the fight unites them in one of the play's few scenes of harmony.[11] The audience first hears of the Louis fight following the exchange which foreshadows the play's tragedy—Floyd parries with Hedley over Buddy Bolden's lyrics, Canewell offers to "cut him [Buddy Bolden] for you" and Hedley responds, "I'll cut him myself"— Canewell interrupts, "Joe Louis fighting tonight. We gonna listen to it on the radio" (40–41). Here, Wilson interjects the possibility of something positive albeit ephemeral as Hedley, Floyd and the others continue to debate God, Toussaint Louverture, and racial oppression. The Joe Louis fight interrupts the characters' battles with each other, providing a pause in their discord. Scene 5 opens with the characters putting aside their differences and uniting to listen to the fight. After Louis wins (as he did in both the 1941 Conn fight as well as the 1948 Walcott fight), the characters celebrate Louis's victory "communally" with the Jump Back dance (Elam 22). According to Elam, this performance serves as a *lieux de mémoire* to mark triumph over oppression (22). But here, readers should remember that Louis's triumph was short-lived. After his 1948 victory, his life continued to trend in a more tragic direction.

Another significant detail from the 1948 fight symbolizes the characters' post-war situation. The 1948 Louis/Walcott fight kept being postponed—from June 23 to 24 to 25—then finally on June 26, Louis won in an 11th-round knockout. The "promise" of the fight kept being postponed as the "promise" for a better life for African Americans post–World War II kept being postponed. Despite African Americans' significant contributions to the war effort and Truman's executive order in 1948, the armed forces were not fully integrated until the 1960s and even then racial tensions continued ("Integration").

By *Seven Guitars*' conclusion, the promise of a better life for the characters has been continually postponed, never fulfilled. Floyd promises not to "jump back" on Vera, but by the end of the play, his turn to crime and his confrontation with Hedley result in his death, thus breaking that promise with resounding finality. The contentiousness within the community, which the Louis fight and its celebration interrupted, returns as Floyd and Red Carter fight over Vera. In the stage directions, Wilson writes, "(*Floyd broods. His brooding darkens the stage*)" (53). Here we see that the paradoxical nature of African American World War II experience—fighting a war on two fronts, one against the enemy overseas and one at home against the enemy racism—has resulted in an internalization of conflict within both the community and the individual. Consequently, African Americans suffered from a unique form of post-traumatic stress disorder. They struggled to reconcile their desires—to believe in themselves and to succeed in America—with their fear that entrenched racism may erase their hopes and dreams, indeed destroy their identities. In Act Two, Scene 3 Floyd voices those desires and fears: "I don't want to live my life without ... [I want to] Have something. Have anything.... If it ain't nothing but peace of mind.... It's a cold world, let me have a little shelter from it" (78). Ultimately, however, Floyd fails to resolve his inner conflict.

From *Seven Guitars*' beginning, the characters' internal conflicts erupt into external confrontations. The play opens with Canewell and Red Carter sparring; Floyd argues with Vera and Canewell; Floyd fights with Red Carter over Vera after the Louis bout. Then, Canewell and Red Carter fight over Ruby. The play ends with "another senseless loss of black life" caused by black on black violence (Elam *Past* 51). This cycle of retributive violence continues in *King Hedley II* with the protagonist and his father representing the interiorization of violence directed against the black community (Pease 71). Here, readers can apprehend the reverberations of the history that produced these conflicts as they appear in the overlap between the decades in which Wilson set his plays.

The tragedy in Wilson's *Seven Guitars* results not only from the racist, discriminatory post–World War II environment but also from the characters' internalization of this racism and their inability to resolve conflicts within and among themselves. Their failure to do so originates, in part, from their incapacity to recognize the significant contexts of their political and cultural histories. Harry Elam contends that Floyd's self-centered ambitions coupled with his "betrayal of the power of the blues and values of the community" result in destroying Vera's trust in him, and ultimately, his own life (*Past* 48, 101). Steven Tracy notes the irony that Floyd's and Hedley's "commodification of culture" in the pursuit of material wealth ends with Floyd dead, Hedley a murderer, and money possessing no value. Audiences may understandably struggle with such a pessimistic conclusion. How are they to understand where Wilson leaves his characters? How are they to see the historical context of the characters' situation as a "as a place to envision the past as it ought to have been in order to understand the present and to achieve a future they desire" (Elam *Past* xi)?

The essential historical contexts for August Wilson's *Seven Guitars* as in the other plays in his cycle, range from the cultural to the political as they overlap decades. However, the play begins and ends in 1948 with African Americans who struggle to move on with their lives, who have not benefitted from the post-war economic boom, but who are fighting still. The characters may be "stalled" in time as Kushner contends (viii) or they may be poised on the point of possibility. They may be moving towards a "'new form of positivity and of sudden redistributions'" (Foucault qtd. in Timpane 69). Or they may be moving towards the destiny of Hedley's "son" and Stool Pigeon (an aged Canewell) in *King Hedley II*. They do not want a future life like that of the post–World War II Joe Louis; they want a life like the pre–World War II victorious Joe Louis. Hedley does not want a future like that of the past Buddy Bolden's (who was institutionalized not for tuberculosis but for alcoholism and mental illness).[12] *Seven Guitars*' characters, then, fit Alan Nadel's description of a "Jazz set" ... with "subversive chord structures [and] competitive rhythms" (*May* 5). At the end of the play, they remain performing in alternating moments of harmony and dissonance with Vera speaking of hope, and Hedley, who crumbles the money like "ashes" or death, suggesting truth.

Notes

1. Wilson's use of the blues in *Seven Guitars* constitutes significant cultural context. See Steven C. Tracy's "The Holyistic Blues of *Seven Guitars* in *August Wilson: Completing the Twentieth-Century Cycle*."

2. For a discussion of Wilson's use of anachronisms see John Timpane's essay in *May All Your Fences Have Gates* and Tony Kushner's Foreword to *Seven Guitars*. I am also indebted to Alan Nadel and to the Wilson conference, August Wilson: The Second Half of the Cycle, for suggested ways of characterizing history and time in Wilson's work.

3. See Shannon's presentation at the August Wilson conference cited above.

4. John Timpane applies James' theory to his reading of Fences.

5. See, for example, Herman Beavers who contends that the 1940s "laid the seeds for the nascent civil rights movement that flowered in the next decade" (115).

6. Harry Elam in his *The Past as Present in the Drama of August Wilson* includes other African American history. He reads Hedley as the "embodiment of the black diaspora [where] the slave trade ... the legacy of colonialism ... the heritage of the native uprisings and Toussaint Louverture all congeal" (67). Elam's explanation of the Great Migration is that it "distanced [African Americans] from their ancestral, cultural, and spiritual foundations" (174).

7. One way to regard the dynamic of promises made and broken is to note the history of social justice causes that Eleanor Roosevelt championed and FDR's response to her advocacy. As Goodwin explains, "Eleanor thought in terms of what *should* be done, Franklin thought in terms of what *could* be done" (163).

8. Once again, Philip Randolph exerted pressure on the president to enact this order.

9. Nineteen years after Johnson became world champion, black boxers were not allowed to fight for the championship because as Louis's biographer, Chris Mead, explains, America hated Jack Johnson.

10. See, for example, the article "Why Joe Louis Must Never be Champion."

11. In January 1948, before the actual fight, the *New York Times* called Joe Louis "the top disappointer."

12. Harry Elam discusses the history of "racial madness," and the Lafargue clinic in his *The Past as Present* 62.

Works Cited

Beavers, Herman. "You Can't Make Life Happen Without a Woman: Paternity and the Pitfalls of Structural Design in *King Hedley II* and *Seven Guitars*." *August Wilson: Completing the Twentieth-Century Cycle*. Ed. Alan Nadel. Iowa City: University of Iowa, 2010. 110–22. Print.

Brooks, Gwendolyn. *Selected Poems*. New York: Harper and Row, 1944. Print.

Capeci, Dominic J., Jr., and Martha Wilkerson. "Multifarious Hero: Joe Louis, American Society and Race Relations during World Crisis, 1935–1945." *Journal of Sports History* 10, no. 3 (Winter 1983). 26 Mar. 2008. http://www.la84foundation.org/SportsLibrary/JSH/JSH1983.

A Chronology of African American Military Service. 13 Mar. 2003. http://www.redstone.army.mil/history/integrate/chron3b.htm.

Elam, Harry J., Jr. *The Past as Present in the Drama of August Wilson*. Ann Arbor: University of Michigan Press, 2004. Print.

———. "*Radio Golf* in the Age of Obama." *August Wilson: Completing the Twentieth-Century Cycle*. Ed. Alan Nadel. Iowa City: University of Iowa Press, 2010. 186–207. Print.

Goodwin, Doris Kearns. *No Ordinary Time/Franklin and Eleanor Roosevelt: The Home Front in World War II*. New York: Simon & Schuster, 1994. Print.

Hietala, Thomas R. *The Fight of the Century: Jack Johnson, Joe Louis, and The Struggle for Racial Equality*. Armonk, NY: M.E. Sharpe, 2002. Print.

Hoyt, Davina. "Tuskegee Airman of World War II." *USD History Department*. 3 Nov. 1996; 13 Mar. 2003. http://history.acusd.edu/gen.

I-Chin Tu, Janet. "The Evolution of '*Seven Guitars*'—August Wilson Surprised Himself with the Twists That Entered His Play, a 40s Blues Saga Opening at the Rep." *Seattle Times*, 25 Dec. 1997. Web. 7 Aug. 2012.

"Integration of the Armed Forces." *African Americans in World War II*. 3 Mar. 2003. http://www.redstone.army.mil/history/integrate/welcome.html.

Joe Louis: America's Hero Betrayed. HBO, 23 Feb. 2008. Television.

Kushner, Tony. Foreword. *Seven Guitars*. New York: Theater Communications Group, 2007. Print.

Lahr, John. "Black and Blues: *Seven Guitars* a New Chapter in August Wilson's Ten-Play Cycle." *New Yorker*, 15 Apr. 1996: 99–101. Web. 25 Feb. 2013.

Morehouse, Maggi M. "World War II." *Encyclopedia of African American History, 1896 to the Present: From the Age of Segregation to the Twenty-first Century*. Ed. Paul Finkelman. Oxford: Oxford University, 2012. Web. 8 Jan. 2013.

Nadel, Alan. "Beginning Again, Again: Business in the Street in Jitney and Gem of the Ocean." *August Wilson: Completing the Twentieth-Century Cycle*. Ed. Nadel. Iowa City: University of Iowa, 2010. 14–29. Print.

———. "Introduction." 2010. *August Wilson: Completing the Twentieth-Century Cycle*. Ed. Nadel. Iowa City: University of Iowa, 2010. 1–14. Print.

———. *May All Your Fences Have Gates*. Iowa City: University of Iowa, 1994. Print.

Nalty, Bernard C. "World War II." *Encyclopedia of African American Culture and History*. Eds. Jack Salzman, David Lionel Smith, Cornel West. New York: Macmillan Library Reference, 1996. Volume 5, 2883–2890. Print.

Pease, Donald. "August Wilson's Lazarus Complex." *August Wilson: Completing the Twentieth-Century Cycle*. Ed. Alan Nadel. Iowa City: University of Iowa, 2010. 71–96. Print.

"Postwar Prosperity, 1946–1973." *Gale Encyclopedia of U.S. Economic History*. Eds. Thomas Carson and Mary Bonk. Detroit: Gale, 2000. Volume 2, 812–815.

Shannon, Sandra. *The Dramatic Vision of August Wilson*. Washington, D.C.: Howard University Press, 1995. Print.

———. "A Transplant That Did Not Take: August Wilson's Views on the Great Migration." *African American Review* 31.4 (Winter 1997): 659–666.

———. "Turn Your Lamp Down Low! Aunt Ester Dies in [King Hedley II] Now What?" August Wilson: The Second Half of the Cycle conference, University of Kentucky Press, Lexington, 4 Apr. 2008.

Sklaroff, Lauren Rebecca. "Constructing G.I. Joe Louis: Cultural Solutions to the 'Negro Problem' During World War II." *The Journal of American History* 89.3 (December 2002): 958–983.

Timpane, John. *May All Your Fences Have Gates*. Ed. Alan Nadel. Iowa City: University of Iowa Press. 1994. 67–85. Print.

Tracy, Steven C. "The Holyistic Blues of *Seven Guitars*." *August Wilson: Completing The Twentieth-Century Cycle*. Ed. Alan Nadel. Iowa City: University of Iowa, 2010. 50–70. Print.

Wilson, August. *Seven Guitars*. New York: Theater Communications Group, 2007. Print.

The Use of Stereotype and Archetype in *Ma Rainey's Black Bottom*

Michael Downing

> I am one of those warrior spirits. The battle since the first African set foot on the continent of North America has been a battle for the affirmation of the value and worth of one's being in the face of this society that says you're worthless.
> —August Wilson

> Here in America whites have a particular view of blacks. I think my plays offer them a different way to look at black Americans.
> —August Wilson

Levee Green, Troy Maxson, Boy Willie Charles, and King Hedley II are character creations of August Wilson that embody the spirit of the warrior archetype. It should come as no surprise that August Wilson himself embraced that designation (Bigsby), especially considering that he fought a protracted battle to resurrect, preserve, and sanction the commonplace customs and rituals of African American culture since he began his career as a playwright. Part of this battle has involved subverting cultural stereotypes historically assigned by whites to blacks and remaking those them into archetypes. By doing so, he forged a new mythology for people of African descent living in America. In a 1991 interview with Wilson critic Sandra Shannon, Wilson said, "The one thing we did not have as blacks was a mythology" (Wilson "Blues, History and Dramaturgy" 545). As a cultural warrior with a goal of changing the way white people "look at black Americans" (*The Paris Review*), Wilson was successful in creating a mythos that has been embraced by African American actors, directors, and audiences across the United States, even into

England and China (see August Wilson Blog: http://augustwilsonblog.wordpress.com/).

August Wilson's role as cultural mythmaker is well established. Trudier Harris claims that Wilson is "in the business of expanding—within established patterns—what African American folklore means and what it does ... he is as much a mythmaker as he is a reflector of the cultural strands of the lore he uses" (49). Michael Feingold argues that Wilson is "a mythmaker who sees his basically naturalistic panorama-plays as stages in an allegorical history of black America" (270). Joan (Fishman) Herrington writes that August Wilson (along with Romare Bearden) "addressed what Wole Soyinka describes as the 'deep-seated need of creative man to recover this archetypal consciousness,' and their art, which shares many characteristics, shares most of all its ability to speak across racial and cultural lines" (145). Pamela Jean Monaco says Wilson "reveals through his writing the beauty and nobility in the struggle to survive. By doing so, Wilson transforms drama from a spectacle observed to a ritual, a ritual that affirms a common vision, thereby elevating the story of local history to the mythical" (89). Referring specifically to *Fences*, Kim Pereira writes, "the search for identity by blacks is an exploration of their individual characteristics, their mythic signification, and their struggle to integrate with society" (52). In an interview with Sandra Shannon, Wilson himself recognizes his own efforts to "keep all of the elements of the culture alive in my work, and myth is certainly a part of it. Mythology, history, social organizations, economics—all of these things are part of the culture" ("August Wilson Explains His Dramatic Vision: An Interview" 119).

One essential aspect of Wilson's mythmaking is to elevate the commonplace into the holy. In an interview with *The Paris Review*, Wilson said, "Blacks see the content of their lives being elevated into art.... They don't always know that it is possible, and it's important for them to know that" (Wilson "August Wilson, the Art of Theater"). This effect is often achieved by portraying an initial pejorative, racist stereotype, unvarnished. From there, additional information is provided, often in the form of monologue, which provides additional perspective on the stereotype from an African American point of view. This allows the stereotype to be reclaimed and reinscribed with meaning that originates from within the African American community rather than from without. The end product is a stereotype that has been converted from one that evokes criticism, suspicion, and scorn into an archetype that evokes empathy, understanding, and compassion, promoting the characters and situations to mythical status.

For example, *The Piano Lesson* opens with Boy Willie Charles and Lymon Jackson, two black men, driving a truck load of watermelon to Pittsburgh. The historical association of blacks and watermelons clearly has been pejorative and racist, but the play does not shy away from this initial depiction and any negative associations that might arise. The stereotype is converted when Boy Willie reveals his plan to sell the watermelons—along with the family's heirloom piano—combine that money with money he already has in order to purchase land down South. In this way, the watermelons represent an opportunity to improve Boy Willie's future, not as a means to insult him and keep him down.

For the purposes of this study, the word "stereotype" is defined as an amalgam of characteristics typically applied externally by one group of people to another. "Pejorative, racist stereotype" means the characteristics are designed to reinforce the alleged superiority of one group over another. "Archetype" is defined according to the concept espoused by mythologist Joseph Campbell in *The Power of Myth*. Here, Campbell describes "archetype" as an "elementary idea" that is deeply rooted in the stories, legends, and rituals of a particular culture, with the "differences in the costumes" being a result of "environment or historical conditions" (61). For Campbell, the warrior archetype, for example, universally manifests itself in all traditions, the only difference being the outward appearance of the character. Wilson himself saw a relationship between the "universal" and the "specific" as evidenced in his interview with *The Paris Review*: "You can be specific as to a time and place and culture and still have the work resonate with the universal themes of love, honor, duty, betrayal, etcetera (Wilson "August Wilson, the Art of Theater").

In *Ma Rainey's Black Bottom*, Wilson's technique of initially depicting a character in stereotypical fashion begins with his portrayal of Ma Rainey herself. Ma does not take the stage until the play is nearly half over, but before she emerges, Wilson has already cast her in a negative light by having Sturdyvant, the record producer, make pejorative remarks about her. Sturdyvant says that he does not want Ma "march[ing] in here like she owns the damn place" (18). He also says he does not want any of that "Mother of the Blues bullshit" (18). In addition to being late for the session, Ma is involved with a white police officer, who is prepared to charge her with "assault and battery" (49); she inexplicably brings her nephew, the stuttering Sylvester, insists that he perform the introduction to her song (75), and she arbitrarily demands a Coke before she will sing (76). Ma barely sets foot on the stage before Wilson casts her as late, allegedly difficult, chaotic, at risk with the law, unreasonable, and evidently not committed to the cause in the same way that the white "businessmen" are.

In *Ma Rainey*, Wilson offers a depiction of Ma that is equally unflattering; however, as the play unfolds, Wilson provides the critical background information necessary to deconstruct the initial stereotype. Ma is late to the recording session because she and her "entourage" were in a car accident on their way to the recording studio. This incident seems serious and dramatic at first—and creates chaos on stage—but then we learn from Irvin that the accident resulted in nothing more than a "scratch" to the car (61). The situation is certainly not as dramatic as it first appeared. Sylvester, who was driving, says, "The man hit me" (49). So Ma and her party were not necessarily at fault. Wilson indicates that the charge of alleged "assault and battery" was a direct result of racism as the white cabbie was trying to prevent Ma, a black woman, from entering his cab. The cabbie's interference, based wholly on race, not only caused him to be knocked down during the altercation, it also made Ma late to the recording session and pulled the police into the situation. All accounts suggest Ma was not at fault, so the initial chaos cannot be fairly attributed to her. In these ways, Wilson presents and then deconstructs several initial stereotypes related to Ma.

By the end of the play, Ma is reconstructed as archetype. She is cast as mother, queen, and goddess. Her relationship to Sylvester is specifically one of archetypal "othermother," which Patricia Hill Collins defines as women "who assist bloodmothers by sharing in the mothering responsibilities" (178). Ma's insistence that Sylvester be included in the production fulfills the function of othermother. Ma says, "I promised my sister that I'd look out for him and he's gonna do the voice intro on the song my way" (62). Ma is prioritizing family. Despite Ma's relative power and determination, Wilson casts her as arbitrarily difficult to underscore the stereotype of the angry black woman. In this case, Ma shows bravery by standing up to those who control the production process. For his part, Sylvester is ultimately successful in recording the intro, despite his stutter. He faces the world bravely and succeeds.

In Act II, Wilson invokes the stereotype again with Ma's arbitrary demand for a Coke, which seems outrageous, particularly for a woman in 1927. However, power and self-determination and is not afraid to cast Ma as arbitrarily difficult in order to do so. The band is about to record the song "Ma Rainey's Black Bottom" when Ma asks for a Coke, saying, "You know I don't sing nothing without my Coca-Cola!" (76). Irvin admits that he forgot the Coke and tries to quell Ma, but then Wilson has Sturdyvant step up and reinforce the stereotype: "Now, just a minute here, Ma. You come in an hour late ... we're way behind as it is ... the band is set up and ready to go.... We're ready to make a record and what? You decide you want a Coca-Cola?" Irvin gives in and offers to call the deli and get a Coke, but he wants to wait until they record one song. Ma resists and tells Sylvester and Slow Drag to go the store on the corner and buy three bottles of Coca-Cola.

The play then evokes empathy by changing its depiction of Ma. Instead of continuing to allow Sturdyvant to drive the narrative, Ma says:

> White folks try to be put out with you all the time. Too cheap to buy me a Coca-Cola. I lets them know it, though. Ma don't stand for no shit. Wanna take my voice and trap it in those fancy boxes with all them buttons and dials ... and then too cheap to buy me a Coca-Cola. And it don't cost but a nickel a bottle [79].

This evokes empathy and enables the character depiction to be altered. Then Ma says, "They don't care nothing about me. All they want is my voice. Well, I done learned that, and they gonna treat me like I want to be treated no matter how much it hurt them.... As soon as they get my voice down on one of those recording machines, then it's just like if I'd be some whore and they roll over and put their pants on" (79). Framed in this context, Ma's request for a Coke is not unreasonable. Instead of being arbitrarily demanding, her request becomes a strategy of self-determination comparable to Wilson's belief in "black self-determination against the hegemony of the white controlled culture industry" (Elam 223). Ma's position can also be seen as an effort to gain symbolic compensation beyond what she and the band will be paid in actual dollars, which, as history has demonstrated, will in no way be enough to adequately reward them for their work.

Once empathy is established for Ma, she is converted into a queen, which was hinted at by Sturdyvant himself early in the play. As queen, Ma not only stands up for herself but for her race and her gender in this economic/social transaction. She is, to use the vernacular, "representin.'" She embodies the empowered African queen archetype. Sandra Shannon recognizes Ma's queenly qualities in her regard for the blues singer as "at once a symbol of the African continuum and a reminder of the resilience and perseverance of Ma's people. She is their queen" ("The Blues on Broadway" 83). Shannon further argues that Ma's role is important "in preserving as well as promoting elements of African American culture" (87). This also has mythic import as it satisfies the "sociological component" of

Joseph Campbell's "Four Functions of Myth," which is to "validate and maintain a certain sociological system: a shared set of rights and wrongs, proprieties or improprieties, on which your particular social unit depends for its existence" (*Pathways to Bliss* 8).

Robert Bly offers a powerful archetype for Ma Rainey in his description of her as "The Woman Who Looks Two Ways" (141). Bly argues that such a woman has "two faces" and the ability to look two ways simultaneously. She has the power to "get the plot of life moving ... [she is also] instigating, up-leaping, fiery, outrageous" (142). Ma has the ability to look two ways. Her role as queen and othermother positions her to deal with white "gods" of the capitalist world, Sturdyvant and Irvin. At the same time, she works to preserve and expand upon a space for herself, her family, and her culture. Doris Davis argues that Ma Rainey, along with Aunt Esther (in *Gem of the Ocean*) and Berniece (in *The Piano Lesson*), "represents Wilson's dramatic archetype of the strong matriarchal female, the bearer of memories and wisdom, whose songs—though varied in nature—are at the center of their lives and provide an anchor for themselves and others" (166). Davis also claims that Ma represents Wilson's "prototype for the assertively voiced female" (173), one who takes good care of Dussie Mae and Sylvester, buying them "clothes, shoes and whatever they need" (173).

In all of these ways, Ma is effectively converted from stereotype to archetype and occupies a place as a self-assertive goddess in Wilson's pantheon. Ma becomes archetypal. She has become a mother, queen, and goddess—one who is able to challenge assumptions about power, gender, and social status. Ma is able to stop time in the studio because she needs a Coke, to find a role for all of her children, including her stuttering nephew.

The character of Levee begins as the stereotypical "angry" black man who contests everything. He argues with everyone on stage. He argues about shoes, the value of reading books, and the style of music the band is playing, which he calls "old jug band" music (repeatedly in Act I). Wilson also depicts Levee as ignorant, which is a pejorative, racist stereotype that Wilson is ready to depict and then complicate: Levee claims to know how to play "real" music, yet when challenged by Toledo to spell the word "music," Levee spells it "M-U-S-I-K," prompting Toledo to tell Levee how "ridiculous" he is (28).

After establishing the initial stereotype, the text provides critical background information on Levee that evokes empathy, diminishes the stereotype, and amplifies Levee's archetypal qualities of warrior/savior.

For example, Wilson describes how an eight-year-old Levee had attempted to intervene as his mother was being attacked and raped by a gang of white men when the family was living in the South:

> My daddy went into Natchez to get some seed and fertilizer.... My mama was frying up some chicken when them mens come in that house. Must have been eight or nine of them. She standing there frying that chicken and them mens come and took hold of her just like you take hold of mule and make him do what you want.... She tried to fight them off, but I could see where it wasn't gonna do her any good, I didn't know what they were doing to her ... but I figured whatever it was they may as well do to me too. My daddy had a knife that he kept around there for hunting and working and whatnot ... I tried my damnest to cut one of them's throat! I hit him in the shoulder with it. He reached back and grabbed hold of that knife and whacked me across the chest with it. (Levee raises his shirt to show a long ugly scar.) That's what made them stop. They was scared I was gonna bleed to death. My mama wrapped a sheet around me and carried me two miles to the Furlow place and they drove me up to Doc Albans [69–70].

In suffering a near-death experience in order to save his mother, Levee proves himself willing to offer the ultimate sacrifice: the spilling of his own blood to save another. In this way, Wilson deconstructs the initial "angry black man" stereotype. When Levee is placed into the context of this story of maternal love and blood sacrifice, his depiction is altered and his archetypal qualities as both warrior and savior emerge.

Levee is a complicated figure, however, and is not defined by the light of archetype as clearly as Ma Rainey. In fact, the interpretation of Levee as savior may seem inappropriate, based on his rant *against* God, late in Act II:

> Cutler's God! Come on and save this nigger! Come on and save him like you did my mama! Save him like you did my mama! I heard her when she called you! I heard her when she said, "Lord, have mercy! Jesus, help me! Please, God, have mercy on me, Lord Jesus, help me!" And did you turn your back, motherfucker? Did you turn your back? ... Turn your back on me, motherfucker! I'll cut your heart out [99].

However, it is imperative to remember that the black and white mythologies within the play are inverted. As Levee utters this "blasphemy," he is directing it toward a "white" god, one who, at best, turns his back on African Americans, and who, at worst, sanctions violence against them. At this point in the play, Levee is experiencing a surge of his ancestral identity, and, as a result, he cries out for all of those souls who have been abused by this "white" god and this "white" mythology. In this sense, Levee can be interpreted as an archetypal figure inhabiting a mythological system that, as the play demonstrates, emerges from a "world that was not of their making, in which the idea of themselves as a people of eminent worth that believed their recent history was continually assaulted" (Preface to *Three Plays*).

As a result of this inverted existence, Levee's unconscious impulses appear to emerge irrationally. His subconscious impulse is to pray, to call out to a higher power. Unfortunately, because he occupies a white mythology whose god is deaf to him, the prayer comes out as a violent rant. Kim Periera writes, "Devoid of their mythological dimensions, [Wilson's] characters, Levee, Troy and Boy Willie, in their separate plays, are merely destructive forces at odds with their world instead of agents of change challenging the status quo and reordering their universe. Within the full context of their cultural ancestry, they are the warrior spirit reincarnations of self-empowered trickster deities, figures which recur in myths from the Yoruba Eshu to the Hindu Krishna" ("Music and Mythology" 65).

Levee needs to find his own mythology—his own "song"—in order for his cry to be heard and answered. Faced with the mythological denial of his spiritual existence, Levee experiences extraordinary confusion concerning his psychic identity, his personal god, and the members of his mythological community. This confusion, according to Pereira, is evidenced when Levee "eschews his own people because he does not recognize them for the real friends they can be and turns instead to the white man as he seeks to fulfill his destiny through a contract with a member of the same race that destroyed his family and cast him adrift in the first place" (22). In the end, Levee's efforts to control his own destiny fall short.

Levee, not able to reconcile his violent past, is doomed to relive it. Sturdyvant's rejection angers Levee, and since Levee is not positioned to gain retribution on Sturdyvant, takes grievous offense at Toledo, who inadvertently steps on Levee's shoe. An argument ensues between Levee and Toledo, and Levee succumbs to his violent past, stabbing and killing Toledo. The character of Levee transforms from stereotype to archetype; however, once he becomes the warrior, his psychic circumstance prevents his success in that role. The warrior lashes out, but lashes out at the wrong target, evoking another ugly stereotype: black-on-black violence.

Sturdyvant's familiar pattern is subverted as he converts the music producer from all-powerful "god" archetype to predatory "white devil" stereotype. The role of Sturdyvant as god begins with his disembodied voice in the very first line, which comes through a speaker from the control booth. The stage directions mention several times how the booth is positioned above the action and only can be reached by a "spiral staircase." He is a businessman and music executive in the 1920s, which means he has a great deal of power and influence. In these ways, Sturdyvant is god-like. Within a capitalist mythology, Sturdyvant is a god because he is able to manipulate the lives of those who enter into his kingdom, which is essentially economic.

As the play unfolds, empathy for Sturdyvant diminishes. His spiritual aspect contracts and he is converted into just another exploitative, capitalist "businessman" who disregards essential human qualities in order to make a profit. Sturdyvant's intention is to steal Ma's voice. He says, "I just want to get her in here ... record those songs on that list ... and get her out. Just like clockwork" (18). Later in the play, he says he just wants Ma to "sign the forms" (105). As such, Wilson depicts Sturdyvant as being disconnected from Ma's concerns, whether those concerns involve providing her with a Coke or inquiring as to her well-being after the automobile accident. In these ways, Wilson diminishes empathy for Sturdyvant and changes his depiction of him from revered god to pathetic cliché.

Furthermore, the all-powerful Sturdyvant is revealed as incompetent. In Act II, once Ma finally sings "Ma Rainey's Black Bottom," Sturdyvant says (over speaker), "Irv! Something's wrong down there. We don't have it right" (86). At first, they try to blame the mishap on Levee, saying he "kicked the plug out" (86). But, ultimately, the problem was a "chewed up" cord (86). Evidently, for all of his music industry prowess, Sturdyvant is not able to ensure that all of the equipment had been tested and functioning properly. Empathy is also erased when it is revealed that Sturdyvant's subconscious does not allow him to conduct his business unfettered. Sturdyvant admits it haunts him by disturbing his sleep:

> STURDYVANT: I don't even know why I bother with this anymore.
> IRVIN: You did all right last time, Mel. Not as good as you did before, but you did all right.... Okay, so they didn't sell in New York. But look at Memphis ... Birmingham ... Atlanta. Christ, you made a bundle.
> STURDYVANT: It's not the money, Irv. You know I couldn't sleep last night? This business is bad for my nerves. My wife is after me to slow down and take a vacation. Two more years and I'm gonna get out ... get into something respectable. Textiles. That's a respectable business. You know what you could do with a shipload of textiles from Ireland? [19].

There appears to be no compelling reason to suspect that Sturdyvant will leave the music business, especially when there are other musicians—like Levee—who seem to be eagerly waiting to be exploited.

Throughout the play, there are numerous examples of Sturdyvant dismissing African American archetypal qualities. For example, he does not appreciate Ma's role as "Mother of the Blues," which he calls "bullshit" (18). Without hesitation, he exploits Levee by asking him to write several Blues songs, which Sturdyvant initially promised to record. At the end of the play, Sturdyvant refuses to record Levee's songs but offers to buy them for five dollars apiece, saying, "Well, Levee, like I say ... they just aren't the kind of songs we're looking for ... but I'll take them off your hands for you" (108). For Sturdyvant, the value of blacks is determined by how much money they can earn for him, and his understanding of Blues music exists only at the level of commodity.

In contrast to this position, Wilson's personal consideration of the Blues is strikingly different. He offers his personal insight into this conflict between African and European perspectives on the Blues when he writes,

> Blues is the best literature we have. If you look at the singers, they actually follow a long line all the way back to Africa.... They are the carriers of culture, carriers of ideas, like the troubadours in Europe ... I found that white America would very often abuse them. [If you destroy the Blues] you're taking away from a people their self-definition. These guys were arrested as vagrants and drunkards and whatever. They were never seen as valuable members of society by whites [Wilson "Blues, History and Dramaturgy" 541].

By the end of the play, the character of Sturdyvant has been converted entirely into a self-interested, money-grubbing stereotypical character. He has no appreciation for any archetypal qualities that the black characters might have. He only values blues music as commodity; he tries to avoid paying Sylvester; he has reneged on his promise to help Levee record his songs; and he ultimately perpetuates the exploitation of black musicians by offering to buy Levee's songs outright, with no consideration of future royalties. Sturdyvant represents all of the heinous and exploitative stereotypes long associated with the "white devil."

Though this paper examines only *Ma Rainey's Black Bottom*, Wilson's technique of constructing and then deconstructing stereotypes—often converting them into archetypes—is evident in every play of his famous Century Cycle. Troy Maxson in *Fences* is initially cast as a garbage man, but he goes on to wrestle directly with Death; Bynum Walker, who is involved with "mumbo jumbo nonsense" and inexplicably kills a pigeon at the beginning of *Joe Turner*, emerges as a shaman who is able to "bind" family together. For August Wilson, confronting all of the elements in the ancestral past of African Americans—positive and negative—is essential in deconstructing and reconstructing an authentic identity that serves as a model for the future. In his own life, Wilson underwent this process of conversion. Born Frederick August Kittel, Jr., Wilson deconstructed his identity and reinvented himself as August Wilson, archetypal sage and storyteller, a warrior spirit who is not afraid to confront the pejorative, racist stereotypes faced by African Americans in his plays. In this way, he fashions a new mythology and a new future for generations of black Americans who experience his work.

WORKS CITED

Berman, Paul. Rev. of *Ma Rainey's Black Bottom*. *The Nation*. December 8, 1984. 626–628. Rpt. in *Contemporary Literary Criticism* 39, 279–281. Print.
Bigsby, Christopher. *The Cambridge Companion to August Wilson*. Cambridge: Cambridge University Press, 2007. Print.
Bly, Robert. *Iron John: A Book About Men*. Reading, MA: Addison-Wesley, 1990. Print.
Campbell, Joseph. *The Hero with a Thousand Faces*. Princeton: Princeton University Press, 1949. Print.
_____. *Pathways to Bliss: Mythology and Personal Transformation*. Novato, CA: New World Library, 2004. Print.
_____. *The Power of Myth*. New York: Anchor, 1991. Print.
Davis, Doris. "'Mouths on Fire': August Wilson's Blueswomen." *MELUS* 35.4 (Winter 2010). Print.
Elam, Harry, Jr. *The Past as Present in the Drama of August Wilson*. Ann Arbor: University of Michigan Press, 2009. Print.
Feingold, Michael. "Romare Bearden and August Wilson." *May All Your Fences Have Gates: Essays on the Drama of August Wilson*. Ed. Alan Nadel. Iowa City: University of Iowa Press, 1993. Print.
Harris, Trudier. "August Wilson's Folk Traditions." *August Wilson: A Case Study*. Ed. Marilyn Elkins. New York: Garland, 1994. Print.
Herrington (Fishman), Joan. "Romare Bearden, August Wilson, and the Traditions of African Performance." *May All Your Fences Have Gates*. Ed. Alan Nadel. Iowa City: University of Iowa Press, 1993. Print.
Hill Collins, Patricia. *Black Feminist Thought: Knowledge, Consciousness, and the Politics of Empowerment*, 2d ed. New York: Routledge, 2000. Print.
Monaco, Pamela Jean. "Father, Son, and Holy Ghost: From the Local to the Mythical in August Wilson." *August Wilson: A Case Study*. Ed. Marilyn Elkins. New York: Garland, 1994. Print.
Pereira, Kim. *August Wilson and the African American Odyssey*. Urbana: University of Illinois Press, 1995. Print.
_____. "Music and Mythology in August Wilson's Plays." *The Cambridge Companion to August Wilson*. Ed. Christopher Bigsby. Cambridge: Cambridge University Press, 2007. 65–74.
Rich, Frank. "A Family Confronts Its History in August Wilson's *Piano Lesson*." *New York Times* 17 April 1990, C-13. Rpt. in *Contemporary Literary Criticism* 63, 456. Print.

Shannon, Sandra. "The Blues on Broadway: *Ma Rainey's Black Bottom*." *The Dramatic Vision of August Wilson*. Washington, D.C.: Howard University Press, 1995. Print.

Wilson, August. "August Wilson." A World of Ideas. Interview with Bill Moyers. 1988. Web.

———. "August Wilson Explains His Dramatic Vision: An Interview." *Conversations with August Wilson*. By Sandra Shannon. Jackson: University Press of Mississippi, 2006. Print.

———. "August Wilson, the Art of Theater No. 14." Interview with Bonnie Lyons and George Plimpton. *The Paris Review*. Web.

———. "Blues, History, and Dramaturgy: An Interview with August Wilson." By Sandra Shannon. *African American Review* (Winter 1994). Print.

———. *Fences*. New York: Penguin, 1986. Print.

———. *Gem of the Ocean*. New York: Theatre Communications Group, 2006. Print.

———. *Joe Turner's Come and Gone*. New York: Penguin, 1988. Print.

———. *Ma Rainey's Black Bottom*. New York: Penguin, 1985. Print.

———. *The Piano Lesson*. New York: Penguin, 1990. Print.

———. Preface. *Three Plays*. Ed. Paul Carter Harrison. Pittsburgh: University of Pittsburgh Press, 1991. Print.

Gem of the Ocean's Fugitive Movements

Isaiah Matthew Wooden

Throughout his twentieth-century history cycle, August Wilson carefully traces distinctions between law and justice. The incommensurability of law and justice recurs as a trope most poignantly, however, in *Gem of the Ocean*, the play that launches Wilson's project to write ten plays, each set in a different decade, that collectively offer a multidimensional portrait of black life in America.[1] In *Gem of the Ocean*, the law is ever-present. It chases folk to their deaths; it barges into places—peaceful homes—where it is neither welcomed nor invited; it repeatedly makes itself known. Justice, on the other hand, proves more elusive. Indeed, for the black residents of Wilson's imagined Pittsburgh, justice is often fugitive. Justice is only ever achieved through radical acts: that is, acts that undercut, subvert, escape, or exceed the law. Wilson's decoupling of the oft-consolidated notions of law and justice in *Gem of the Ocean*, I contend, opens critical space to investigate a history that sees the law consistently reconfigured and reorganized to criminalize the black: that is, a history that pits blackness against the law, a history that archives the necessary alignment of blackness with the fugitivity of justice. More significantly, the disentanglement of law from justice in *Gem of the Ocean* invites a serious consideration of the question: Why is justice so fugitive, particularly for the black?

This question has animated a number of critical projects and popular discussions in recent years. Scholars Stephen Best and Saidiya Hartman, for example, offer it up for reflection in their introductory essay to the special issue of the journal *Representations* dedicated to the concerns of the Redress Project.[2] In the essay, Best and Hartman, much like Wilson, look across time to evidence the inadequacy of courtrooms and legislative chambers—i.e., the law—as sites for seeking justice on behalf of the slave, the ex-slave, and their descendants. They cite the story of Callie House, a Tennessee seamstress and co-founder of the National Ex-Slave Mutual Relief, Bounty and Pension Association, who, along with her colleagues, petitioned the United States Congress "to pass Senate Bill, No. 1718, introduced June 6 1898, by Senator Mason, of Illinois, Providing pension for Freedmen, etc." (qtd. in Best and Hartman 6). In the written request, House and her counterparts declared, "We believe it *just* and right to grant the ex-slave a petition" (qtd. in Best and Hartman 6; emphasis added). Congress, of course, defeated the petition, along with five other pension bills that came before the body between 1890 and 1903. Best and Hartman go on to recapitulate several cases in which blacks turned to the law to seek redressive action for the injuries of slavery and note the futility of those efforts. Despite multiple appeals to the law across time, justice for the slave and her descendants remained on the run.

More recently, the shooting death of seventeen-year-old Trayvon Martin illuminated just how little had changed vis-à-vis the inadequacy of courtrooms as sites for seeking justice in the years since House and her colleagues issued their petition. A trip to the convenience store to purchase candy and iced tea in February 2012 quickly turned deadly for Martin. George Zimmerman, a neighborhood watchman in the gated Sanford, Florida, community where Martin's father lives, determined that the boy was suspicious and reported his presence to the police upon seeing him. And despite instructions from a 911 operator not to follow Martin, Zimmerman proceeded to do so anyway. The details of what happened next are murky. What's certain is that when police arrived onto the scene, Martin was dead. Zimmerman shot him once in the chest; he claimed he did so in self-defense. Zimmerman was taken into custody, questioned for five hours and ultimately released without being charged with a crime by police. That he could profile, follow and shoot Martin with impunity sparked a national outcry. Protesters around the United States echoed Martin's parents' calls for Zimmerman's arrest and shared their desire to see justice served for the death of their son. It would take nearly six weeks before a special prosecutor would charge Zimmerman with murder, however. It would take more than a year before the case would go to trial. Throughout that time, Martin's character remained under attack. Indeed, during the trial, Zimmerman's attorneys boldly claimed that Martin "did, in fact, cause his own death."[3] In the end, a jury of six women, five white and one Hispanic, found Zimmerman not guilty of all charges. Martin's parents' appeal to the law to seek justice for the death of their son, in other words, proved futile. For the Martins and their many supporters, justice once again remained on the run.

In the aftermath of Zimmerman's acquittal, many have taken up Best and Hartman's charge to interrogate rigorously the fugitive nature of justice, of blackness, and of justice for the black. A close examination of *Gem of the Ocean* reveals that Wilson's dramaturgy shares a similar interest in exploring and scrutinizing this fugitivity. To be sure, what's at stake in *Gem of the Ocean*, to echo Fred Moten, is fugitive movement: that is, movement whose "relation to law is reducible neither to simple interdiction nor bare transgression" (179). Wilson scripts fugitive movements in *Gem of the Ocean*, in part, to bear witness to the vast chasm that exists between law and justice for the black. More than that, he scripts fugitive movements to ponder the question: What is justice for those folks who have been declared and/or who relish being a problem? Set at the dawn of the twentieth century and just a few decades after the end of chattel slavery and the subsequent Reconstruction period, Wilson peoples *Gem of the Ocean* with such folk.

Gem of the Ocean, in fact, unfolds against a backdrop of fugitive movements—of migrations northward—in search of oft-escaping freedom, justice, and equality. A gripping exchange between Citizen Barlow and Aunt Ester early in the play details these fugitive movements. In the exchange, Citizen recounts for Aunt Ester how he snuck out of Alabama where "they had all the roads closed to colored people" to come North in the hopes of finding greater opportunities (22). Citizen, in other words, arrives in Pittsburgh a lawbreaker. Of course, what Citizen encounters in the North are the doubles to the systems of exploitation and dehumanization he attempts to dodge by fleeing the South. In the North, as in the South, the project of emancipation remains unfinished. What distinguishes the two geographical locations, however, is that, in the North, the mill replaces the plantation and a brutal black hand, the hand of Caesar Wilk's, substitutes for the white face of the law. Justice remains fugitive in both spaces. Indeed, for Citizen, questions about the time of slavery and the fugitivity of justice become ever more urgent in the North.

Wilson's fashioning of a Pittsburgh community in which former slaves, Aunt Ester, Eli, Solly Two Kings, and people born "after freedom came," Citizen and Black Mary, commix adds to this urgency (26). In addition to reemphasizing the critiques Wilson levies throughout the *Pittsburgh Cycle* against historiographical practices that privilege a linear, chronological sense of temporality and that envision the past replaced by a purportedly more enlightened present, this commixing opens critical space to make legible the histories—of slavery, of discrimination, of injustice—that haunt the theatrical now and, crucially, the political present. These histories offer myriad examples of the role that the law has played in perpetuating injustices against the black. They also offer myriad examples of the ways that the black, much like Citizen, have initiated fugitive movements to circumvent the law in their quests to seek justice.

Citizen repeatedly moves against the law in a search of justice in *Gem of the Ocean*. Knowledge of the gap between his imaginings of the North and the reality of his experiences there, along with a cognizance of the fugitive nature of justice for the black, compels him to perform a radical act of subversion soon after his arrival in Pittsburgh, in fact. In a confessional exchange with Aunt Ester, he describes the act and the circumstances that brought it about: "I stole a bucket of nails. The mill wouldn't pay me so I stole a bucket of nails" (44). Citizen re-narrates his lifting of the bucket of nails from the mill as a *just* act. The absence of equity for the mill worker, he contends, spurred his movement toward "being a problem," toward becoming a fugitive. Wilson's selections of a bucket of nails as the object of Citizen's theft may, at first, seem a curious choice. On its own, a bucket of nails lacks consequential value. It holds little promise for profit. Indeed, it will not repay the debt that the mill owes to Citizen. Still, within the context of an industrial mill, that very same bucket of nails is at once essential and invaluable. Its contents carry the potential to unite, bind, and hold together disparate materials for the production of goods, for the generation of profits, and, consequently, for the successful operation of the mill. In many ways, the bucket of nails is symbolic of the black mill workers in *Gem of the Ocean*. Like the bucket of nails, they are consistently undervalued both within and outside of the mill; and yet, they are absolutely crucial to the mill's proper functioning. When they go missing, much like the bucket of nails, mayhem ensues.

Citizen's theft of the bucket of nails sparks a spate of fugitive movement, movement aimed at escaping the repressive action of the law and staking a claim for justice, in *Gem of the Ocean*. In response, the law activates its police power. The law, Best and Hartman write, produces fugitive identities "to justify [the use of] police power, to justify the exercise of the power to kill (10).[4] In *Gem of the Ocean,* the character of Caesar Wilks, the local constable and opportunist who instills fear in the residents of Pittsburgh's Hill District through the threat of police action and, more often, violence, represents and embodies the law. To maintain his position and power, Caesar considers everyone under his jurisdiction—namely, the blacks—a criminal. In his first interaction with Citizen, for example, he threateningly warns, "I don't want to catch you stealing nothing. I catch you stealing something I'm gonna put you in jail" (31). Later, when Citizen rebuffs his advice and returns his gift of twenty-five cents, Caesar asserts, "I can see you one of them hardheaded niggers. You have to bust you upside the head a couple of times. Then you straighten up. You watch yourself. See, 'cause you just got on my list. I told you I'm the boss man around here. Ask anybody. They'll tell you who Caesar is" (32). Caesar casts Citizen as a "hardheaded nigger" in order to justify his use of force, his use of police power, to bring him under the control of the law. Through the character of Caesar, Wilson interrogates a set of discourses that insist the subjugated remains as such because they have not yet fully come into or earned the right to claim their positions as modern (or post-modern) citizens. What Caesar's engagements with these discourses evidence are the lengths to which those in power go to maintain that power, including exercising the power to kill.

Moreover, in giving the law a black face, Wilson makes salient the ways in which ideologies of white supremacy sometimes exceed the boundaries of racial categories and seep into the consciousness of the very subjects that such ideologies aim to subjugate. Access to the slightest sliver of power encourages the interpellator to perform vigorously their duties to maintain the white supremacist social order. Caesar is a vigorous performer. The character recalls a fraught history of black overseers who, at the behest of white slave owners, wielded violent hands on plantations as a way to prevent the fugitive movement of fellow slaves.[5] Solly, in an exchange with Black Mary, notes this resemblance: "Caesar's the kind of people I would want working for me. If I ever get me a plantation I'm gonna hire him to keep my niggers in line" (14). Moreover, the name Caesar, Harry Elam argues, conjures thoughts of Julius Caesar (or Caesar Augustus) as well as "the blaxploitation film of 1973, *Black Caesar*, written and directed by white film director Larry Cohen and featuring Fred 'the Hammer' Williamson in which the figure of Black Caesar, with the help of a corrupt white police office, became the power broker, ruling over Harlem" (Elam, "Redemptive Power" 82).[6] To be sure, Caesar is a surrogate for and a synecdochical representation of the white repressive legal system that persists, at least for the black, as a structure that takes—lives, freedom, justice—with impunity in *Gem of the Ocean*.

The law, in fact, is partially responsible for taking the life of Garret Brown, a worker at the mill made fugitive by Caesar, in the play. Caesar chases Brown into the local river, accusing him of stealing the bucket of nails that Citizen purloined from the mill. Eli recounts Brown's death for Rutherford Selig, the white traveling salesman who frequents Aunt Ester's home, when the latter man observes that the mill at the center of the play's economy is shut down for the day. He explains, "They had a man named Garret Brown who jumped into the river. Caesar chased him and he jumped in and wouldn't come out. They say he stole a bucket of nails. He say he didn't do it. They having his funeral today" (11). Brown's dive into and refusal to come out of the river—this, as Aunt Ester remarks, in an effort to die in truth rather than live in a lie—signifies on the history of fugitive slaves and their descendants who "wade in the water" to escape the bloodhounds of the law on their way to freedom, in their search for justice.[7] The spectacularity of Caesar's pursuit of Brown, Brown's ultimate death, and Caesar's campaign to prevent Brown from having a church burial proves galvanizing. Like the theft that precedes and produces them, these spectacles spur a series of resistive actions and fugitive movements: most significantly, the shuttering of the mill and its eventual burning down.

In *Gem of the Ocean*, the mill represents the asymmetrical relations— that is, the relations of exploitation—inherent in systems of capitalism for the black. Much like the plantation, the mill produces incredible profits for its proprietors. At the same time, however, its very structure prevents those who labor in its confines from benefiting from the profits that their efforts generate. For the mill workers in Wilson's imagined Pittsburgh to live, as Eli instructs at the play's end—that is, to live fully and freely—the mill has to burn down. Solly Two King intimates as much when he admits to starting the blaze: "Yeah, I burned it down! The people might get mad but freedom got a high price. You got to pay. No matter what it cost. You got to pay. I didn't mind settling up the difference after the war. But I didn't know they was gonna settle like this. I got older I see where I'm gonna die and everything gonna be the same" (75). What Solly highlights here is the incompleteness of the project of emancipation, the ultimate failure of the project of Reconstruction, and the endurance of the project of slavery. He imagines his burning down of the mill as a kind of curtain call—as a bow to justice. Significantly, the act offers a reminder that, for some, the pursuit of justice and freedom requires fugitive movement: that is, movement against the law.

Solly serves as a great champion for justice across *Gem of the Ocean*. Not surprisingly, he is also the character for whom Wilson scripts the most extensive history of fugitivity. In fact, up until his death at the hands of the law near the play's end, Solly remains on the run and, while there, he vigilantly grapples with questions about the temporality of slavery and the fugitivity of justice. After handing Citizen a piece of chain link, he relays that his journey as a fugitive began in 1857, five years before the signing of the Emancipation Proclamation:

> That's my good luck piece. That piece of chain used to be around my ankle. They tried to chain me down but I beat them on that one. I beat them on a lot of things. I beat them when I got away. I had some people who helped me. They helped show me the way and looked out for me. I got all the way to Canada. There were eight us. I was in Canada in 1857. I stood right there in Freedomland [57].

Standing in freedom with the knowledge that thousands remained in bondage proved too overwhelming for Solly. What good is freedom, he wonders, if you can't do anything with it? (28). Having stepped foot into Freedomland, albeit briefly, and having experienced the similarities between the air there and the air in bondage, he returns with the conductors who guided him northward and commits to replicating their generosity by aiding others dodging the law in pursuit of freedom and justice. In other words, he dedicates himself to living a life for the people. He joins the Underground Railroad *to do something* with his freedom.

The two objects that Solly first appears with and often carries throughout *Gem of the Ocean*—his walking stick and basket of pure—archive the time he spent as a transporter of the fugitive. Indeed, both function as souvenirs that catalogue those instances in which Solly undermined the law in pursuit of justice. His walking stick, he tells Citizen, not only served as a tool to assist his journeying on unfrequented paths but also as a site to mark, to notch his successes in carrying people to freedom. Showing Citizen the stick, he explains pridefully, "That's sixty-two notches. That's sixty-two people I carried to Freedom. I was looking to make it sixty-three when Abraham Lincoln come along and changed all that" (57). The law, of course, labels the walking stick as a weapon, as a symbol of criminality.[8] Upon seeing Solly with his walking stick, Caesar comments, "I see you still carrying that stick.... Well now they got laws against that now. I told you that.... They got laws against carrying a stick in Pittsburgh. That's a weapon" (34). The walking stick's potential, especially in the hands of the black, to operate outside the grasp of the law prompts the law to illegalize it. A perennial outlaw, Solly, citing Abraham Lincoln and General Grant's propensity for carrying walking sticks, replies to the implicit threat of imprisonment in Caesar's statement by exclaiming, "The law can go to hell if you telling me I can't carry a walking stick!" (34–35). The brief exchange recalls a long history in which activities deemed "black" have come under greater scrutiny and, indeed, have been subject to harsher punishments under the law. Wilson repeats with revisions this history to surface the ways that, too often, the law has been reworked to criminalize black expressivity.[9]

If Solly's walking stick marks him as a fugitive in *Gem of the Ocean*, then the basket of pure with which he travels marks him as an outlier. Wilson does not offer an explicit narrative to explain how Solly, as Caesar puts it, "come to picking dog shit up off the street" (35). He does, however, offer a possible hint in a single line late in the play. While telling Citizen about his time as a "dragman"—that is, as the person who guarded the rear on the Underground Railroad—Solly remarks that he often had to fight with the hounds sent by the law to chase after the scents of fugitive slaves. He remembers, "A dog tried to tear my leg off one time. I got a big part of my arm missing. Tore out the muscle and everything. He was going for my throat." After recounting this violent encounter, he goes on to say, "It was a good thing I found that pure otherwise I'd have to kill every dog I see" (58). Seeing in the dog a productive, not destructive potential permits Solly to reorient his relationship to the species and, more importantly, to the violence of his past: violence sanctioned by the law. In other words, the collection and distribution of pure gifts him a new way of seeing and relating that reminds him that, as Aunt Ester remarks, "ain't nothing in God's creation that ain't good" and that it is "man who sometimes gets in the way of God's creation and turns it over to the devil" (16, 21). This clarity of vision, of course, is what previously allowed Solly to carry fugitive slaves to freedom.

Through the character of Solly, Wilson remembers multiple histories of fugitive warriors, those documented in the archive and those left to ghost, who fought tirelessly to make freedom and justice mean something. Indeed, Solly's death in the final scene of *Gem of the Ocean* does not mark an ending, but instead a beginning. As Elam writes, Eli's benediction, "So live," over Solly's body serves as "a noble petition of hope for the future of the gathered community and [as] a purposeful plea for African Americans to live a life founded on personal integrity and committed to the collective struggle for truth" (Elam, "Redemptive Power" 75). Through Solly, we learn that freedom often has a cost. We also learn, however, that the fights for freedom and for justice, whether waged against the law or not, are ultimately noble fights.

It is through the character of Aunt Ester, the formidable figure around whom most of *Gem of the Ocean*'s plot pivots, that Wilson makes explicit this latter point. Though she ghosts several of the works in the *Pittsburgh*

Cycle—notably, *Two Trains Running, King Hedley II,* and *Radio Golf*—*Gem of the Ocean* is the only play in which Wilson explicitly calls for Aunt Ester's embodiment on stage. Put differently, as Barbara Lewis writes, Wilson gives her "a body, a substance, a materiality, and a future" in the play (145). Indeed, he fashions Aunt Ester, like Solly, as a conductor of sorts. She guides members of the community to freedom. Furthermore, she activates in them a sense of self-empowerment that allows for the repair of the injuries troubling their souls.

Aunt Ester relishes being a problem, and from her first appearance in the play's prologue, Wilson invites a consideration of the ways she engages fugitive movements. As Eli prepares to retire for the evening in the play's opening, drawing shades and extinguishing lights in the 1839 Wylie Avenue home that he shares with Aunt Ester and Black Mary, a knock at the door startles him. An agitated Citizen greets Eli when he responds to the knock's insistent call. Citizen explains to the older man that he has traveled to the house to visit Aunt Ester. He hopes that she can wash his soul. Eli directs Citizen to return to the house on Tuesday when Aunt Ester will be accepting guests. At once confused and unsatisfied by this advice, Citizen pushes his way into the residence, declaring, "I ain't going nowhere till I see Aunt Ester" (7). Citizen's movement and declaration compels Eli to grab him and to shove him towards the front door. A tussle ensues. In the midst of the melee, Citizen loses his hat and both men knock over a lamp. The commotion draws Aunt Ester out of her bedroom. Her arrival onto the scene immediately restores peace in the house. After picking up Citizen's hat, brushing it off, and handing it to him, Aunt Ester asks, "Didn't he say Tuesday, baby? Go on I'll see you on Tuesday?" (8). Citizen, calmed by her presence, accepts the hat and exits the house as he entered it, a fugitive on the move. He plants himself across the street from the address, where he waits: for Tuesday, Aunt Ester, and the chance at justice and redemption that a meeting with her promises. What Citizen glimpses in this early encounter and later discovers fully is that Aunt Ester is the ultimate fugitive.

Indeed, Aunt Ester exists outside of the law. She embodies a site where the past, present and future coalesce; she evidences the ways that one informs the other. To echo Lewis, she "mediates between those gone before, those here now, and those waiting to join the living—being conversant with each and holding each in tandem so that the entirety can be strengthened by the interstitial flow" (146). She carries their memories along with her own: she feeds the memories and remembers them out loud. Significantly, she crosses the borders of time and space to access powers that exceed the boundaries of rationality. In other words, she at once concretizes and catalyzes a movement of escape—liberatory movements—that resists the restrictive logics of circumscription. For as she tells Black Mary, "Life is a mystery.... It ain't all for you to know. It's all an adventure. That's all life is. But you got to trust that adventure" (42–43). Part of what she energizes in the people who appeal to her for remedy—often, from the law—is a trust in the adventure.

Aunt Ester understands the pursuits of justice, freedom and redemption as adventures: that is, as fugitive movements that exceed the law. Before telling Citizen about the City of Bones and journeying with him there, she directs him to go upriver and search for two pennies lying side by side on the ground. Later, when Black Mary asks what the two pennies are for, Aunt Esther explains that she sends Citizen on the adventure to give him something to do:

> He think there a power in them two pennies. He think when he find them all his troubles will be over. But he need to think that before he can come face to face with himself. Ain't nothing special about the two pennies. Only thing special about them is he think they special. He find two pennies then think he done something. But, he ain't done nothing but find two pennies [46].

Citizen arrives at 1839 Wylie Avenue a fugitive from the law searching for meaning and a means to restructure his given reality. Given this, Aunt Ester charges him with performing the acts of finding and securing the two pennies so that he might begin to develop a different orientation to his past and present and, crucially, so that his future might be marked by newfound freedom from the law. Upon Citizen's anxious return to the house with his handkerchief full, Aunt Esther declares, "Some people don't like adventure, Mr. Citizen. They stay home like me. I done seen all the adventure I want to see. I been across the water. I seen both sides of it" (52). The disclosure, which foregrounds Aunt Ester's own journey across the water during the Middle Passage, serves as a prelude to her vivid descriptions of the City of Bones, a half mile by half mile place at the bottom of the ocean to which she has traveled. Aunt Ester has seen its inhabitants who have burning tongues that not even the water can extinguish. She narrates it as a kind of refuge for those who engaged fugitive movement as a way to escape slavery, to escape the law.

As Elam writes, the City of Bones "actively remembers the loss of those that did not make it across the [Middle Passage]." He continues, "In a proactive act of reconstructing history at the bottom of the sea, those seemingly forgotten black travelers—those who were too informed for the journey, those who mounted unsuccessful insurgencies, those who jumped into the cold, uncertain water rather than face the cold uncertainties ahead—have built a city" (Wilson, "Redemptive Power" 79). Aunt Ester remembers them and their fugitive movements out loud for Citizen and, in so doing, she resurfaces the histories of violence—physical, emotional and epistemic—committed against the black on both sides of the water, often in the name of the law, as well as the history of their resilience in the wake of death and despair.

For Citizen, the psychic plunge below the surface of the water to confront these histories as well as his own past ultimately proves redemptive. Indeed, his journey to the City of Bones with Aunt Esther, Eli, Black Mary and Solly permits him to see afresh that he "got a duty to life" (68). He emerges from the journey reborn, no longer a prisoner of the law. He also emerges with a greater sense of justice. After making his way through the storm of the Middle Passage and witnessing people with his visage repeatedly sing, "Remember me," Citizen arrives at the gates to the City of Bones. There are twelve gates and twelve gatekeepers, Black Mary and Solly inform. Citizen, Aunt Ester instructs, must pay the gatekeeper with the two pennies he collected on his earlier adventure before he can enter the gates. The gatekeeper is Garret Brown. When Citizen hedges at the sight of Brown, Aunt Ester insists:

> You got to tell him, Mr. Citizen. The truth has to stand in the light. You got to get your soul washed.... You got to tell him, Mr. Citizen. Otherwise you'll never be right with yourself. Peter denied Christ three times. You might not get lucky like Peter to have three chances. You got to tell him now [69].

Citizen does tell him: he states his name and confesses to stealing the bucket of nails. In doing this, he opens the gate so that the hand of justice can pass through. Moreover, in confessing, Citizen does justice to Garett Brown, the man who sacrificed his own life for the sake of Citizen's. Indeed, through the character of Aunt Ester and Citizen's voyage to the City of Bones, Wilson attempts to do justice to all of the ancestors who sacrificed their lives so that their descendants might live. So live. What Aunt Ester helps to reveal is that living, and making it mean something, is the ultimate form of justice.

In many ways, *Gem of the Ocean* anticipates the necessity for fugitive movement across the twentieth century for the black. Wilson ends his *Pittsburgh Cycle*, in fact, where it begins: with a fugitive on the move in search of justice. In the final scene of *Radio Golf*, the play that concludes the cycle, Harmond Wilks, a descendant of Caesar, dawns face paint and picks up a paint brush—an object that, within the play, carries similar significance as Solly's walking stick—to signal a battle against the law and the injustices that it has perpetuated. Indeed, the vast chasm between law and justice are matters that Wilson revisits throughout his twentieth-century history cycle. As Elam writes, "While the law serves the interest of whites and the white power structure, there is the potential and hope within these works that the power of faith, hope and struggle can bring justice to African Americans" (Elam, *Past as Present* 239). In *Gem of the Ocean*, the law is made to stand in the light. What ultimately gets revealed are the ways that justice is made fugitive by the law and the various strategies the fugitive have had to deploy to achieve justice. Some folk, the play makes salient, relish being a problem. Necessarily, for those folk, the quest for justice requires an engagement with fugitive movements.

Notes

1. All references to Wilson's *Gem of the Ocean* are cited in the text parenthetically with page numbers.

2. Convened first by Best and Hartman in the fall of 2004 at UC Berkeley, the Redress Project is "a group of scholars and activists devoted to questions of slavery, fugitive forms of justice, and the role of history in the political present."

3. Zimmerman attorney, Mark O'Mara, stated this during the defense's closing arguments on Friday, 5 July.

4. Here, Best and Hartman offer an introduction to and summary of the arguments that Bryan Wagner puts forth in his essay, "Disarmed and Dangerous: The Strange Career of Bras-Coupé."

5. For a more detailed analysis of this history, see Claude Nolen's *African American Southerners in Slavery, Civil War, and Reconstruction*.

6. The name also brings to mind the Christian use of "Caesar" as a metonym for the government or for the law. In the New Testament of *The Bible*, Jesus instructs his followers to "give unto Caesar what is Caesar's and to God what is God's" (Matthew 22: 21 NIV).

7. In his exegesis of four decades of influential black popular music, Scholar Craig Hansen Warner notes this history. Elucidating this point, he writes, "'Wade in the Water,' one of the most common slave songs and gospel standards, provided literal escape instructions for slaves pursued by bloodhounds" (Werner 7).

8. When Caesar comes to arrest him for burning down the mill, Solly does turn the walking stick into a bone breaker, hitting him on the knee before fleeing (Wilson, *Gem* 70–71).

9. A glaring contemporary example of this is the increasing criminalization of "sagging pants." Black, urban youth, namely those engaged with the hip-hop scene and culture, adopted the practice of "sagging" their pants in the 1990s. In recent years, several lawmakers have emerged to proclaim that the practice poses a public danger. They couch their assertions, of course, in the rhetoric of decency. Though

the practice has essentially gone global, the laws that police it disproportionately affect black, urban youth.

WORKS CITED

Best, Stephen, and Saidiya Hartman. "Fugitive Justice." *Representations* 92.1 (Fall 2005): 1.15. Print.
Elam, Harry Justin. "*Gem of the Ocean* and the Redemptive Power of History." *The Cambridge Companion to August Wilson*. Ed. Christopher Bigsby. Cambridge: Cambridge University Press, 2007. 75–88. Print.
____. *The Past as Present in the Drama of August Wilson*. Ann Arbor: University of Michigan Press, 2004. Print.
Lewis, Barbara. "Miss Tyler's Two Bodies: Aunt Ester and the Legacy of Time." *August Wilson: Completing the Twentieth-Century Cycle*. Ed. Alan Nadel. Iowa City: University of Iowa Press, 2010. 145–151. Print.
Moten, Fred. "The Case of Blackness." *Criticism* 50.2 (Spring 2008): 177–218. Print.
Nolen, Claude H. *African American Southerners in Slavery, Civil War, and Reconstruction*. Jefferson, N.C.: McFarland, 2001. Print.
Wagner, Bryan. "Disarmed and Dangerous: The Strange Career of Bras-Coupé." *Representations* 92.1 (Fall 2005): 117–151. Print.
Warner, Craig Hansen. *A Change Gonna Come: Music, Race, and the Soul of America*. New York: Plume, 1998. Print.
Wilson, August. *Gem of the Ocean*. New York: Theatre Communications Group, 2006.
____. *Joe Turner's Come and Gone: A Play In Two Acts*. New York: Theatre Communications Group, 2008. Print.
____. *King Hedley II*. New York: Theatre Communications Group, 2008. Print.
____. *Radio Golf*. New York: Theatre Communications Group, 2008. Print.
____. *Two Trains Running*. New York: Theatre Communications Group, 2008. Print.

Reclaiming the Mother: Women, Documents and the Condition of the Mother in *Gem of the Ocean* and *Ma Rainey's Black Bottom*

Jesslyn Collins-Frohlich

Sandra Shannon asserts that in his century cycle Wilson writes "around, through and against recorded history in order to give voice to the nameless masses of Africans in America" ("Framing" 27). Wilson's narrative of those excluded from official histories is dominated by men who struggle to find a place in the world. Yet it also includes female characters whom Harry Elam considers "repositories for blackness" (*Gem* 77) and who Doris Davis claims provide "the rudder of self-knowledge" (167) required to keep Wilson's characters from finding themselves "adrift." In *Gem of the Ocean* Wilson introduces Aunt Ester, who he declares is the mother of all of the characters,[1] and in *Ma Rainey's Black Bottom*, Ma is the self-styled "Mother of the Blues." As "mothers" to their communities, both women are part of a complicated past and conflicted present that recalls the systematic exclusion effected by the legal premise of the "condition of the mother," which stated that a person's freedom or bondage depended upon the status of their mother.[2] As a result of this law, the bodies of black women came to physically and legally recreate the slave condition. The "condition of the mother" coupled with the illegality of education for slaves made black culture matriarchal and its history largely oral. In this way, the "condition of the mother" not only determined legal status but also served as a way to set distinct boundaries between the black community and the patriarchal, white community where history was written and lives were documented. The contemporary ramifications of constructing such boundaries appear in *Gem of the Ocean* and *Ma Rainey's Black Bottom* in two documents: Aunt Ester's bill of sale and Ma's recording contract.

In a post-emancipation world that demands blacks fit themselves and their cultural histories into a patriarchal, white world that relies on paper documentation, both documents define the two women and their communities as outside of the white world. Therefore, in Wilson's plays, written documents become problematic reminders of the past as well as troubled markers of the contemporary status of blacks who, having moved out of the realm of being property, are no more capable of fair interactions with the white power structure than they were as slaves. In this paper I maintain that for Aunt Ester and Ma Rainey, the key to successfully navigating the matriarchal/patriarchal and oral/written dichotomies that mark their exclusion is the creation of a counterinsurgent literacy[3] that reclaims the once repressive idea of the "condition of the mother" as a vital tool for maintaining communities and ensuring cultural continuity in the face of increasing pressure to conform to dominant, white values.

The term "counterinsurgent" carries decidedly military connotations, but at its core it denotes a fight for the relevance and beliefs of a community. Officials at the U.S. State Department define insurgency as "the organized use of subversion and violence to seize, nullify, or challenge political control of a region. As such, it is primarily a political struggle in which both sides use armed force to create a space for their political, economic, and influence activities to be effective" (2). Thus counterinsurgency seeks to maintain the political control of a region through a combination of military and civilian efforts that reduce the political, economic and social influence of insurgents while bolstering support for the governing party (2). I use the term "counterinsurgent" to describe Aunt Ester and Ma Rainey's approach because they use the "condition of the mother" to read documents in a way that makes them political and cultural tools that create space for their ideas, enforce the legitimacy of their roles in the black community, and empower others to resist the insurgent forces of the white power structure.

When *Gem of the Ocean* opens, Pittsburgh's Hill District in 1904 is a space overcrowded with "displaced Southern black people struggling to survive in a hostile Northern urban environment" (Adell 52). Despite gaining civil rights and relocating to the North, the relationship of the black individual to white society remains largely unchanged because race is still used "as criteria for inhuman treatment" (Nadel, "Boundaries" 88). Stripped of their humanity, black lives are valued by white society for their production value. Likewise, though laws theoretically recognize the rights of blacks, in reality they discriminate and oppress. The discrepancy between theory and experience leads to dissonance and violent fracture within the community. In the Hill District, many such conflicts are perpetrated by the black constable Caesar Wilks. As an agent of the law, Caesar compounds the hardships of life in the North by evicting people when they cannot pay their rent and then arresting them for vagrancy. He also causes disruptions by turning to violence when he is unable to make members of the black community to obey the white man's laws. Thus, when Garrett Brown refuses to come out of the water and let Caesar arrest him for a crime of which he is innocent, Caesar attempts to bribe him with warm clothes and soup. When the bribe fails, he resorts to hitting Brown with a two-by-four (12). Violence in the name of the law breeds conflict within the community and places it at further odds with the white power structure. For individuals trying to negotiate the difficulties of being black in America, Aunt Ester's home at 1839 Wylie Avenue is a haven, a place to go to find perspective and an identity.

Aunt Ester's ability to provide perspective is rooted in her belief that the disunity and violence found in the black community and its members results from an inability to reconcile the matriarchal, oral past with the patriarchal, written world of the present. In short, neither the individual nor the community knows where they fit because they do not know who they are. As a surrogate "mother" who helps her "children" to understand the world and their role in it, Aunt Ester begins resolving the conflict by approaching documents in a way that reclaims the "condition of the mother" as a powerful bridge between past and present instead of a barrier.[4] In a discussion with her protégé Black Mary, Aunt Ester explains the process through which she gained her role as memory keeper:

> I was nine years old. That's how old I was when my mama sent me to live with Miss Tyler. Miss Tyler gave me her name. Ester Tyler. I don't tell nobody what I was called before that. The only one know that is my mama. I stayed right on there with her till she died. Miss Tyler passed it on to me. If you ever make up your mind I'm gonna pass it on to you.... If you don't want it I got to find somebody else. I'm getting old. Going on three hundred years now. That's what Miss Tyler told me. Two hundred eighty-five by my count [43].

Aunt Ester's explanation reveals several details that reshape the meaning of her role and the bill of sale that confirms her identity. The role of memory keeper is two hundred eighty-five years old, but Ester is not. The current Aunt Ester inherited the name and document with the job. Consequently, the role, name, and bill of sale become symbolic of the passing of history. As such, the bill of sale is powerful because it documents the continuation of black history and culture. In this role its strength and validity is no longer dictated by the white power structure that wrote it, but by the black women who pass it from generation to generation.

The transfer of history from woman to woman through the role of Aunt Ester also reverses the original intentions of the document by reclaiming "the condition of the mother" and the matriarchal inheritance it created as a tool for continuity and regeneration. Each new Aunt Ester ensures black history is a living entity that carves out a powerful role for women and a shared past within the community. It also creates a moment of inclusion for the black community because the action of providing a written document as the proof of the transmission of their history reconfigures the relationship between the written and the oral, for Aunt Ester has inscribed upon a written document the oral history of her community. She has aligned the patriarchal, written present with the matriarchal, oral past in a way that creates a productive, inclusive overlap. By reclaiming the power of the "condition of the mother" and the document that stipulated it, Aunt Ester creates a space for her belief that to make sense of the present or future, one must look to and embrace the past.

Following this mantra, Aunt Ester uses her bill of sale to create within the black community a group of individuals who are able to fight the restrictions they face. Aunt Ester facilitates this by literally folding her bill of sale into a paper boat that symbolically transports Solly, Black Mary, Citizen Barlow and others to the City of Bones and back. By building her boat out of her bill of sale, Aunt Ester shows that the power of documents comes from their ability to be shaped and reshaped by those who discern their true purpose. So, when Aunt Ester shows Citizen Barlow the boat and asks, "You see that, Mr. Citizen. That's a boat. You gonna take a ride on that boat. Do you believe you can take a ride on that old boat Mr. Citizen?" his response, "This a piece of paper" (54), proves his lack of understanding. In his experience, documents serve the white power structure, not the black community, and are a means of controlling the population. Even when a black man like Caesar becomes an agent of the law and gains access to documents, he is incapable of using them to do anything other than oppress the black community because he sees paper documents as a means of gaining another sort of paper-money. Due to his inability to either literally or figuratively read a document, Citizen Barlow fails to grasp how a black woman can use history to transform a document into a means of creating and sustaining a community.

Citizen Barlow's illiteracy means that he remains critical of Aunt Ester's boat because he does not understand how the pieces come together. To explain the document out of which the boat is made and its history, Aunt Ester reasons that "a boat is made out of a lot of things. Wood and rope.... Wood and rope and iron. The workmen with their hammers ringing. A boat is something. It takes a lot of men to make a boat. And it takes a lot of men to sail a boat" (64). Aunt Ester explains the process of boatbuilding in this way to help Citizen Barlow understand that regardless of whether a vessel is made of boards or a document, what matters is the community that creates it. Through the material of her boat, Aunt Ester evokes the Middle Passage and slavery so that both are defined as communal acts. It took an entire country to build and reinforce slavery, and it took the power of community to survive it.

Following Aunt Ester's reasoning, reclaiming the history represented by her bill of sale must also be a communal act that reconnects individuals with their shared slave and African ancestry. Therefore, Citizen Barlow cannot travel to the City of Bones without the support of the community. Only after hearing the experiences of others who have made the journey does Citizen Barlow believe in the paper boat. Citizen Barlow becomes a citizen only when he is able to comprehend the shared past and read it onto his future. He can then join those who have taken the trip to the City of Bones and, as demonstrated by his picking up of Solly Two King's staff, find a valuable role in the community. Citizen Barlow and others find communal and individual identities because Aunt Ester renegotiates the power and purpose of a document in a way that creates space for ideas of shared heritage and interconnectedness.

In *Ma Rainey's Black Bottom*, Ma builds upon Aunt Ester's counterinsurgent literacy by using her contract and release to reconcile the oral and the written and emphasize communal identity. Set twenty-three years after *Gem of the Ocean*, in Chicago in 1927, *Ma Rainey's Black Bottom* introduces another mother whose relationship with documents is strikingly similar to Aunt Ester's. As the self-styled "Mother of the Blues," Ma's title and her function as the voice through which black experience is recorded allude to the "condition of the mother" and the complex connections between ideas of written and oral histories. Ma creates her legacy, not through the reproduction of flesh and blood children, but through songs that tell of black life. In an explanation of her role that echoes Aunt Ester's view of her own position, Ma explains that the blues are "a way of understanding life" that "help[s] you get out of bed in the morning ... knowing you ain't alone." It is her responsibility to take the "emptiness" of life "and try to fill it up with something" (82–83) that gives the black community a shared identity and knowledge of itself. Yet Ma's role also highlights the continued problems faced by the black community.

Though Ma has "displaced the traditional positioning of women within the music industry's hierarchy" (Elam, *Past* 92), her ability to connect to her community and ensure a legacy depends upon recordings that are governed by releases and contracts with a white recording company that seeks to make her songs and identity into pieces of merchandise to be bought and sold. So, even as Ma claims a voice and a position unavailable to her slave ancestors (Nadel, "Ma Rainey" 110), she is bound by the power of the written word and white men. Like Aunt Ester, Ma's relationship to the white power structure is controlled by a document that seeks to define her as a way of improving the economic situation of the white men who own her. Ma's ability to pass along the "understanding of life" offered by the blues depends upon her redefinition of the documents that control her voice and the positions available to her. Her contract presents the possibility of making the written, recorded world acknowledge the oral, communal significance of the blues by creating a productive overlap. Therefore, Ma's goal and the motivation for her actions in the play is ensuring that her contract allows her to record songs that validate her role as "Mother of the Blues" and tell of the shared African history of her community. To make this happen, she must contend with the racism built into her contract and relationship with the recording company.

The conversation had by the white producer Sturdyvant and Ma's white agent Irvin prior to her arrival suggests there is a fundamental difference between their understanding of a contract or release and Ma's. For Ma, the contract is a deal with the devil made to cement her legacy. She views the contract as giving the recording company the rights to her voice but not to her whole being. However, the record company views the contract as granting them the right to make Ma do as they please, and they see the release as merely a part of making a record and collecting the money they earn for making Ma a star. If anything, they reason Ma should be indebted to them for the opportunity to record and the financial security it brings, even if they make decidedly more money from the contract than she does. To Irvin and Sturdyvant the diva-like behavior Ma exhibits at each session is entirely unjustified, so before Ma arrives they fight over how to control her behavior.

> STURDYVANT: She's your responsibility. I'm not putting up with any Royal Highness ... Queen of the Blues bullshit!
> IRVIN: Mother of the Blues, Mel. Mother of the Blues.

STURDYVANT: I don't care what she calls herself. I'm not putting up with it. I just want to get her in here ... record those songs on that list ... and get her out. Just likeclockwork, huh? [18].

In this exchange Irvin and Sturdyvant decide that the worth of Ma's recordings does not cover the costs of dealing with her. Their misunderstanding of Ma's behavior and scoffing at her title also illustrate the unequal conditions upon which they offer the contract. Ma is worthy of a recording—not because of who she is as a person or even her musical skills but because they stand to turn a profit from her by appealing to a race records demographic. Ma explains, "If you colored and can make them some money, then you all right with them. Otherwise, you just a dog in the alley" (79). Despite her relative success, Ma must still sell her identity to a white man through a contractual agreement that reinforces economic and social inequalities.

In order to challenge such exploitive transactions and the racism that informs them, Ma employs her counterinsurgent logic to create space for her own ideas and the black community she represents by using her role as a contracted singer to dictate the actions of her white manager and producer. As she explains to her bandleader Cutler, "They don't care nothing about me. All they want is my voice. Well, I done learned that, and they gonna treat me like I want to be treated no matter how much it hurt them" (79). Accordingly, Ma acts in a way designed to force Irvin and Sturdyvant to acknowledge her humanity and let her record the music she wants. Ma begins by making them wait. As Shannon explains, waiting had long been used by dominant, white culture as a tool for "perpetuating racial oppression." Ma's delayed arrival emphasizes the "damage that prolonged periods of waiting have caused the Afro-American artist" ("Long Wait" 136) and temporarily grants her control of the situation by reversing the racism of waiting. She makes white men wait on a black woman. When she finally enters the studio followed by a police officer, Ma builds on the power she gains through making them wait by demanding Irvin tell the cop who she is even though she knows her name means nothing to the officer. It is an exercise in controlling Irvin and making a white man acknowledge her worth to another white man in order to validate "her independence and self-determination" (Elam, *Past* 93). Later in the play when Ma delays the session by demanding they turn up the heat, get her a Coca-Cola, and play her version of "Ma Rainey's Black Bottom," she emphasizes her disdain for the situation by referring to herself in the third person.

Not only is Ma's use of third person an indication of the conflict she experiences between her private and public life,[5] it too is part of an elaborate contract negotiation in which Ma interrogates the value of a document that creates a divide between the personal identity she constructs for herself and the abstract name created by the contract, records and releases. Like Aunt Ester, Ma realizes that, historically, stripping a contract of a person's the flesh and bone identity turns people into property by denying their humanity. Repeating her name allows Ma to remind them of her identity and give that identity power in the negotiations. It also mocks the validity of documents that define a person as only a name. Ma knows that a person is more; he or she is a product of shared history, experience, and community. Thus, the contract, release and her records are spiritually and culturally worthless if they do not acknowledge the person and community behind the name and voice.

As a "mother" in the black community, Ma is the transmitter of a legacy, a lineage, a history. So, when her recording contract fails to account for her whole identity, she threatens to invalidate it by making a full retreat into the oral realm. When Irvin suggests she sing Levee's version of the song, she tells him, "Levee ain't messing up my song with none of his music shit. Now if that don't set right with you and Sturdyvant ... then I can carry my black bottom on back down South to my tour, 'cause I don't like up here no ways" (63). She employs the same threat when Irvin complains that they do not have enough time to wait for Sylvester to get through the intro without stuttering. Again Ma says, "I can walk out of here and go back to my tour. I got plenty fans. I don't need to go through all of this" (74). For Ma the tour confirms her value to people outside the recording industry, and gives her the tools she needs to shift the power dynamics of her contract.

Ma's threat to return to the community undermines the contract by highlighting the reality that, in the music industry, making money depends entirely upon having an audience. As Cutler confirms, "The colored folks made Ma a star. White folks don't care nothing about who she is" (95). While Ma can return to the community who made her significant and continue to perform without the help of records, Irvin and Sturdyvant are entirely dependent upon recordings and the salability of Ma's status as "Mother of the Blues" as a way to gain an audience and make a profit. By reminding them that no recording is successful without an audience, and that she understands the audience best, Ma uses the "condition of the mother" to reverse the power structure of the contract from one controlled by white men, to one she controls through the collective power of the black community. She makes a space for her music and a shared history by transforming her contract into a document that uses the recorded word of white men to validate the oral, matriarchal structure of the black community.

Once Aunt Ester and Ma Rainey use documents to establish the power of shared, black history, they can then employ their counterinsurgent literacy to lend legitimacy to their own roles in the community and reduce the influence of insurgent white ideologies. When Caesar shows up at Aunt Ester's door with an arrest warrant for Solly, he expects cooperation because he thinks the document has power. But what he gets is a defiant Aunt Ester who uses her bill of sale to question his authority and the warrant's validity.

> AUNT ESTER: I see you got a piece of paper. I got a piece of paper too. Black Mary, get my piece of paper over there. Sit on down there, Mr. Caesar, I want to show you something.
> *(Black Mary takes the paper boat out of the drawer and hands it to Aunt Ester. She unfolds it and hands it back to Black Mary.)*
> Give that to Caesar, let him take a look at it.
> *(Black Mary hands Caesar the paper.)*
> Tell me how much that piece of paper's worth, Mr. Caesar.
> *(Caesar reads the bill of sale aloud.)*
> CAESAR: I wouldn't give you ten cents for it.
> AUNT ESTER: Then how much you think your paper's worth? You see Mr. Caesar, you can put the law on the paper but that don't make it right. That piece of paper say I was property. Say anybody could buy or sell me. The law say I needed a piece of piece of paper to say I was a free woman. But I didn't need no piece of paper to tell me that. Do you need a piece of paper, Mr. Caesar?

Aunt Ester's first step in countering Caesar's warrant is to devalue both documents by labeling them pieces of paper. Reducing her bill of sale and the warrant to mere paper is her way of showing that documents derive their power from a shared, communal meaning that engenders willing compliance. Without this, they are simply sheets of paper. For Aunt Ester, the warrant's irrelevance stems from its disassociation from the community. It is the law put on the page, but since she and the black community are largely excluded from the systems that write and determine the meaning of the law, the warrant cannot force her to act. Aunt Ester also emphasizes the warrant's worthlessness when she transforms her bill of sale from the boat back into a piece of paper before she hands it to

Caesar. This gesture not only reminds the audience of her power to transform documents, but it shows her contempt for Caesar whom she deems incapable of the deeper knowledge of history and documents implied by the boat. She flattens and simplifies it so Caesar might understand.

Aunt Ester further challenges Caesar by showing how the law fosters the inhuman treatment of blacks. Her asking Caesar if he needs a piece of paper to tell him who he is points to the irony and danger of Caesar's position. He not only bears the name of the crown,[6] but he also upholds its laws without recognizing that that they mark him—not as a man in control of his own life, but one controlled by and made a tool for the forces that oppress. His failure to comprehend this is highlighted in his assertion that "these ain't slavery times no more, Miss Tyler. You living in the past. All that done changed. The law done changed and I'm custodian of the law. Now you know, Miss Tyler, you got to have rule of law otherwise there'd be chaos. Nobody wants to live in chaos" (78).

Caesar returns to a white sanctioned understanding of documents that seeks to disconnect past and present. According to Caesar the wrongs of the past cannot be repeated because a black man now serves as custodian of the law. He disregards the fact that plantation owners often used slaves as overseers—a point not lost on Solly, who says, "Caesar's the kind of people I would want working for me. If I ever get me a plantation I'm gonna hire him to keep my niggers in line" (14). Solly's comment and Caesar's admonishment that "these ain't slavery times no more" (78) hint to the dangers of forgetting history. Caesar repeats the mistreatment of the past by visiting on his own people the same impersonal interpretation of the law and documents that whites used to enslave them. He lacks the connection to the past and understanding of himself that Aunt Ester claims is required to accurately read or value to a document. Therefore, she challenges Caesar and the white power structure he represents by countering with black history.

Aunt Ester also uses her counterinsurgent literacy to empower Black Mary to speak against her own brother in a way that reclaims family and community as networks of people who share a common interpretation of the past. Black Mary fights back when Caesar arrests Aunt Ester by telling him that Aunt Ester's house is a sanctuary. When Caesar says he knows nothing about a sanctuary and has an obligation to arrest those who break the law wherever they are, Black Mary counters with spiritual law.

> The Bible say, "A place of refuge shall be given unto you and whosoever seeketh counsel therein shall he be made also clean, for I have given unto the master of that abode a place above the law, for the law is a punisher of men, and I seeketh their redemption" [79].

Caesar responds by producing his copy of the Commonwealth of Pennsylvania penal code and citing it chapter and verse. He even goes so far as to confirm the signature of the duly elected Judge Homer S. Brown. The relative inequality of these two texts is immediately apparent to everyone except Caesar, who once again fails to realize the irony of his upholding laws he is unable to write and supporting judges that he is unable to vote into office. Though Caesar can read the words on the page, he cannot comprehend their intent or impact. Thus Caesar continues to enforce the law by any means necessary, which eventually leads to his shooting Solly for burning down the mill. It is at this moment that Black Mary challenges Caesar's authority by reminding him of his own past.

> I remember you when you was on the other side of the law. That's my brother. The one selling hoecakes off the back of a wagon. The one that helped Mrs. Robinson and the kids when nobody else would. That's my brother. The one who used to get out of bed every morning to take me to school. The one who believed everybody had the same right to life ... the same right to whatever there was in life they could find useful. That's my brother. I don't know who you are. But you are not my brother. You hear me Caesar? You are not my brother [84].

Black Mary's disavowal of Caesar because she no longer knows him is more than a family disagreement. Through her actions Black Mary transforms the idea of family from one of shared biology to shared history. Black Mary's insistence on shared history combined with Aunt Ester's use of documents, further redefines the "condition of the mother" by making it a tool for exclusion as well as inclusion. Aunt Ester and Black Mary become "mothers" only to those who are willing to share their history and believe that a bill of sale is a boat to the City of Bones. The "condition of the mother" becomes a tool for creating a family, a community, and protecting it from those outside forces that could rip it apart.

Ma also uses her contract to, at least temporarily, fend off insurgent ideas. Being "fully aware that her signature on the release ... marks the end of her power" (Kubitschek 183–184), Ma withholds her written consent until her nephew Sylvester has recorded his part and the songs have been played her way. Both stipulations give her the opportunity to reinforce her view of how documents derive power and ensure that her legacy is preserved. Throughout the play, Ma is seen protecting those individuals whom she considers to be part of her community. Her insistence that her nephew Sylvester introduce the song is not merely a chance to defy Irvin and Sturdyvant, it is a family matter. She tells Sturdyvant, "Ma listens to her heart. Ma listens to the voice insider her. That's what counts with Ma"

(63). In this explanation of her motives, Ma directly contradicts the financial concerns that drive Irvin and Sturdyvant by pointing to a deeper concern over family and community. She wants Sylvester to do the part so that when he gets paid he can "send some of it home to [his] mama. Let her know [he's] doing all right" (61). Ma is taking care of her family by seeing that the exchange of money facilitated by her contract returns to the community that supports her.

Ma also cares for her family by creating cohesion and empowering others. Ma's relationships with her band members are based on a shared history and understanding of their indebtedness to the black community. The band is to back Ma who uses her fame and her voice to negotiate a place for the blues and the black community from which they stem. So, when Levee threatens to jeopardize these connections, the band must defend their community. As the newest and youngest band member, Levee is painfully unaware of the music industry's racism or the collective effort needed to fight it. Therefore, when the set list written by Irvin contradicts the one Ma discusses with Cutler, Levee interprets the band's unwillingness to play his version as a personal slight instead of an effort to present a united front. Cutler tries to stifle Levee's anger and offer an explanation by reminding him of his place in the heirarchy. Cutler explains, "You trying to tell me what we is and ain't gonna play. And that ain't none of your business. Your business is to play what I say" (34). Instead of acquiescing to the established roles of the band or Ma's authority, Levee demands that Cutler "look at the paper! Get the paper and look at it! See what it say!" Cutler responds, "We ain't talking about the paper. We talking about you understanding where you fit in when you around here" (34). Levee's insistence that the answer to the problem is found on the paper and that if Culter only "looks" he will "see" it emphasizes his dependence upon both the written word and the white man for validation.

Confronted with an individual whose reliance on the approval of whites, the band counters with an explanation of the industry that confirms the relevance of Ma and a communal identity. Cutler reprimands Levee's insistence on the power of Irvin's list by saying, "The sooner you understand it ain't what you say, or what Mr. Irvin say ... it's what Ma say that counts." He is interrupted by Slow Drag who confirms Cutler's stance by asserting, "Don't nobody say when it comes to Ma. She's gonna do what she wants to do. Ma says what happens with her" (37). When Levee still fails to comprehend the true nature of the situation, Toledo warns, "As long as the colored man look to white folks to put the crown on what he say ... as long as he looks to white folks for approval ... then he ain't never gonna find out who he is and what he's about, He's just gonna be what white folks want him to be about" (37). Cutler, Slow Drag and Toledo's responses highlight the necessity of turning to Ma and the community she harnesses to find an independent, black identity. Their words also seek to explain to Levee the impossibility of a black man finding himself or a justification of his ideas on a piece of paper or in the words of a white man. Sticking together and playing their role has brought success in spite of the white men who would reduce the blues as a commodity.

Therefore, Ma fires Levee not only because he challenges her authority but because his music is of the moment and disconnected from the community and history. Like the white folks Ma ridicules, Levee fails to recognize the blues as more than a music trend and trades his community and history for the promise of economic reward and recognition from the white power structure without understanding what such a transaction will actually cost him. As the play closes Levee is a lone, "muted trumpet struggling for the highest of possibilities and blowing pain and warning" (111). Levee, like Caesar, does indeed serve as a warning that placing too much faith in documents, white power structures, or one's individual abilities leads to violence and loss. These men also come to embody the challenge, particularly for Wilson's male characters, of determining how to function in a world they do not fully comprehend.

Thus, in the end, the counterinsurgent literacy Aunt Ester and Ma use to transform documents and reclaim the "condition of the mother" also evokes the question of identity and history that seems to haunt Wilson and his plays. In *Ma Rainey's Black Bottom* Toledo voices this concern when he asks, "Now what's the colored man gonna do with himself?" once he realizes he's "a leftover from history" (57). Wilson himself posits two possible answers: "Do we assimilate into American society and thereby lose our culture, or do we maintain our culture separate from the dominant cultural values and participate in the American society as Africans rather than blacks who have adopted European values?" (130). Wilson's options repeat the notions of oral/written, matriarchal/patriarchal, and past/present used to set boundaries on black identity. However, the answer provided by Aunt Ester and Ma is to use the "condition of the mother" to establish a history and new literacy that dissolve dichotomies by embracing dualities.

As mothers whose power is in part derived from their connection to white society, Aunt Ester and Ma know that wholesale adoption or rejection of the dominant culture causes an internal rift because either option means denying a vital part of their past and present. Both women rely on the liminal space created by the overlapping of cultures and time as a source of their power. Without this space and the fusion of past and present, Aunt Ester cannot transform a bill of sale into a boat, and Ma cannot be a successful singer because they cannot overcome the barriers placed on their identities. Thus the vision of black identity and history offered by Aunt Ester and Ma is recursive. A document or a song that tells of the past can be used to help generations of people find their identities because each offers insight into the present. One must simply read it correctly.

When examined as recursive processes, Aunt Ester's use of her bill of sale and Ma's manipulation of her release are part of a new literacy that reverses the exclusivity of traditional literacy by focusing not on the ability to comprehend or repeat words on a page but to understand and revise actions in the present. Thus Toledo's assertion that the black man "is a leftover" (57) proves he is illiterate. Though he can read words on a page, he cannot see that to be a leftover is to accept the dominant culture's view of history as a linear path. He has not learned that "knowing who you are and where you've been"[7] hinges on the ability to read the matriarchal, oral past of the black community and the written, patriarchal present of the dominant culture simultaneously. Ultimately, the ability to acquire the literacy promoted by Aunt Ester and Ma allows the black community to fight for a distinct identity in two ways. It protects and nurtures black history and identity, and it creates a space for the idea that it too is a legitimate, dominant culture.

NOTES

1. In the preface to *King Hedley II*, Wilson writes, "Aunt Ester has emerged for me as the most significant persona of the cycle. The characters, after all, are her children" (x).

2. The legal construct of the "condition of the mother" comes from a 1662 Virginia statute that defines the legal status of children of Englishmen and black women. The statute states that "all children born in this country shall be held bond or free only according to the condition of the mother."

3. Literacy, as used in this essay, refers to the ability to read and write as well as the shared cultural practices that help one to function in society, achieve goals and develop knowledge.

4. My understanding of Wilson's view of the connection between the past and present draws upon Harry Elam, Jr.'s assertion that in his plays "Wilson is not simply reviewing this past and reevaluating history. His project is so much more provocative, as he considers how this past now impacts on the African American present" (233). It is also informed by Wilson's repeated assertions in interviews, articles and his speech "The Ground on Which I Stand" that moving forward requires one to return to their past.

5. Sandra Shannon argues that Ma's switch between third person in exchanges with Irvin and Sturdyvant and first person in conversations with her band, Sylvester and Dussie Mae shows the extent to which Ma experiences conflict between her private and public life ("Ground" 154).

6. Caesar's evokes historical rulers whose faces graced the official currency of the realm as well as the practice of naming slaves after white, historical figures. Caesar's name marks his adoption of white values and lack of connection to the black community.

7. In an interview with Kim Powers Wilson explains, "The importance of history is simply to find out who you are and where you've been. It becomes doubly important if someone else has been writing your history" (5).

Works Cited

Adell, Sandra. "Speaking of Ma Rainey/Talking about the Blues." *May All Your Fences Have Gates.* Ed. Alan Nadel. Iowa City: University of Iowa Press, 1994. 51–66. Print.

Davis, Doris. "'Mouths Afire': August Wilson's Blues Women." *MELUS* 34.4 (Winter 2010): 165–185.

Elam, Harry, Jr. "Gem of the Ocean and the Redemptive Power of History." *The Cambridge Companion to August Wilson.* Ed. Christopher Bigsby. New York: Cambridge University Press, 2007. 75–88. Print.

____. *The Past as Present in the Drama of August Wilson.* Ann Arbor: University of Michigan Press, 2006. Print.

Kubitscheck, Missy Dehn. "August Wilson's Gender Lesson." *May All Your Fences Have Gates.* Ed. Alan Nadel. Iowa City: University of Iowa Press, 1994. 183–199. Print.

Nadel, Alan. "Boundaries, Logistics, and Identity: The Property of Metaphor in *Fences* and *Joe Turner's Come and Gone*." *May All Your Fences Have Gates.* Ed. Alan Nadel. Iowa City: University of Iowa Press, 1994. 86–104. Print.

____. "Ma Rainey's Black Bottom: Cutting the Historical Record, Dramatizing a Blues CD." *The Cambridge Companion to August Wilson.* Ed. Christopher Bigsby. New York: Cambridge University Press, 2007. 102–112. Print.

Powers, Kim. "An Interview with August Wilson." *Conversations with August Wilson.* Eds. Jackson R. Bryer and Mary C. Hartig. Jackson: University of Mississippi Press, 2006.

Shannon, Sandra G. "August Wilson Explains his Dramatic Vision: An Interview." *Conversations with August Wilson.* Ed. Jackson R. Bryer and Mary C. Hartig. Jackson: University of Mississippi Press, 2006.

____. "Framing African American Cultural Identity: The Bookend Plays in August Wilson's 10-Play Cycle." *College Literature* 36.2 (Spring 2009): 26–39. Print.

____. "The Ground on Which I Stand: August Wilson's Perspective on African American Women." *May All Your Fences Have Gates.* Ed. Alan Nadel. Iowa City: University of Iowa Press, 1994. 150–182. Print.

____. "The Long Wait: August Wilson's *Ma Rainey's Black Bottom*." *Black American Literature Forum* 25.1 (Spring 1991): 135–146. Print.

United States. Department of State. Bureau of Political-Military Affairs. *U.S. Government Counterinsurgency Guide*. Department of State, January 2009. Web.

Wilson, August. *Gem of the Ocean*. New York: Plume, 2003. Print.

———."The Ground on Which I Stand." *Callaloo* 20.3 (1998): 493–503.

———. *King Hedley II*. New York: Plume, 2005. Print.

———. *Ma Rainey's Black Bottom*. New York: Plume, 1985. Print.

A Century Lacking Progress: The Fractured Community in *Gem of the Ocean* and *King Hedley II*

CHRISTOPHER B. BELL

August Wilson's fidelity to the Hill District is almost painful. The Hill is the predominantly African American neighborhood in Pittsburgh where Wilson lived, with a few interruptions, until his early thirties. At one point in Wilson's life, this one square mile boasted fifty-five thousand black residents. When Wilson died in 2005, the number was less than five thousand. In 2001, Wilson fondly recalled the Hill in the 1960s: "The avenue shimmered. Hundreds of people on the sidewalk. Life going on" (Lahr 40). Today, no trace of such an existence remains apparent. When asked in 1989 about what had happened to the Hill of his youth, Wilson recalled,

> [The] same thing that's happened to most black communities. Most of it is no longer there. At one time it was a thriving community, albeit a depressed community. But still there were stores and shops all along the avenue. They are not there anymore. It has become an even more depressed area than it was [when I grew up there] [Moyers 67].

A systematic effort by the city planners of Pittsburgh to revitalize the substandard living conditions contributed to the Hill's dissolution. Laurence Glasco and Christopher Rawson note that in 1961 the Civic Arena was built in the Lower Hill, not far from where Wilson grew up at 1727 Bedford Avenue. Pittsburgh's professional hockey team, the Penguins, was given a new home. However, eight thousand residents were displaced and over four hundred businesses closed. Despite promises to the contrary, residents, mostly African Americans, were not given assistance to find new housing. Subsequently, they crowded into the Middle Hill. Over time, cramped conditions and the neglect of city planners led to a demoralized and paralyzed state (Glasco and Rawson 38–40). Wilson himself left the Hill permanently in 1977. Shortly after the playwright began his celebrated Pittsburgh Cycle, a series of ten plays that chronicles the African American presence throughout the twentieth century, nine of which are set in the Hill.

By situating the bulk of his literary output in the Hill, Wilson offers a microcosm of the poor, urban African American experience in the twentieth century. When looked at chronologically, the dissolution of the neighborhood becomes steadily apparent. For example, in *King Hedley II*, the plight reaches its apex, and the community teeters on the brink of annihilation. Knowing the history of the Hill, one may be inclined to agree with Robert Brustein, who argued that Wilson's cycle merely depicts "black martyrdom" and is "monotonous, limited, [and] locked in a perception of victimization" (par. 3). However, the playwright finds that the African American community itself is at least partially culpable for its own demise. In fact, in 1991, the playwright told Christopher Bigsby, "These kids today ... don't even know about [their ancestors]. They know nothing about that part of their lives and their connection to it. I think this is a flaw in African American culture. The connection is broken" (212). The responsibility of the community for its state of ruin depicted *King Hedley II* is juxtaposed by the promise of freedom from oppression in the cycle's first play, *Gem of the Ocean*, set in 1904. Aunt Ester, a 366-year-old conjure woman who serves as the spiritual center of the Hill, serves as Wilson's manifestation of this promise. She offers succor for the spiritually deprived and psychologically maimed. For Wilson, Aunt Ester was

> the most significant persona of the cycle. The characters, after all, are her children. The wisdom and tradition she embodies are valuable tools for the reconstruction of their personality and for dealing with a society in which the contradictions, over the decades, have grown more fierce, and for exposing all the places it is lacking in virtue [Wilson, *King Hedley II* x].

By following her wisdom and adopting her values, individuals can find peace within themselves, and, collectively, the community can thrive. However, *King Hedley II* depicts the failed realization of Aunt Ester's vision. In this play, she dies, as does the play's protagonist. When looked at in tandem, *Gem of the Ocean* and *King Hedley II* illustrate that, despite the external forces that crippled the Hill district (such as the decision to build the Civic Arena), the ultimate dissolution of the neighborhood rests at least equally on the shoulders of those within the community who turned their collective backs on the example set by its most vital member. Ultimately, only a human sacrifice that promises Aunt Ester's resurrection can serve to help repair the broken community.

To write that the black community seen in *Gem of the Ocean* has more potential than the one depicted approximately seventy years later is a bold statement indeed. Wilson depicts a group suffering from the aftershock of slavery's demise some forty years prior. Tranquility remains elusive for blacks this play. At the beginning of the play, Citizen Barlow brings conflict to Aunt Ester's doorstep at 1839 Wylie Avenue. Citizen steals a bucket of nails to protest working conditions at the local steel mill that employs the majority of blacks in the Hill. However, a man named Garret Brown is accused of the theft. Rather than admit guilt for a crime he has not committed, Brown jumps in the river and drowns, effectively committing suicide. In protest, the workers go on strike, threatening calamity. Caesar, the local constable, comments on the potential negative result of the strike.

> Close down the mill and ... a hundred niggers is going to jail for trying to steal something. ... A hundred niggers is going to jail for loitering. A hundred niggers is going to jail for trying to disturb the peace after they get mad and start fighting each other. Five hundred babies is gonna go hungry. You gonna have a hundred new prostitutes. People gonna be living on the streets begging for a dime [Wilson, *Gem of the Ocean* 34].

Furthermore, the discord within Pittsburgh is a microcosm of the kind of trouble blacks suffer from throughout the land. For instance, another character, Solly Two Kings, receives a letter from his sister in Alabama, telling him that "the white peoples is gone crazy and won't let anybody leave" (Wilson, *Gem of the Ocean* 15). We learn later in the play that Citizen himself escaped these conditions, but he finds an equal amount of trouble in Pittsburgh. Such is the combustible nature of the play.

Wilson contrasts the bleak conditions of the black community with a harmonious atmosphere that infuses Aunt Ester's home at 1839 Wylie. Harry Elam notes that the play "is a noble petition of hope for the future of the gathered community and a purposeful plea for African Americans to live a life founded on personal integrity and committed to the collective struggle for truth" ("*Gem of the Ocean* and the Redemptive Power" 75). The characters who congregate at 1839 Wylie live a philosophy, articulated by Aunt Ester herself, that a whole human being is one who lives life with dignity, independence, and integrity, while serving to help others within the community find self-worth. Two elderly characters best exemplify this philosophy, Aunt Ester and Solly Two Kings. Importantly, part of the tension Wilson crafts in *Gem of the Ocean* centers on the need for Aunt Ester and Solly Two Kings to find young individuals within the community to become heirs to their respective thrones.

First, Aunt Ester's role within the community bears scrutiny. As noted above, her age is among her most important traits. Her more than three hundred year presence on the Hill provides a stability amidst the chaotic conditions for blacks on the hill. However, although most critics write about Aunt Ester as a single figure, it is important to note that Aunt Ester is part of a lineage. Certainly, in a sense, there is only one Aunt Ester. The one who assumes the role inherits the collected memory of African American existence in America. Barbara Lewis explains this succinctly, noting, "Who she was in the past no longer matters because her person pas has died so that she can take on the collective past of all the prior Aunt Esters.... As a lineal role revivified each generation, Aunt Ester sustains threads of collective memory, replicating the principle of royal and papal succession: the head does not die, but rather regenerates with a new face" (146). But Aunt Ester has a corporeal presence. The human herself can die. What if Aunt Ester is unable to secure an heir before death? Again, Aunt Ester's need to secure an heir in *Gem of the Ocean* serves as a source of tension. Without an Aunt Ester, the memories of the black community are lost. Wilson centers the conflict on Aunt Ester and Black Mary. When the play opens, Black Mary has been living at 1839 Wylie for three years. The audience learns Black Mary struggles to accept the role of Aunt Ester. Unlike the current Aunt Ester, who has lived at 1839 since she was seven years old, Black Mary is approximately thirty. One senses the anxiety Aunt Ester feels about Black Mary's reticence. In Act One, the following exchange occurs:

> AUNT ESTER: If you ever make up your mind I'm gonna pass [my name] on to you. People say it's too much to carry. But I told myself somebody got to carry it. ... If you don't want it I got to find somebody else.
> BLACK MARY: I ain't say I didn't want it.
> AUNT ESTER: You act like it. Run from it all the time. I told myself Black Mary got to make up her mind. I don't know how much time I got left [Wilson, *Gem of the Ocean* 43].

The dynamic between the two characters is of paramount importance to the African American community. If Aunt Ester cannot secure an heir, the memories of the community will be lost. The tension increases throughout the play. As noted above, Aunt Ester preaches individual self-worth. What Black Mary fails to do early in the play is assert her independence. Understandably, she feels intimidated not only by the role of Aunt Ester, but the woman herself, who holds court at 1839 Wylie with a sense of grace and humor that belies the magnitude of her responsibility. Throughout the play, Aunt Ester and Black Mary quarrel. Ostensibly, the audience sees that Aunt Ester seeks to mold Black Mary in her image, what with her constant harping on how to properly cook food, serve visitors, and wash the laundry. In actuality, the old woman attempts to have Black Mary assert her will. Until she does, she can be nothing more than what her brother Caesar thinks she is, "a washerwoman" for a woman who has "both feet in the grave just waiting for the body to follow" (Wilson, *Gem of the Ocean* 35). The climax of this conflict occurs near the end of the play. Aunt Ester tells Black Mary that her fire in the kitchen is too high, making the room too hot and the food unpalatable. Black Mary defends herself, and, in one of Wilson's most splendid lines, Aunt Ester exclaims, "You be done burnt down the place ... turn it down!" Finally, Black Mary stands up for herself.

> Here! You cook it! You turn it down! I can't do everything the way you want me to. I'm not you. You act like there ain't no other way to do nothing. I got my own way of doing things. I like the fire high. That's the way I cook. You like it down. That's the way you cook. If you ain't cooking you ain't got nothing to say about it. All you got to worry about is the eating.... It's been three years now I can't do nothing to satisfy you. I may as well lay down somewhere and forget about it. You got something to say about everything. Turn the fire down. Wash the greens in the other pot. Shake that flour off the chicken. Tuck in the corners of the sheets. That too much starch. That ain't enough salt. I'm tired of it! Your way ain't always the best way. I got my own way and that's the way I'm doing it. If I stay around here, I'm doing it my way [Wilson, *Gem of the Ocean* 74].

Instead of assuming matriarchal authority, Aunt Ester simply replies, "What took you so long?" and exits the scene (Wilson, *Gem of the Ocean* 74). At this point, the audience understands that Aunt Ester's role is secure. Having asserted her independence, Black Mary shows she has learned the meaning of Aunt Ester's counsel. Not until she asserts her independence is she prepared to assume the role of Aunt Ester. The importance cannot be understated. Again, without an heir to Aunt Ester's role, the memories of the community are lost. In a sense, there is a collective sigh of relief, as the metaphorical foundation of the Hill District, Aunt Ester, remains intact at the end of the play. Ultimately, that foundation crumbles eighty years later in *King Hedley II* when Black Mary dies, having failed to secure an heir.

Before turning to *King Hedley II*, one must also note the relationship between Citizen Barlow and Solly Two Kings, as it mirrors that between Aunt Ester and Black Mary. Whereas Aunt Ester grooms Black Mary to assume her position, Solly Two Kings serves as a model male figure in the community for Citizen to aspire to be like. Solly Two Kings is a former Underground Railroad worker and a model of strength and dignity, "a character who represents the strength and courage of African Americans" (Spencer and Chambers 12). Importantly, Solly carries a piece of iron that had been part of the shackles that bound him as a slave: "That's my good luck piece. They tried to chain me down but I beat them on that one." He also carries a walking stick, which he proudly shows Citizen. "Look at that.... That's sixty-two notches. That's sixty-two people I carried to freedom" (Wilson, *Gem of the Ocean* 57). Solly, in fact, still seeks to emancipate those blacks he believes remain in bondage, despite the passage of the Fourteenth Amendment nearly sixty years prior to the play's setting. The old man is in the midst of preparations to travel to Alabama to rescue his sister from the whites holding her in captivity, as noted in the letter mentioned earlier in this essay. The chain and walking stick illustrate Solly's devotion to freedom, which he believes most African Americans have neither attained or understand. Before he leaves for Alabama, however, Solly learns Citizen will take a trip to the City of Bones, he offers a toast to the young man, and recites the second verse of W.C. Bryant's poem "Thanatopsis":

> So live, that when thy summons comes to join
> The innumerable caravan which moves
> To that mysterious realm, where each shall take
> His chamber in the silent halls of death,
> Thou go not, like the quarry-slave at night,
> Scourged to his dungeon, but, sustained and soothed
> By an unfaltering trust, approach thy grave
> Like one that wraps the drapery of his cough
> About him, and lies down to pleasant dreams.

Importantly, Solly hands Citizen his link of chain before the journey begins, heeding Aunt Ester's insistence that he needs a piece of iron for the journey. The scene mirrors the relationship between Aunt Ester and Black Mary. Just as Aunt Ester has taught Black Mary her role, Solly symbolically hands his to Citizen, although the connection is not entirely clear at this point.

Before Solly's and Citizen's relationship can completely manifest, the latter must travel to the aforementioned City of Bones, arguably Wilson's most magnificent imaginative creation, the symbolic territory at the bottom of the Atlantic Ocean made from the bones of the Africans who did not survive the Middle Passage, what the playwright calls "the largest unmarked grave in the world" (Wilson, Preface X). Elam comments on the importance of the city: "Its construction is an act that reunites or remembers the collective black body, those old bones making them into a unified structure, a communal site, a city that joins past to present and that overcomes loss by recuperating and actively maintaining a living African American history" (81).

Elam shows that by constructing the City of Bones, and reconstructing history, Wilson creates a locale by which African Americans can reconnect with their lost ancestry. For the playwright, African American history is one of loss, dislocation, and rupture. The community itself is unaware of a collective history. And Aunt Ester is the conduit for those who seek redemption, which is reflected when Citizen arrives at the City of Bones and confesses his sin to Garret Brown, the former's personal gatekeeper. Having cleansed himself, Citizen is *"reborn a man of the people"* (Wilson, *Gem of the Ocean* 70).

Having completed his journey, Citizen, like Herald Loomis at the end of *Joe Turner's Come and Gone,* stands on his own two feet for the first time. What Citizen will do with his life remains to be seen. In short, Wilson forges a spiritual bond between Citizen and Solly. When the group returns from the journey to the City of Bones, Caesar comes looking for Solly, knowing the freedom fighter has burned down the mill to stoke the fire of the protest alluded to earlier. When Solly strikes Caesar with his walking stick, the constable swears personal vengeance. At the end of the play, after Caesar shoots Solly, the old man dies in Aunt Ester's kitchen. As the characters carry Solly from the kitchen to be buried, Citizen, who already possesses Solly's chain link noted earlier, *"takes off his coat. He puts on Solly's coat and hat and takes Solly's stick. He discovers the letter from Solly's sister in the hat"* and exits, headed to Alabama to free Solly's sister and earn the sixty-third notch on the walking stick (Wilson, *Gem of the Ocean* 85). Just as Black Mary assumes the role of Aunt Ester, so does Citizen assume the role of Solly. While the end of the play is marred by sadness over the freedom fighters' death, the birth of the new one is a moment of triumph, a promise of hope for the community.

As we fast forward to *King Hedley II*, set in 1985, the optimism for the black community at the end of *Gem of the Ocean* has been erased. In the former play, Wilson depicts a desolate, forgotten community. In the stage description, Wilson notes, "The setting is the backyards of a row of three houses. One of the houses is missing." Also, the playwright notes that across the street from the houses is "an old advertisement for Alaga Syrup featuring Willie Mays ... painted on one of the buildings" (Wilson, *King Hedley II* 6). Mays endorsed Alaga Syrup in the mid-sixties, making the billboard approximately twenty years old, and it is unlikely the company actively seeks revenue from the endorsement of a Hall of Famer eleven years retired at this point in time. The missing house and old billboard illustrate how marginalized the inhabitants of this community have become. And while the quiet non-removal of a twenty year old billboard suggests external indifference, the slow decay of an entire house reflects an internal disregard for one's existence. In *The Past as Present in the Drama of August Wilson,* Elam offers a compelling analysis of the play's backdrop: "Internal ruptures are the focus for the fateful vision of the African American community in the 1980s that Wilson presents in *King Hedley II.* Wilson depicts a black wasteland devastated by black-on-black violence and crime ... internalized oppression [and] self-destructive violence" (69). Notice Elam's emphasis on internal disregard. The community has turned against itself. Aunt Ester's guidance is absent, and, amidst this despair, she dies of grief. Incidentally, this Aunt Ester is the former Black Mary from *Gem of the Ocean.* Unlike her predecessor, the current Aunt Ester failed to secure an heir before she died. As a result, "[t]he lessons of black suffering, terror, and survival have been forgotten and the way into the future blocked as a result" (Elam 69).

Unlike the elderly figures in *Gem of the Ocean,* the older characters in *King Hedley II* are essentially ignored by the younger generation. Even before Aunt Ester's death is announced in Act One, Stool Pigeon says, "the path to her house is all grown over with weeds, you can't hardly find the door no more" (Wilson, *King Hedley II* 8). In essence, one sees through Stool Pigeon, who is approximately seventy years old, the attitude toward the elderly. First of all, he is shunned by the community. His birth name is Canewell, but he is given the moniker Stool Pigeon because he informed to the police about who murdered Floyd Barton, events that occur at the end of Wilson's play set in the 1940s, *Seven Guitars.* In *King Hedley II,* Stool Pigeon refers to himself as a truthsayer and is a preserver of the history the community itself ignores. He collects newspapers, stacked so abundantly in his house that Ruby, his neighbor, threatens to call the police. Stool Pigeon remains unmoved by Ruby, and when a character asks him why he collects the papers, he answers, "See I know what went on. I ain't saying what goes on ... what went on. You got to know that. How you gonna get on the other side of the valley if you don't know that? You can't guess on it ... you got to know" (Wilson, *King Hedley II* 27). Stool Pigeon's desire to preserve history is a tough fight indeed. In addition to Ruby's threat to call the police because of the potential firetrap in his home, he suffers violence. In Act Two, Scene One, Stool Pigeon enters after having been accosted by a local gang of youths, who take sixty-three dollars and burn his papers. Interestingly, Stool Pigeon is not concerned about the money. He says, "I wasn't gonna fight them on that sixty-three dollars but I tried to fight them on my newspapers.... They burned up their history. They ain't gonna know what happened. They ain't gonna know how they got from tit to tat. You got to know that. They ain't gonna know nothing" (Wilson, *King Hedley II* 69). Elam notes, "Stool Pigeon suggests that you cannot move into the future without knowing the past. Through his preservation of the newspapers, he holds onto history and protects the knowledge of what went on before." Furthermore, "[t]he animosity expressed by Ruby toward Stool Pigeon reflects the fragmentation present with Wilson's picture of the black community in the 1980s" (*The Past as Present* 70). As for his experience with the gang of youths, we see a generational chasm that separates Stool Pigeon from those who do not care about their own history. Unlike Citizen Barlow in *Gem of the Ocean*, who feels a guilt so burdensome over the death of Garret Brown, the violence depicted in *King Hedley II* is perpetrated with a callous indifference in regard to its after effects.

Despite the bleak tone that permeates *King Hedley* II, Wilson offers a solution to the problems depicted in the play. For the playwright, the way to correct the damage within the black community is to metaphorically reset the clock. Enter King, the central figure in the play, the one who can ostensibly right the ship. On the surface, King appears to be another young, directionless black thug. Shortly before the play's beginning, he is released from prison, having served time for murdering another young black man, Pernell. King works construction for a local contractor named Hop, but only sporadically, and, it appears, strictly for cash. He also sells stolen refrigerators with his friend Mister. Although his desire to open a video store with Mister is endearing, he commits armed robbery to add to his savings. Beneath the surface, however, King is more complicated. Importantly, he shares a connection with Aunt Ester. As a young man, he cut the weeds in her backyard, keeping the path to her door clear. He also fetched her medicine each week. Most importantly, Aunt Ester once gave King a key ring. Stool Pigeon tells him, "You see, the key belongs to the righteous. Aunt Ester gave you the key ring, that means you got to find the key" (Wilson, *King Hedley II* 21).

Wilson further distances King from the stereotype of a violent young black man by illustrating that he lives a Spartan lifestyle. He does not spend his money on flashy clothes, jewelry, or cars. In fact, the most charming aspect of King's character is his desire to grow a garden of flowers for Tonya. When Ruby tells King he needs "good dirt" for the seeds to grow, King replies "This is the only dirt I got. This is me right here" (Wilson, *King Hedley II* 10). As the play progresses, the seeds grow. When another character, Elmore, inadvertently steps on them at the end of Act One, King persists and continues to grow them. Despite the "bad dirt," the flowers grow, as does King. He expresses remorse for murdering Pernell, whom he learns late in the play was a father like he will soon be. He stops grieving over his old flame, Nessie, and appears ready to fully commit to Tonya.

Through his personal growth, despite his surface flaws, we see in King the root of an individual willing to put others' needs ahead of his own, the kind of character Aunt Ester would encourage to work for the better of the community. Instead of becoming the common "warrior" figure in a Wilson drama, however, King emerges instead as the community's final hope for redemption. After Aunt Ester dies, so does her cat. Stool Pigeon buries it in the yard between his and King's house. He claims, "[a]ll you need now is some blood. Blood is life. You sprinkle some blood on there and if she ain't used up her nine lives Aunt Ester coming back" (Wilson, *King Hedley II* 69). In short, Stool Pigeon seeks a sacrifice, which turns out to be King. At the end of the play Elmore and King two engage in a crap game that escalates into a fight. The two draw weapons on each other, but neither uses them. Amidst the chaos, however, Ruby, King's mother, enters the house and returns with her gun. She means to shoot Elmore, but King walks toward the house as she fires the gun and the bullet hits him. As he dies, his blood flows over Aunt Ester's cat's grave, and Stool Pigeon rejoices at the sacrifice. Indeed, a cat's meow is heard as the lights go dark, promising Aunt Ester's resurrection, or at least its potential. Importantly, the filicide that ends the play further emphasizes that the black community plays an unfortunately crucial role in its own demise. King, and all the other characters for the matter, are truly at the margins of society, yet their actions continue to push them further from the mainstream. Yet with the potential resurrection of Aunt Ester, the ignored legacy of the black community featured in *King Hedley II* may be erased by a renewed spirit that embraces the strength of that community, the kind of spirit celebrated by the promise of a vital cast of characters at the end of *Gem of the Ocean*.

WORKS CITED

Bigsby, Christopher. "An Interview with August Wilson." *The Cambridge Companion to August Wilson.* Ed. Christopher Bigsby. Cambridge: Cambridge University Press, 2007. 202–213. Print.

Brustein, Robert. "The Lesson of *The Piano Lesson*." *The New Republic* 21 May 1990: 28–30. *Literature Resource Center.* Web. 15 May 2012. Print.

Elam, Harry. "*Gem of the Ocean* and the Redemptive Power of History." *The Cambridge Companion to August Wilson.* Ed. Christopher Bigsby. Cambridge: Cambridge University Press, 2007. 75–88. Print.

_____. *The Past as Present in the Drama of August Wilson.* Ann Arbor: University of Michigan Press, 2006. Print.

Glasco, Laurence, and Christopher Rawson. *August Wilson: Pittsburgh Places in His Life and Plays.* Pittsburgh History & Landmarks Foundation, 2011. Print.

Lahr, John. "Been Here and Gone." *The Cambridge Companion to August Wilson.* Ed. Christopher Bigsby. Cambridge: Cambridge University Press, 2007. 28–51. Print.

Lewis, Barbara. "Miss Tyler's Two Bodies: Aunt Ester and the Legacy of Time." *August Wilson: Completing the Twentieth Century Cycle.* Ed. Alan Nadel. Iowa City: University of Iowa Press, 2010. Print.

Moyers, Bill. "August Wilson: Playwright." *Conversations with August Wilson.* Eds. Jackson Bryer and Mary Hartig. Jackson: University of Mississippi Press, 2006. 61–80. Print.

Spencer, Vivian Gist, and Yvonne Chambers. "Ritual Death and August Wilson's Female Christ." *August Wilson: Completing the Twentieth Century Cycle.* Ed. Alan Nadel. Iowa City: University of Iowa Press, 2010. Print.

Wilson, August. *Gem of the Ocean.* New York: Theatre Communications Group, 2006.

_____. *King Hedley II.* New York: Theatre Communications Group, 2005. Print.

_____. Preface. *King Hedley II.* By August Wilson. New York: Theatre Communications Group, 2005. vii–xi. Print.

"He gonna give me my ham": The Use of Food as a Symbol for Social Justice

Psyche Williams-Forson

During a 2002 interview, playwright August Wilson stated: "Anthropologists, they want to know what you eat, they want to know why you eat what you eat, they want to know your social manners, how your community is organized, how you court, whatever it is" (Roberts xi). Wilson shares a similar sentiment in an interview with David Savran, when he explains, "I try to approach people with an anthropologist's eyes. That's why I make constant references to food. If you study culture, you want to know what people eat, what their social organization is" (34). Because food carries cultural and spiritual meaning, signifies social relationships and creates/reflects a sense of identity, it has the ability to mediate human relationships (Counihan 7). It is, as Wilson intimates, part of the social organization to which people ascribe. So central are food interactions in everyday life that it can be argued foodways plays a constitutive role in shaping cultural, social, and ethnic traditions. In other words, what is consumed and the choices made surrounding that consumption speak volumes about individual and community identity.

African American literature has been the one place where black people have been able to define themselves with and against the order of the day. As a result, literature provides one of best sites to locate African American food traditions. Though largely acts of imagination, these are also spaces of revelation. The signs of cultural hegemony, food politics, and delineations of power are omnipresent. Often embedded in the language that describes food relations are deeper insights into how these rituals are emblematic of cultural survival and continuity. Equally entrenched in African American literature are food events that provide an abundantly rich source for finding black women's acts of self-definition.

In Wilson's dramas, food is pervasive in its reflection of African American expressive culture—from Bertha's boardinghouse biscuits in *Joe Turner's Come and Gone* to the Coca-Cola in *Ma Rainey's Black Bottom*; Boy Willie's watermelon holla' in *The Piano Lesson*, to Louise's double entendre-laden ballad cry of "try my cabbage" in *Seven Guitars*. These everyday food-related performances speak to the ways that African Americans use food to indicate group affiliation. Food not only celebrates belonging, but in black communities it represents resourcefulness and ingenuity even as it nourishes, fulfills, and sustains. The setting and foodways interactions in *Two Trains Running* make it especially useful for exploring foodways as a central aspect of African American expressive culture. This essays examines select food events—or situations wherein food activities take place—that take place in the play, to glean a range of meanings that emerge from African American economic, political, social and cultural traditions. Risa's unhurried diner service and Hambone's continued ardent cry, "He gonna give me my ham," for example, illustrate the power of food to illuminate cultural sustainability and survival. Moreover, by considering the ways that Wilson's characters engage in a variety of food-related activities—from obtaining, preparing, and serving to consuming food—this essay emphasizes the importance of cultural spaces where women work and play. Lastly, this discussion reveals how these cultural arenas allow a sense of agency to emerge, particularly in the lives of black women.

Often when Wilson writes women into his plays he has them performing roles typical of gender norms or performing in ways conventionally thought by society to be associated with their gender. These women support and serve men; they care for children, and most of all, these women cook. Wilson brings to the stage women who, in the words of Harry Elam, "either through their own volition or as the result of external social pressures, ultimately conform to traditional gender roles and historical expectations" (*May All Your Fences Have Gates* 165). For this portrayal Wilson makes no apologies. Rather, he explains in a 1996 interview with Nathan Grant: "I do create some black women characters and try to be honest in their creation, but it's very hard to put myself in their space" (179). In an earlier interview with Sandra Shannon, Wilson similarly expresses,

> I doubt seriously if I would make a woman the focus of my work simply because of the fact that I am a man, and I guess because of the ground on which I stand and the viewpoint from which I perceive the world, I can't do

that although I try to be honest in the instances in which I do have women. I try to portray them from their own viewpoint as opposed to my viewpoint ["The Ground on Which I Stand" 106].

This analysis considers whether or not it is always necessary to read the women characters in Wilson's plays in relation to the men. It seems that if we do this, we run the risk of primarily noticing their lack of voice and seeing them as insufficiently developed. Viewing women characters from this point of view can also lead to a failure to appreciate their personal and communal complexities, particularly when using food.[1]

Risa's role in the diner of *Two Trains Running* opens up a plethora of ways to read women's empowerment on a culinary cultural landscape. To fully grasp Risa's acts of agency it seems some background about the diner is in order. Against the setting of economic upheaval, change, destruction, and rapid gentrification in Pittsburgh, we find a semi-functioning diner where everyday performances with food unveil social and psychological survival. The setting is a diner located adjacent to a meat market and a funeral home. Patricia Gantt remarks that this location is a symbolic placement between "life (Lutz's Meat Market) and death (West's Funeral Home)" (83). Though Gantt's observation is understandable, in many ways the diner is surrounded completely by death. The restaurant will be torn down and removed along with the already vanished supermarket, drugstores, the five and ten, and the local shoe store. Inside the diner, the patrons are few and more recently the jukebox has ceased to work. In short, the diner is located in a place surrounded by blight or what some food scholars have labeled a food desert.[2]

Diner architecture during the play's time period was minimal containing a counter (which usually ran the length of the place), a row of densely packed stools, and a few tables or booths lining the front wall or packed in tightly at the end of the space (Hurley 1285). In *Two Trains Running,* the diner landscape is similar. It is small and simple encompassing four stools, a counter, and three booths lined against one wall. The tight space means that conversations take place within close proximity to one another. This level of intimacy creates the conditions to overhear one another's conversations allowing for constant disruptions and the lack of privacy. The menu further emphasizes the diner's minimalism; it is not only scarce but also hastily scribbled on a blackboard behind the counter. This kind of eatery held the social function of serving cheap but familiar and hearty food mostly to men working in factories, during the immediate post–World War II era. In places like Baltimore, Maryland, Newark, New Jersey, and Pittsburgh, diner eateries flourished because they catered primarily to these working class men. The 1940s brought with it the addition of women, like Risa, as waitresses. Restaurateur James Mears explained to *Diner Magazine*, "Women belong in restaurants as waitresses, hostesses and cashiers. They give an atmosphere to your place which encourages the family trade" (Hurley 1298).

Diners owned and operated by African Americans, like Wilson's fictional Memphis Lee's Home Style Restaurant, were essential in the era of Jim Crow segregation. Similar to barber shops, beauty salons, poolrooms, bars, and churches, these haunts or "third places" served as gathering spaces with immense social, cultural, and psychological value. Bruce Johansen explains, "these sites may provide a spiritual or traditional connection between past and present ... help give a disempowered group back its history, or provide an essential reference point in a community's identity or sense of itself.... They may shape some aspect of community behavior or attitudes ... they are accessible to the public, offering the possibility of repeated use to build up associations and value to the community of users, or they might be places where people gather and act as a community" (Johansen 24–25). August Wilson's life experience tending grill, from time to time, gave him first-hand knowledge of small restaurant flow— from the food to the verbal exchanges and the gender encounters. Given this overview, seemingly, it would be a mistake to overlook Risa's role in community building as less than central to the play, an argument the remainder of this essay will seek to explain.

In the play *Two Trains Running*, Risa uses food not only to self-express but also to unsettle the male domain of Memphis' Diner. One of the ways that we learn about Risa's personality is through her participation in ritualized verbal playing such as specifying and signifying. Signifying, and playing or "doing the dozens," are rooted in African American oral traditions. One of the many aspects of African American expressive culture found in *Two Trains Running*, this kind of verbal play has long been considered a male bonding ritual (Major 51). But, women play too. In *Dust Tracks on a Road*, Zora Neale Hurston explains that one of her landladies had a way of "specifying" or "putting [her] foot up" on people. Hurston writes,

> it is all right to go to the house of your enemy, put one foot up on his steps, rest one elbow on your knee and play in the family. That is another way of saying play the dozens, which is also a way of saying low rate your enemy's ancestors and him, down to the present moment for reference, and then go into his future as far as your imagination leads you. But if you have no faith in your personal courage and confidence in your arsenal, don't try it. *It is a risky pleasure* [Walker 57].

As Hurston indicates, signifying comes from a place of "courage" and it involves a level of "confidence." To "get at" the meanings behind a waitress' involvement in this "risky pleasure" seems to require that we broaden our thinking around when the "dozens" is played, by whom, and in what context. Expanding allows for recognizing when this strategy is being used by women to effect self-expression.

Risa is quick to offer verbal quips when she wants to "put one foot up on [a man's] steps." When Memphis, the diner's owner talks with Wolf, a customer, about his wife leaving him, Risa does not hesitate to interject her thoughts into the conversation: "Maybe [your wife] didn't like the way you was treating her." Memphis responds, which prompts Risa to rejoin: "Maybe she don't see it like that. She had to leave for something" (4–5). Having said her piece Risa fades into the background until the next time that she has something to say, all the while keeping pace with her food service. Despite the fact that her comments might be hurtful, Risa "talks shit" to Memphis about his wife and does so with confidence stating to her friend and customer, Sterling (who questions her insubordination), "I ain't worried about getting fired" (18). The warning of Hurston's landlady that "lowrating" and "playing the dozens" is "risky" if one's arsenal is not full, seems to elude Risa who plays the talking game with aplomb. Risa's behavior illustrates what Geneva Smitherman says is the way some black women "play the Dozens, and 'talk shit'"—they signify or cleverly convey serious messages through oral jesting (241).

Risa engages in the diner's chitchat when she pleases and when she chooses not to do so she slides back into the kitchen. In a long verbal exchange between Risa and Memphis in which they go back and forth about cooking food for a customer, Risa balks at every command Memphis barks:

MEMPHIS: Hey Risa
RISA: What?
MEMPHIS: What you mean, "what?" You see the man sitting there. Wait on him. That's what you here for.
RISA: I was trying to clean the chicken.
MEMPHIS: The man want to eat now...
RISA: We ain't got no chicken. And we ain't got no meat loaf. We ain't got no hamburger either. We just got beans and corn bread.
MEMPHIS: You got some hamburger back there.
RISA: It's all frozen.
MEMPHIS: Well, take it out the freezer, thaw it out...
RISA: You want some beans? [16–17].

This banter continues with Memphis insisting that Risa hurry and finish preparing the food. Finally, Risa yells, "I'm frying it!" Having made this statement Risa exits to the kitchen. Quite possibly, had there been a door Risa would have slammed it shut!

In the public space of the diner Risa enjoys a relative amount of self-actualization and self-awareness through the camaraderie, celebration, and competition that permeates the verbal play. Considering black women's participation in the public sphere—the street, the school, the church, the city, the coffee shop, barbershop, and the salon—kitchens make sense as a necessary addition (Black Public Sphere Collective 2–3). Blacks have never had access to the public sphere in the same ways as whites and by extension black women have been limited in their access to many male spaces. Though restricted, women have always participated in the public sphere for their own sakes, for uplifting the race and community, and for their families. In the legacy of those African American women before her, Risa manipulates and uses to her advantage verbal/nonverbal cues, along with silence, to insert her voice. In *Check It While I Wreck It: Black Womanhood, Hip-Hop Culture, and the Public Sphere*, Gwendolyn Pough explains that black women use the concept of the cipher—a place where people gather to create knowledge and simultaneously a process of continuous motion—to get across their point. Pough goes on to say that black women make use of everything "to bring wreck" (41).

In the public culinary cultural landscape of the diner Risa uses a variety of objects associated with her profession—foods, auxiliary implements (such as kitchen utensils, brooms, mops), and even her body (a point to which I will momentarily return) to play "the culinary dozens" (Williams-Forson 135). Verbal facility, skill, and quickness in speech are all characteristics of doing the dozens. And, though not required, public space often is useful because it assures the players that there will be some kind of audience. Because an aspect of the dozens almost always involves some element of negative valuation and recitation on mothers, men tend not hesitate to use this tactic. One day, while Risa is sweeping the floor she swipes the broom over the feet of Wolf, the number runner. This causes him to exclaim: "Don't sweep me with that broom, girl. Ain't your mama never taught you nothing?" Risa replies, "Well, move your feet out of the way then" (90). Disregarding Wolf's jab at her "mama" Risa again sweeps over his feet and then simply tells him to move, which he soon does. Risa is undaunted by Wolf's reference to her mother or superstition, suggesting that she is deliberate about entering the arena of insult. Perhaps it was always her intention to get Wolf to move out of her way. She is effective in doing so by playing the nonverbal/verbal game of dozens using the broom along with her wit.

It is easy to overlook the moments when Risa, too, "brings wreck"[3] because they are sometimes subtle and occluded by our focus on the male network in the diner. But Risa uses great skill in performing the culinary dozens—play that does not involve references to someone's mother, but generally always involves the manipulation of food objects. Almost daily, West—the local undertaker—comes into the diner for his coffee and requests "let me get a little bit of sugar here, Risa." Shortly after Holloway, another patron, makes the same request, Sterling, then a relatively new visitor to the diner, asks Risa, "How come you don't give nobody no sugar? You make them ask for it." To this Risa responds, "I give it to them. All they got to do is ask. West asks for sugar and then half the time don't use it. You watch him. First thing he do is ask for sugar and then it look like he change his mind" (50). Clearly, it should be of little interest to Risa whether her patrons use the sugar or not. But Risa is aware of her seemingly subordinate position in the diner as the only woman in a largely male domain. Writing along these lines Harry Elam, borrowing from Patricia Hill Collins' "outsider within" concept, argues, "Risa's location within the restaurant's labor system, but outside the male network of conversation and associations provides her with a unique perspective on the men as well as her own subordination" (*The Woman Question* 100). To a large extent this is certainly true. It is equally true that Risa exercises a degree of control over the men by forcing them to ask her for the confection.

When analyzing *Two Trains Running*, most critics focus on Risa's unhurried service and her refusal to provide sugar to customers who request coffee unless they also specifically ask for the confection. To be sure, Risa's deliberately slow service in the diner can be read as an act of resistance against the male establishment who insists day in and out that she "give them some sugar." The double entendre of the phrase is no doubt intended as Risa withholds two kinds of sugar—the sweetener but also attention to her physical body—to which a great deal of critical attention also has been given. Wilson writes, "I felt I was right in having [Risa] refuse to be defined by her genitals [through self-scarification] ... but I couldn't go beyond that into making some heavier interior psychology of it. Not that I didn't want to, I guess, but I don't know it" (Grant 110). However, Wilson invites readers to "go beyond" his reading, to resist the urge to see Risa primarily as a scarred and maimed woman with little voice. When Risa moves at her own pace while cooking food, refuses to serve necessary condiments until asked, and talks back to the customers (all of whom are men), she forces them to interact with her on *her* terms. Pough would describe Risa's behavior as "moments when Black women's discourses disrupt dominant masculine discourses, break into the public sphere, and in some ways impact or influence the U.S. imaginary, even if that influence is fleeting" (76). It seems important that we give place to the instances when Risa situates and inserts herself into the conversations of the male-dominated diner, especially when they do not directly involve food.

Risa joins in the time-honored tradition of playing the numbers without putting in any money. Though she tells her admirer Sterling that playing the numbers is "throwing away" your money she does offer to give him a number to play:

> STERLING: I'm trying to get twenty-five hundred dollars. I wouldn't mind taking a chance on that if I had me a good number.
> RISA: Play seven eighty-one.
> STERLING: How you come up with that?
> RISA: I got seven scars on one leg and eight on the other.
> STERLING: Where you get the one from?
> RISA: That's my business.
> STERLING: One what?
> RISA: Go on, Sterling, I ain't playing with you.

While we do not know how or from where Risa derives the "one" we can use our imaginations to figure any number of reference points. Perhaps it speaks to her vagina, the single space that exists between "seven scars on one leg and eight on the other." Or, maybe she is simply referencing herself. Both observations are plausible given Sterling's remark, "What? I just say, 'where you get the one from?' You getting all embarrassed. What you getting embarrassed about? I ought to play seven eighty-two. We can put one and one together" (48–49).

Here, it seems, is another instance where Risa employs a kind of verbal play on the culinary landscape. Risa is coy about the origins of the number one in her configuration. Similar to the double entendre in Louise's ballad cry of "try my cabbage" in Wilson's *Seven Guitars*, Risa makes the men in the diner repeatedly ask her for some sugar. It is possible then, that she is employing a similar coquettish stance by wanting Sterling to play the guessing game with the proffered number. The game, perhaps, is another way Risa asserts control in the male-dominated space. To be sure, a number of interpretations are possible. But it seems that an empowering reading of Risa's character ensues when we do not foreclose on the numerous crafty ways that women often engage the male network of conversation especially when using food and in kitchens.[4]

Despite Wilson's statement that he could not go beyond what he knew to write Risa's character, such behaviors and conversations stemming from the kitchen were not lost on him. Wilson believed that the content of his "mother's life—her myths, her superstitions, her prayers, the contents of her pantry, the smell of her kitchen, the song that escaped from her sometimes parched lips, her thoughtful repose and pregnant laughter—are all worthy of art" (x). As such, it is believable that Wilson had some familiarity with the ways that women behave in and around kitchens. Wilson's depiction of Risa suggests he understood, to some extent, the critical ways in which African American women act as cultural workers with or involving food. It is no wonder, then, that Risa is effectively engaged in the political action of *Two Trains Running*.

Like many African American women, Risa's involvement in social action is threatened with being overlooked because it does not reside in places of overt politics. Yet, Risa's participation in the daily acts of taking orders, preparing, and serving food is significant for what it suggests about the critical ways in which African American women act as cultural workers using food. Food preparation, as "women's work" is often seen as an extension of a woman's way of being or her femininity (DeVault 180). Not only are women in Wilson's plays important for their role as nurturers as Sandra Shannon has observed, but also for their role as entrepreneurs and cultural workers, as exemplified by Bertha Holly in *Joe Turner's Come and Gone* (*The Ground* 162). For example, as Shannon notes, Bertha nurtures her tenants and seems genuinely concerned with their well-being (162). But more than a caretaker, Bertha is also a cultural worker. On this role, Bernice Johnson Reagan writes,

> Women were the heads of their communities, the keepers of tradition. The lives of these women were defined by their culture, the needs of their communities, and the people they served ... they accepted the responsibility when the opportunity was offered—when they were chosen. There is the element of transformation in all of their work.... These women, however, became central to evolving the structure for resolving areas of conflict and maintaining, sometimes creating, an identity that was independent of a society organized to exploit natural resources, people, and land [168–169].

Risa also serves as a cultural worker in and beyond the landscape of the diner.

When Memphis returns to the diner from visiting Aunt Esther, he notices a sign on the menu board that announces the funeral of Hambone, the mentally disabled man who appeared at the restaurant every morning. Risa, who acts as Hambone's caretaker, immediately responds to Memphis that Hambone died in his sleep (109). For nine and a half years Hambone would show up and shout, "I want my ham. He gonna give me my ham." Hambone was told he would be given a ham if he did a good job painting the fence at Lutz's Meat Market, the white-owned grocery adjacent to the diner. When Hambone completed the job he was given a chicken instead. Hambone refused the substitute. Every morning after that day Hambone would appear at the owner's doorstep to demand his ham.[5] During his visits to the diner, Risa feeds and clothes Hambone, despite protestations by Memphis that she get back to work. Ignoring Memphis and others who ridicule the mentally impaired man, Risa slips him cornbread and beans as if he is a paying customer. By helping the mentally unstable Hambone, a role few of the men seemed to relish or invite, Risa contributes to uplifting her community. Her unwavering support of his repeated cry, "He gonna give me my ham" speaks to Risa's belief that Hambone was as normal as she but in need of extra support instead of criticism.

Aside from the social justice implications of Hambone's struggle—refusing to accept anything other than what was owed to him—Risa contributes to bringing about a modicum of stability in Hambone's life. For all intents and purposes, Risa is Hambone's sole familial support and the diner serves as a surrogate home. Risa and Hambone's relationship is further solidified by the shared discrimination and oppression they experience from the wider community—Risa because she is a woman (and black), Hambone because he is mentally ill. Both are stigmatized by society and they bear the psychological and physical scars to reflect their isolation—real or imagined. Though the negative self-images that usually accommodate such stigmatisms could limit their ability to live full lives, both Risa and Hambone embrace the challenge. Risa confronts life's limitations with daily verbal and non-verbal interruptions in the diner and Hambone is defiant with his disruptive cry, "he gonna give me my ham!"

When Hambone dies, it is Risa who insists that West's Funeral Home lay him out in something other than a pauper's casket. Such care is socially engendered to women and is generally most always devalued. But, ethical care of others can challenge us to see this attribute as one of human strength, akin to acts of justice. Taking this analytic one step further, black feminist thought suggests we understand Risa in her role as a cultural worker. Not only is she a "keeper of tradition" by caring for the mentally infirm, but also, as Reagan suggests, Risa "accept[s] the responsibility [of caring for Hambone] when the opportunity was offered—when [she was] chosen" (168). Like countless other African American women before her who were bound by various social, personal, and familial restraints Risa too mobilizes herself and others in the community to effect change on a local—and often considered insignificant—level.

Risa's work with Hambone goes beyond the gustatory to encompass the realm of the emotional and cultural as well as the spiritual and transformational. In her analysis of the performativity of black women's faith and its radical implications for resistance, Telia Anderson asserts, "Black women *church*. As modern day apostles, they speak to and from the church within themselves…. Black women can and do have church anywhere: in beauty parlors, in the street, on the dance floor, around the kitchen table" (126). Anderson goes on to state that spirituality moves and functions outside of institutional worship halls "in a more public and secular declaration of self and identity." In other words, Risa illustrates her connection with the Divine through her acts of care. Anderson maintains that black women like Risa who call the spirit in this way "[occupy] a place of disclosure, rather than a place of reference." This kind of cultural performance—using food and other elements to show care toward a mentally ill person—

> [evokes] a transcendent model, evoke[s] a transgressive one, which breaks through sedimented meanings and normative traditions, plunging us back into the vortices of political struggle … black women subvert the prescribed order by invoking the church attainable within their individual bodies…. Although black women may not crush the vise of racism … by calling on the spirit in whatever idiom, they subvert the totality of its hold. It is not that black women are completely free to perform as they wish within a given hegemonic arena, but rather that they communicate with a force beyond their particular circumstances to salute the divinity within that propels and energizes their performances [Anderson 127].

Cultural workers often became central "to sometimes creating, an identity that was independent of a society organized to exploit natural resources, people, and land" (Reagon 169). Perhaps it is this transformative energy, or his fondness for Risa and Hambone, or maybe even Risa's insistence that overcomes Sterling who risks going back to jail when he breaks into Lutz's store and takes the long sought after ham. Though Hambone will be unable to enjoy it because he is dead, Sterling gives the ham to West Funeral Home to be placed in Hambone's casket. This climactic ending can be read as confirming the notion that African Americans are only able to seek justice upon death. However, by reading the ending as justice obtained through community action Risa's transformative work in and beyond Memphis' eatery is highlighted.

Food has the ability to convey a multitude of meanings because food performs, speaks, and acts (Kirshenblatt-Gimblett 1). In the setting of Memphis' diner food takes on multiple meanings. The culturally familiar beans, cornbread, chicken, collard greens, potato salad, macaroni and cheese, meatloaf, mashed potatoes, and green beans offer nourishment, and provide memories, comfort, and security. But in this space, where food, memory, and business activities intersect, some social boundaries collapse while others remain intact. For example, because Risa is the only female in a male-dominated space the focus could lean toward the predictable issues of sexuality and femininity. Left unexplored, but present nonetheless, are the daily acts of agency, contributions to social justice, and transformative work (large and small) that women perform in and out of the kitchen. Additionally, it is possible to miss the myriad ways in which black women's work and play in the kitchen using a variety of foodstuffs represent a valid form of self-expression, self-assertion, and self-possession.

NOTES

1. With this argument I am pushing back against arguments waged by the important theatre scholars like Kim Marra who suggests that Wilson invites a feminist critique because he positions his female characters as "other." I do not disagree with Marra but suggest a different kind of engagement with Wilson's work, one that enables a broader reading of his female characters. See Marra "Ma Rainey and the Boyz: Gender Ideology in August Wilson's Broadway Canon."

2. Food deserts are generally considered places that are devoid of any kind of full service grocery store. For more, see Steven Haider and Marianne Bitler, "An Economic View of Food Deserts in the United States," National Poverty Center (March 2009).

3. Pough defines this in a hip-hop context as inhabiting great skill or being outstanding in one's rhetorical greatness. I'm using the concept in this discussion to relate to times that Risa dishes out as much flack as she has received.

4. In the Plume edition of the play the cover has a picture of the restaurant with Risa inside and all of the men on the outside. In her hand is a cup of coffee and a plate. Looking into the restaurant with obvious longing are all of the male characters.

5. Normally, the particular food object is not necessarily as important as its implications. However, it is absolutely fitting that Hambone would reject the chicken given its stereotyped associations with African American people. In a further display of rebuke, Hambone demands payment because so many before him had been denied their "forty acres and a mule" and he insists that the promise made to him be fulfilled.

WORKS CITED

Anderson, Telia. "'Calling on the Spirit': The Performativity of Black Women's Faith in the Baptist Church Spiritual Traditions and Its Radical Possibilities for Resistance." *African American Performance and Theater History: A Critical Reader.* Eds. Harry Elam, Jr., and David Krasner. New York: Oxford University Press, 2001. 114–131. Print.

The Black Public Sphere Collective, ed. *The Black Public Sphere: A Public Culture Book.* Chicago: University of Chicago Press, 1995. Print.

Counihan, Carole. *The Anthropology of Food and Body: Gender, Meaning, and Power.* New York: Routledge, 1999. Print.

DeVault, Marjorie. "Conflict and Deference." *Food and Culture: A Reader.* Eds. Carole Counihan and Penny Van Esterik. New York: Routledge, 1997. 180–200. Print.

Elam, Harry. "August Wilson's Women." *May All Your Fences Have Gates.* Ed. Alan Nadel. Iowa City: University of Iowa Press, 1994. 165–182. Print.

———. "The Woman Question." *The Past as Present in the Drama of August Wilson.* Ann Arbor: University of Michigan Press, 2006. 88–126. Print.

Gantt, Patricia. "Ghosts from 'Down There': The Southernness of August Wilson." *August Wilson: A Casebook.* Ed. Marilyn Elkins. New York: Routledge, 2000. 69–88. Print.

Grant, Nathan. "Men, Women, and Culture: A Conversation with August Wilson." *Conversations with August Wilson.* Jackson: University Press of Mississippi, 2006. 172–187. Print.

Haider, Steven, and Marianne Bitler. "An Economic View of Food Deserts in the United States." Washington, D.C., National Poverty Center (March 2009). Web. 2 May 2013.

Hurley, Andrew. "From Hash House to Family Restaurant: The Transformation of the Diner and Post-World War II Consumer Culture." *Journal of American History* 83.4 (March 1997): 1282–1308. Print.

Johansen, Bruce. *Imagined pasts, imagined futures: Race, politics, memory, and the revitalization of downtown Silver Spring, Maryland.* Dissertation, University of Maryland College Park. Proquest UMI, 2005. (Publication No. AAT 3202411.)

Kirshenblatt-Gimblett, Barbara. "Playing to the Senses: Food as a Performance Medium." *Performance Research* 4. 1 (1999): 1–30. Print.

Major, Clarence. *Dictionary of Afro-American Slang.* New York: International, 1970. Print.

Marra, Kim. "Ma Rainey and the Boyz: Gender Ideology in August Wilson's Broadway Canon." *August Wilson: A Casebook.* Ed. Marilyn Elkins. New York: Garland, 2000. 123–160. Print.

Pough, Gwendolyn. *Check It While I Wreck It: Black Womanhood, Hip-Hop Culture, and the Public Sphere.* Lebanon, NH: Northeastern University Press, 2004. Print.

Reagon, Bernice Johnson. "African Diaspora Women: The Making of Cultural Workers." *Women in Africa and the African Diaspora.* Eds. Rosalyn Terborg-Penn, Sharon Harley, and Andrea Benton-Rushing. Washington, D.C.: Howard University Press, 1987. 167–180. Print.

Roberts, Brian Henry. *Can you tell me how to get to the crossroads? A Cultural Analysis of Community Rituals in Five Major Plays by August Wilson.* Dissertation. Indiana University of Pennsylvania. Proquest UMI, 2002. (Publication No. AAT 3066017.)

Savran, David. *In Their Own Words*. New York: Theatre Communications Group, 1988. Print.
Shannon, Sandra. "Developing Character: *Fences*." *The Dramatic Vision of August Wilson*. Washington, D.C.: Howard University Press, 1995. 89–118. Print.
———. "The Ground on Which I Stand: August Wilson's Perspective on African American Women." *May All Your Fences Have Gates*. Ed. Alan Nadel. Iowa City: University of Iowa Press, 1994. 150–164. Print.
Smitherman, Geneva. "Testifyin, Sermonizin, and Signifyin: Anita Hill, Clarence Thomas and the African American Verbal Tradition." *African American Women Speak Out on Anita Hill–Clarence Thomas*. Detroit: Wayne State University Press, 1995. 224–242. Print.
Walker, Alice, ed. *I Love Myself When I Am Laughing: A Zora Neale Hurston Reader*. New York: The Feminist Press, 1979. Print.
Williams-Forson, Psyche. "*Say Jesus and Come to Me*: Signifying and Church Food." *Building Houses Out of Chicken Legs: Black Women, Food, and Power*. Chapel Hill: University of North Carolina Press, 2006. 135–163. Print.
Wilson, August. *Two Trains Running*. New York: Plume, 1992. Print.

Resurrecting "phantom limb[s] of the dismembered slave and god": Unveiling the Africanisms in *Gem of the Ocean*[1]

Artisia Green

"It's not potentially destructive at all. To say that I am an African, and I can participate in this society as an African, and I don't have to adopt European values, European aesthetics, and European ways of doing things in order to live in the world...."
—August Wilson, *Conversations with August Wilson*

"You will understand *Gem* through Olokun."
—Julianna Sarr, personal interview

At the helm of the August Wilson 20th century cycle is *Gem of the Ocean* (2003). On the surface, this play chronicles the first generation of the post-emancipation era and the first family of the Wilson Cycle—Aunt Ester and her protégé, Black Mary; the formidable Eli and Solly Two Kings, the harbinger of justice; Caesar Wilks, the town constable; and the determined Citizen Barlow. The year is 1904 and the black heirs of the Constitutional promissory notes entitling them to life, liberty and the pursuit of happiness are attempting to cash out. The search has begun for the fruits of freedom (King). After 250 years of enslavement, notions of liberty meant non-restricted movement and access to education. It represented the reuniting of families, the acquisition of land, and labor that produced a living-wage. However, in *Gem* Wilson argues that "so far, [freedom] doesn't mean very much" (Dezell 254) describing its injustices and resultant grief as "a mighty big ocean" (Wilson, *Gem* 60). Despite the abolishment of slavery, African Americans continued to suffer from discrimination and destabilization. Anti-black violence and quasi-slavery legislation formed the basis of an ensuing tide of white-supremacy which demoralized newly freed African Americans. Structural injustices—sharecropping, merchant liens, peonage systems, and Jim Crow—prevented many African Americans from migrating North and West in the hopes of escaping legal, political and economic subjugation.

In spite of these tensions, Wilson has been quoted as saying that "[these characters] figure out how to live in the world." He continues on by explaining that at the center of [Gem] is the incredible spirituality of African people who honor their ancestors. They have concepts of God—trees that have spirits. All of these things have been part of their belief system" (Dezell 254). It is this belief system—the character of their African cultural heritage—that should be wholly embraced lest they fall victim to the limitations of the law and the trappings of American materialism.

As all of these ideals blend into art, *Gem* offers a duality for the masses. On the one end its dramaturgy is fashioned after the paradigm of the West, "the age-old dramaturgy handed down by the Greeks and rooted in Aristotle's poetics" (Lyons). However, within Wilson's poetic form lies the "phantom limb[s] of the dismembered slave and god" (Okediji 3). Beneath *Gem*'s Judeo-Christian tropes and pseudo-American patriotism is a Yoruban cosmology situated within the characters and the architecture of the text. Yoruban ideals instilling historical and ancestral pride not only offer equality for the black self-image, but further propel the black psyche beyond the limits of the oppressor into the realm of deities.[2] Wilson's employment of such an African aesthetic—Òrìṣà archetypes, sacred objects and spaces, and Yoruban temporal coordination—positions *Gem* as one of his "spirit-centered texts" [with a] primary function of [evocating and dramatizing] spiritual conditions and spiritual activity" (Rahming 36). This essay seeks to illuminate the play's spiritual potency by first discussing the characterizations informed by Òrìṣà archetypes while simultaneously noting significant objects and spaces, followed by comments on the temporal coordination of the architecture of the play.

Òrìṣà Archetypes, Sacred Objects and Spaces

Wilson describes *Gem*'s characters as "a series of tributary streams ... linked back to the ocean from which they find impulse" (Wilson, "Sailing"). This "impulse" is shaped by one of the four defining B's of his dramaturgy—Romare Bearden's collage technique, most particularly his juxtaposition of African masks and African American faces (Herrington

23). Wilson's employment of Òrìṣà archetypes marries each character with an expression of a Yoruban divine consciousness. Olarosa, Ògún, Òṣun, Aganjú / Ṣàngó, and Òṣóṣì are the Òrìṣà archetypes that shall be discussed in this section of the essay.

Olarosa, or "the god la stands at the door," is the guardian of homes. Situated at the homes' entrance and armed with a sword or stick, he keeps watch for impertinent and unknown entities. For the past twenty-five years, Eli has stood watch at 1839 Wylie Avenue, declaring to each unknown guest and those who he believes enter with ill intent that, "This is a peaceful house" (Wilson, *Gem*, 7). His protection over the house also extends to the outside of the domain. As a function of his status as helper and guardian, he spends the better part of Act I building a wall "to keep Caesar on the other side" (Wilson, *Gem* 14). The construction of the wall is significant. Among Yoruba creation stories is the belief that when the Òrìṣàs descended from Ilé-Ifé to earth, what remained of their existence were rocks—òkúta or all seeing eyes—which contained their àṣẹ or "power to bring ideas and desire into being" (Washington 14). In the Ifá/Òrìṣà tradition, worshippers collect the rocks from natural places associated with particular deities. In *Gem*, it is Rutherford Selig who collects these rocks for Eli during his travels along the river. Òṣun—the deity associated with rivers, lakes and streams—is the Òrìṣà most invoked in this instance. Wilson draws upon a material element in one of her creation stories, her association with honey, when he writes about Aunt Ester's house. It is Harmond in *Radio Golf* (2005) who calls our attention to the sweetness of the home:

> HARMOND: You should feel the woodwork. If you run your hand slow over some of the wood you can make out these carvings. There's faces. Lines making letters. An old language. And there's this smell in the air.
> ROOSEVELT: That's them mothballs....
> HARMOND: No.... The air in the house smells sweet like a new day [Wilson, *Radio Golf* 61–62].

Undoubtedly the sweetness of 1839 Wylie Avenue is related to the àṣẹ invoked by the building of the wall with rocks collected from Òṣun's river. Eli says, "I want a wall.... The way [Caesar] going he gonna have everybody in jail (Wilson, *Gem* 14). The wall is Eli's determination to make the home an asylum, a fact which Black Mary makes clear to Caesar in Act II:

> BLACK MARY: 1839 Wylie Avenue is a house of sanctuary. It ain't up

to you to decide. The Bible say, "A place of refuge shall be given unto you and whosoever counsel therein shall he be made also clean, for I have given unto the master of that abode a place above the law, for the law is a punisher of men, and I seeketh their redemption" [Wilson, *Gem* 79].

The design and implementation of the wall is Eli's attempt at creating environmental harmony between tensions that become evident over the course of the play, tensions between Òṣun's sweetness, a function of her preference for peace, diplomacy and negotiation, and the resolute enforcement of the law by Òṣósì (who shall be discussed elsewhere). The wall is also the theoretical demarcation between the material and spiritual realms with Aunt Ester's house as the metaphysical site of accessing such spiritual transcendence.

In *Radio Golf* (2005) we learn that the door to 1839 Wylie Avenue is red. Although not specifically mentioned in *Gem*, the red door is as Olarosa and the wall—a hindrance to "death, sickness, tragedy, loss and obstacles" (Neimark 10). Red noted by Robert Farris Thompson "is the supreme presence of color" (Thompson 6) and is known for its ability to avert malevolent forces as attested to by two Yoruba parables. One says, "The original three cloths of the Egungun were of the color red. They terrorized the witches. They terrorized the forces of pestilence. Afterwards, whenever important elders died, these powerful cloths were added to their corpse and the body rose up as Egungun" (Thompson 219). Another states:

> "Once there was an epidemic, we are not certain what it was, we only know what the god of divination says it was—a dreaded illness that killed thousands, leaving deadly little spots broken out on people's bodies. Diviners told us to carry three red cloths, called eku [cloths of salvation], to a certain spot and sacrifice there, to save the city. At this place the carriers of the cloth met the spirits of disease. The latter fled at the sight of the three red cloths" [Thompson 219].

Thus, the color added to the door of the house protects those who live within and in conjunction with the wall, speaks to a spatial landscape influenced by Yoruban cosmology.

Assisting Eli with the building of the wall is the refuge seeking Citizen Barlow. He evokes the archetype of Ògún, the machete wielding deity of creation and destruction who sits at the forefront of industrialization. The guardian of truth, Ògún is responsible for clearing internal and external obstacles from the path that would impede spiritual growth. Ògún's steady determination to see a task through to completion is evidenced in several ways through Citizen—he makes his own way from Alabama to Pennsylvania even though all the roads were closed and returns to Alabama to see Solly's sister, Eliza's safe passage to the North. Both Citizen and his archetypal forefather, Ògún became victims of their misdirected anger and as a result caused innocent men to die. Note the following praise story of Ògún which speaks of their similar fate:

> Having defended the village of Onire from destruction, Ògún walked to the well for a drink of water. As the people of Onire saw him walk through the streets of their village they pleaded with him to leave. In rage, Ògún raised his àdá, and the water from the well turned red.
> When he realized that he had killed the people of his own village, Ògún felt ashamed and went to live in a hole in the ground. As he made his way into the Earth, he left a chain dangling from the hole and told the people of Onire that they could summon him by pulling the chain [Fatunmbi, *Ogun* 14].

With wounded pride, Ògún massacred his own community because they failed to recognize his humanity. However, they did not recognize him as he was covered in the evidence of his recent battle. In a similar vein, the mills' failure to recognize Citizen's humanity (through insufficient pay and room and board arrangements) sparked his anger which led to a series of events for which he was directly responsible—the death of Garret Brown and the subsequent fragmentation of Mr. Brown's family, an uprising at the mill, and its eventual closure. The guilt and shame he experiences from theft, lying by omission, and murder drive him to climb through Aunt Ester's window (his attempt to circumvent Eli who delayed his audience with her at the front door).

The bucket of nails, a lasting symbol of his crime, is another symbol of importance. The nails are an expression of the ironwork of Ògún, referencing both his industrialism and his function of clearing blockages. Citizen states, "I stole a bucket of nails. The mill wouldn't pay me so I stole a bucket of nails. They say Garret Brown stole it he ran and jumped in the river. I told myself to tell them I did it but every time I started to tell them something got in the way" (Wilson, *Gem* 44). His fear of consequence became his blockage. In appropriating the bucket of nails, Wilson draws upon minkisi phenomenology—the Nkondi. The Nkondi is a particular type of Kongolese spiritual medicine in the form of a figure, activated to enforce oaths, affect illness or cure, and hunt and punish transgressors of harmony. Activation is usually caused by the insertion and striking of a nail within the figure, but it can also be effected by burial curses, striking the earth or driving wood into the earth's surface. If the Nkondi is invoked to enforce justice, the perpetrator can be punished with many things including chest pains or pressure. Citizen references the void he feels at his center twice in Act I; "I feel like I got a hole inside of me," (Wilson, *Gem* 23) and again, "It's like I got a hole inside me. If I ain't careful seem like everything would leak out that hole" (Wilson, *Gem* 44). Thus, Citizens' misdemeanor invokes a figurative Nkondi. The nails, becoming a source of guilt, continuously strike at his center, becoming the crisis which sends him agitatedly to Aunt Ester and subsequently, the womb of the spirit realm in search of renewal.

Upon meeting Citizen, Aunt Ester likens him to one of her sons saying, "Junebug ... a good boy. Just a rascal of a man" (Wilson, *Gem* 20). This symbolic descriptor stands as a proverbial Chekovian gun. The Junebug or Scarabaeus Sacer is a sacred insect to the Egyptians. A dung beetle, it repeats a cycle of collection, underground storage, and reproduction in animal excrement. As such, the Egyptians likened it to their Sun god, Khepri ("He who is coming into being")—the god of creation, the movement of the sun, and rebirth. In likewise fashion, it was Ògún who descended into what Wole Soyinka calls the "chthonic realm, the seething cauldron of the dark world will and psyche, the transitional yet inchoate matrix of death and becoming" (Soyinka 142). As his predecessors, Citizen travels to the City of Bones, where "[his] void is filled with matters in fusion. This [journey becomes the new] beginning ... of [his] time and life" (Fu-Kiau 22–23).

His search for renewal does not immediately begin with the descent to the City of Bones. Aunt Ester first sends him on a search for two pennies—an extension of an idea raised in another play of the Wilson cycle, *Two Trains Running* (1990)—that each man must participate in his own liberation. In *Two Trains*, West recounts his experience of going to see Aunt Ester to find out if his wife was in heaven. His question goes unanswered because of his refusal to throw twenty dollars into the river. He is chided by Holloway who retorts, "That's what your problem is. You don't want to do nothing for yourself. You want somebody else to do it for you. Aunt Ester don't work that way. She say you got to pull your part of the load" (Wilson, *Two Trains*, 76). In the following exchange of *Gem*, Wilson reiterates the idea that freedom does not come without a cost:

BLACK MARY: What's the two pennies for? Why he got to find two pennies?

AUNT ESTER: That's only to give him something to do. He think there a power in them two pennies. He think when he find them all his trouble will be over. But he need to think that before he can come face to face with himself [Wilson, *Gem* 47].

Aunt Ester sends Citizen upriver to retrieve these necessary ritual items. The location (upriver) and the material element (copper) evoke Òṣun, the divinity, as stated earlier, associated with small bodies of water as well as copper, brass and gold. Her mirror, which she is also known to carry, represents the surface of the river, an element that can be used for self-reflection. Citizen has to "wake up," come face to face with himself in this mirror, and learn to see himself through the light of his own eyes. To illustrate this point, Aunt Ester invokes the ancestral Garret Brown as a model of inspiration. "He didn't care if anybody else knew if he did it or not," she says. He knew. He did it for himself. He say I'd rather die in truth than to live a lie. That way he can say that his life is worth more than a bucket of nails. What is your life worth Mr. Citizen? That's what you got to find out" (Wilson, *Gem* 45).

Only Citizen himself can determine the value of his life. Such singularity is captured in the symbolism of the single piece of iron—the other necessary ritual item—Aunt Ester asks him to retrieve from Jilson Grant. "The iron," she says, "would have made [him] strong ... of heart" and given him favor with God (Wilson, *Gem* 62). This ritual item evokes the Odù of which Ògún was birthed, Ògúndámẹ́jì. The ninth of 256 Holy Scriptures in the Ifá orature, Ògúndámẹ́jì speaks of the "fighting, disputes, imminent hostility ... financial problems and opposition from enemies" he would face in the adventure of his life. The Odù also reassures Ògún that by making the appropriate sacrifice (which happens to include a single chain link) he would never die (Epega 35–38).

Besides Aunt Ester, it is also her protégé Black Mary who assists Citizen in his discovery of self and spiritual renewal. In the first of two isolated moments between herself and Citizen, he tries to arrange a late night rendezvous, suggestively encircling Black Mary's waist from behind. In pushing him away, Wilson draws a parallel between this moment and lines from a praise chant of Òṣun:

> Òṣun (embodiment of grace and beauty)
> The preeminent hair-plaiter with the coral beaded comb
> Powerful controller of the estuary
> Propitiator-in-chief of Èkó (the City of Lagos)
> A copulent woman
> Who cannot be embraced around the waist [Abiodun 10].

Black Mary intently demands a level of accountability Citizen has yet to experience. Thus, the play is not solely about his search for the just rewards of citizenship but, also about his developing manhood—his becoming. She states, "You got a woman in your hands. Now what? What you got? What you gonna do? Time ain't long, Mr. Citizen. A woman ain't but so many times filled up. What you gonna do? What you gonna fill me up with? Love? Happiness? Peace? What you got, Mr. Citizen? I seen it all. You got something new? ... Something I ain't seen?" (41). In archetypal fashion of Òṣun, Black Mary becomes the "impulse" of attraction and unification, an impulse Wilson captures here but also suggests in an earlier stage direction in Act I, "Citizen and Black Mary stare at each other" (Wilson, *Gem* 26). However, just as the estuary regulates the river's flow into the ocean, Black Mary polices this encounter by refusing his manner of physical communication—grasping her from behind—as the lack of intimacy prevents him from seeing the fullness of her womanhood and places the weight of their would-be encounter on her. He becomes another taker. Regarding all the former takers in her life, Leroy, John, Cujoe, Sam and Robert, she says, "they use you up and you can't hold them. They all the time taking till it's gone. They ain't tried to put nothing to it. They ain't got nothing in their hand. They ain't got nothing to add to it. They too busy taking. They taking 'cause they need." (Wilson, *Gem* 42). However, the momentary romantic tussle in the sheets he seeks will not assuage his loneliness nor fill his feelings of insufficiency—the hole inside of him. Everyone who comes to see Aunt Ester comes with the need for restoration. Thus, with what will Citizen fill Black Mary up? During this gentle and nurturing confrontation, Black Mary hints at what she makes soundly clear in Act II, "You got to be right with yourself before you can *be* [emphasis mine] right with anybody else" (Wilson, *Gem* 73). As he prepares to escort Solly back to Alabama, Citizen recalls her challenge asking, "Black Mary, is you right with yourself? 'Cause if you is I believe when I come back down from Alabama I'd come by and see you. If I was still right with myself. Then maybe we could be right with each other" (Wilson, *Gem* 76). Black Mary like Òṣun inspires, sparks the desire to create, and generates the passion that seeks abundance (of knowledge, money, love, sweetness, etc.). She becomes Citizen's inclination to be better.

Aunt Ester's oneiromancy provides clues about Black Mary as her protégé and further evidences the ways in which her character is shaped by Òṣun. Aunt Ester says,

> She had seventeen rings and I give her a dime for each one of them. That was in a dream I had about Black Mary before I known her. I had that dream and the next day Black Mary knocked on the door and asked me if I had any laundry that needed washing. I told her to go upstairs and make that bed 'cause anybody willing to do laundry was welcome to stay here. That's three years ago. She been here ever since [Wilson, *Gem* 18].

The seventeen rings is another manifestation of Òṣun, who was the seventeenth Òrìṣà to descend from heaven to earth (the other sixteen were male). This is confirmed in the Odù, Òṣẹtúrá of Ifá sacred orature:

> It was divined for the sixteen Odù
> Who were coming from heaven to earth
> A woman was the seventeenth of them....
> They never knew she was an àjé.
> When they were coming from heaven,
> God choose all good things;
> He also chose their keeper,
> And this was a woman.
> And all women are àjé.
> And because all other Odù left Òṣun out,
> Nothing they did was successful [Abiodun 16].

In "Hidden Power: Òṣun, the Seventeenth Odù," Rowland Abiodun states, "[Òṣun] is believed to have the power to influence the destinies of men, women, and the [Ò]rìṣà, and that Òṣun's presence is crucial to the sustenance of life and order on earth" (Abiodun 11). Black Mary manages the daily affairs of Aunt Ester's way station and is her student assistant in all the rituals performed. Thus, the dream prophesies that Black Mary stands to become Aunt Ester's ultimate promise of survival and evolution—that is, if Black Mary decides that she wants to do so. Aunt Ester spends the majority of the play awaiting a decision that finally comes in Act II. Black Mary agrees to change her name to Ester Tyler but, declares she will negotiate the role on her own terms. She tells Aunt Ester, "Your way ain't always the best way. I got my own way and that's the way I'm doing it. If I stay around here I'm doing it my own way" (Wilson, *Gem* 74). As stated earlier, it is Black Mary (Òṣun) who controls how the river flows into the ocean.

Solly Two Kings is another character determined to act under his own principles. A self-emancipated slave, he changed his name from Alfred Jackson to Solly Two Kings and declared the former dead. As referenced in the text, it is tempting to read this labeling as a type of Christian figuralism—the referencing of two Old Testament Kings, Solomon and David. However, what lies beneath this naming is the conjuring up of two Òrìṣà archetypes—Aganjú (the way Solly functions) and Ṣàngó (the disposition he carries). His embodiment of the archetype of Aganjú is first suggested in his leadership of the Underground Railroad but, also as owner of "the hand of justice" that set fire to the mill. Aganjú is believed to be a primordial Òrìṣà or irúnmọlè associated with Saint Christopher under the syncretism of Yoruba religion with Catholicism. Aganjú is a mediator of the earth's mysteries. He resides at the open mouth of a volcano and is the spirit of the ensuing wilderness and new life that forms after the eruption. He is known primarily for his intermediary role as the ferryman who safely transits departed souls from one plane to another. As a conduit of hope, Aganjú is the ancient one that freedom seekers call upon to assist in navigating troubled waters. A comment by Baba Raul Canizares, author of *Aganjú, Santeria and the Spirit of the Orishas of the Volcanoes and Wilderness* bears repeating in full here:

> According to Roman martyrology, Christopher's [Aganjú's Catholic avatar] birth name was Offerus, the son of a heathen king. It is said that Offerus grew to over seven feet tall. He decided to put himself at the service of the most powerful man on earth. He first served a king said to be the most potent in the world, but the king was terrified of the Devil. Offerus then sought out the Devil, only to find out that Satan was afraid of Christ. He then declared his allegiance to Christ, in time [becoming] the disciple of a hermit who told him he should give himself in service to Christ. The hermit baptized Offerus, changing his name to Christopher (Christ bearer) ... he took up the task of carrying people across a raging stream as his duty to Christ. He [became] the Patron of travelers.... It is thought that his hour is sun rise, for he is thought to be one with the sun. This association with the rising sun makes Aganjú an Òrìṣà people seek when they need hope, when they literally need to experience the dawn of a new day [21–22].

Christopher's name change and his status as liberator and progenitor of new possibilities become part of the Yoruba mythology Wilson draws upon in developing Solly's character. When he burns down the mill, Solly as his Aganjú archetype, becomes "the hand of justice" smiting oppression with a cleansing fire (Wilson, *Gem* 24) invoked in Act I by the Reverend Tolliver. When Aunt Ester admits to her no-confidence in the veracity of Solly's implication in the mill arson, he enters from her room and declares the truth. Solly says,

> Yeah, I burned it down! The people might get mad but freedom got a high price. You got to pay. No matter what it cost. You got to pay. I didn't mind settling up the difference after the war. But I didn't know they was gonna settle like this. I got older I see where I'm gonna die and everything be the same. I say well at least goddamn it they gonna know I was here. The people gonna know about Solly Two Kings [Wilson, *Gem* 75].

His last statement signifies the majestic disposition he carries in the manner of his Ṣàngó archetype. The fourth ruler of the Oyo kingdom, lover of dogs, and women, Ṣàngó is a deified ancestor and another primordial

Òrìṣà. Ṣàngó is known for his virile temperament, volatile personality, dignified walk, and his fierce commitment to enforcing justice. Believed to be the only Òrìṣà besides Olódùmarè and Òrúnmìlà to rule the skies, he strikes with thunder and his lightning rod is truth's illumination. Wilson draws upon Ṣàngó literature through Solly's associations with pure collection, his talk of two women—"one for each arm" (Wilson, *Gem* 18) and his walking stick—the metaphor of both the àṣẹ, Ṣàngó's double-headed axe of liberation and destruction, as well as Aganjú's wooden staff, the oar of his ferry boat. When Caesar comes to arrest Solly for arson, Solly strikes him on his knee and in the warlike manner of a titan he proclaims, "I'm under *God*'s sky, mother-----r! That's what I'm under!" before running out of the door (Wilson, *Gem* 70). The walking stick (a reference to both his atavistic forefathers as with it he directs and strikes) is also a testament to his liberation of others. Inscribed on it are sixty-two markings, narrating the number of individuals he and Eli led to freedom on the Underground Railroad. At the beginning of the play, Solly is planning his last rescue mission to Alabama for his sister, Eliza. She would mark sixty-three or nine when reduced to a single digit, which in Yoruba numerology is the number of both Aganjú and Oyá, who represent transitions and endings.

After stowing away on Selig's wagon and getting as far as West Virginia, Citizen tells Aunt Ester that Solly decided to return to Pittsburg and "bust [the people that were arrested] out of jail," as "he didn't feel right being free and rest of the people in bondage" (Wilson, *Gem* 82). Upon spotting Selig's wagon, Caesar starts shooting to Solly's eventual demise. As Solly slips in and out of consciousness on Aunt Ester's floor repeating, "So live" (Wilson, *Gem* 81) Aunt Ester's prophetic dream in Act I is recalled. She says,

> I dreamed you had a ship full of men and you was coming across the water. Had that stick and you was standing up in this boat full of men. You come and asked me what I was doing standing there. I told you I wanted to go back across the ocean. I asked you to take me. You said you had some work to do but that you would come back. Told me you had a magic stick and when you come back you would part the water so I could walk across. You come on back and all your men had drowned and the boat was sinking. You said you was going to get another boat and some more men. Said you would come back and smote the water. Then you walked off with that stick. Said you was going to Alabama [Wilson, *Gem* 18].

As he is moved to the kitchen table, Solly's life force drains as he begins to traverse the twelve gates of the City of Bones. Successfully passing through each of the gates, he initiates another earthly return. The evidence of his reincarnation is implied through the stage directions which read, "Citizen takes off his coat. He puts on Solly's coat and hat and takes Solly's stick. He discovers the letter from Solly's sister in the hat. Eli pours a drink and raises it in a toast," saying, "So live." Citizen exits without a word (Wilson, *Gem* 85). The play has taken a circuitous journey, ending where it began with Eli and Citizen. Yet, in this structurally Sankofic moment, the *Gem of the Ocean* sails to the height of its spiritual power as does Citizen before walking out into world. Renewed with a sense of purpose and ever so thoughtful of his "duty to life" (Wilson, *Gem* 68). Citizen exits heroically.

Seeing events through to the end is a trait of Òṣósì, the guardian of the forest and protector of the environment. He is archetypally portrayed in Caesar, the town constable. Òṣósì, who works closely with Ògún, identifies the shortest and most meaningful route to an individuals' spiritual evolution and gets to core of any situation, speaking the truth about that which hinders progress, spiritual and otherwise. He is known as the enforcer of the law and guardian of the path of ethical behavior. An oríkì or praise story of Òṣósì speaks of leaving his favorite bird in the care of his grandmother while hunting for food for his family. When he returned several months later, he discovered that the bird had been eaten. Enraged, he charged one of his arrows of precision to strike the heart of the offender. It was his grandmother he heard cry out several moments later (Fatunmbi, *Ososi* 6). Wilson echoes this story, alluding to the eventual demise of Caesar's familial and social relationships due to his strong principles. Through his staunch maintenance of the American legal system Caesar, as does Òṣósì, makes his ethics and position clear in the following statement: "People don't understand the law is everything.... There ain't nothing above the law. Everything come under the law. You got to respect the law. Unless you dead" (Wilson, *Gem* 36). However, Òṣósì's end goal of righteousness, as the oríkì teaches, did not justify the means he employs to enforce it. Suffering lies in the wake of his consciousness about murdering his grandmother as it does for Caesar when Black Mary declares, "I don't know who you are. But you not my brother. You hear me, Caesar? You not my brother" (Wilson, *Gem* 84). Killing children who steal bread, evicting (underpaid) families who are late on rent, and using religion subversively to deny, control or enforce actions demotes him as a proverbial "brothers' keeper." Black Mary denies him the benefit of the family bond and leaves him with the law he praises.

This provides an entry point for discussing Aunt Ester, the physical embodiment of the ancestors. Nearing three hundred years old, Aunt Ester already defies the laws of man and as she impresses upon Citizen, determines for herself what has value. In the following didactic moment between herself and Caesar, who has come to arrest her for aiding and abetting Solly, she speaks on the matter of papers, their value, and the law he represents:

> I see you got a piece of paper. I got a piece of paper too.... It say on there Ester. That's a Bill of Sale for Ester Tyler. That's me ... Mr. Caesar, you can put the law on the paper but that don't make it right. That piece of paper say I was property. Say anybody could buy or sell me. The law say I needed a piece of paper to say I was a free woman. But I didn't need no piece of paper to tell me that [Wilson, *Gem* 78].

She repurposes her Bill of Sale as the *Gem of the Ocean*, a boat which provides Solly, Black Mary (whose previous journeys were alluded to in the text) and Citizen the necessary means of passage to the City of Bones. Wilson, as he has done in other plays, appropriates a song title for the boat's moniker but revises its meaning. *Columbia, the Gem of the Ocean*, is not simply a 19th century battle hymn but, a legal document of servitude, now emblematic of a barge of freedom. "Whatever happen you hold on to that boat. You hold on to that boat and everything will be all right," she says (Wilson, *Gem* 63). In "*Gem of the Ocean* and the redemptive power of history," Harry Elam states, "the medium of enslavement becomes now the method of transcendence" (Elam 82). Not only is the journey on this vessel transcendental but, by insisting that he hold on to the *Gem*, Aunt Ester reminds Citizen of the black American historical condition Wilson spoke of in his Bill Moyers interview and the need for remembrance:

> it [is] criminal that after hundreds of years in bondage, we do not have a thing like the Passover, where we sit down and remind ourselves that we are African people, that we were slaves.... Part of the problem is that we don't know who we are, and we don't recognize the value of claiming that, even if there's a stigma attached to it [Moyers 74–75].

For Wilson, holding the *Gem* becomes "a thing like the Passover" and a 19th century American war ode becomes a praise chant for situating oneself on the ancestral shrine of their African origins—the City of Bones. While the lyrics to David T. Shaw's 1843 song are not explicitly sung in the text, Wilson invokes them in the titular of the play and name of Aunt Ester's Dumasian ark (Dumas 1974)—"O Columbia! the gem of the ocean, the home of the brave and the free, the shrine of each patriot's devotion, a world offers homage to thee" ("Columbia, The Gem of the Ocean") It is in the realm of the Òrìṣà, Olókun, the owner of the ocean, where author Patrick Bellegard-Smith writes:

"These fragmentary remains stood ... dismembered bodies discarded on the ocean's floor—the residue, the 'collateral damage' from the trade between three continents: Africa, the Americas, and Europe. The depth of the ocean is still the domain of Olòkun, a Yoruba diety transmogrified by some in the Americas as the 'patron saint' of the black race. The bones were laid thick; they made a brittle carpet upon which slave ships glided and memories derailed" [Bellegarde-Smith 1–2].

Referring to the historical archive that is her narrative quilt, Aunt Ester describes the City of Bones as "half mile by a half mile.... Pearly white bones ... the center of the world" (Wilson, *Gem* 52). The City of Bones is approximately 1600 meters in circumference, the size of four average running tracks. A sacred number in Ifá, sixteen represents the original number of Òrìṣà who descended to earth, the primary number of Odù within Ifá sacred orature, and references the Sixteen Truths of Ifá. The sacred corpus, as other religious texts (written or orally maintained), narrates "epic and cosmological myths about gods, goddesses and antecedents" (Ogunyemi 82). It describes human encounters with the divine and speaks to a variance of experiences that one may confront over the course of their life in the material realm—joys; challenges and their solutions; and notions of destiny. Thus, it can be argued that the City of Bones—the material evidence of the ancestors as a source of spiritual wisdom—is an embodied sacred text or what Vincent Wimbush calls a signifying scripture, an "elevated object [imbued with 'spiritual and metaphysical meaning'], symbol, ritual, place, person or activity that helps [humans] focus attention on issues critical to the human experience: explore where they came from, deal with lack of knowledge or power, address the unknown, [and] manage trauma and pain and the other ongoing challenges of their existence" (The Institute for Signifying Scriptures). Rather than written vernacular, their guidance which must be actively sought is a narrated book whose orature (sometimes falling on deaf ears) is delivered by culture bearers of the Wilsonian Cycle—Aunt Ester, Bynum, and Stool Pigeon for example. In *Joe Turner's Come and Gone* (1986), Wilson reminds us that by 1911, few were consulting the book. In the preface to the play Wilson tells readers that, "newly freed African slaves wander into the city. Isolated cut off from memory, having forgotten the names of their gods, only guessing at their faces, they arrive dazed and stunned"? Seventy-seven years later, the book seems to be largely forgotten. Stool Pigeon in *King Hedley II* (1999) says:

> The people wandering all over the place. They got lost. They don't even know the story of how they got from tit to tat. Aunt Ester know. But the path to

her house is all grown over with weeds, you can't hardly find the door no more. The people need to know that. The people need to know the story. See how they fit into it. See what part they play [Wilson, *King Hedley II* 8].

Gem's positionality within the cycle is Wilson's redress to the slow death of Aunt Ester—the ancestral presence—in the material world and the consequential wandering black Americans in his cycle faced between 1911 and 1988. He goes back to pick up the dropped ball (Wilson, *Two Trains* 109) to strengthen the link between Africa and the characters.

Temporal Coordination

Gem of the Oceans' plot line, limited locale, cast size, and well-made resolution are signifiers of a climactically structured play. Such a play begins late in the plot, working towards the climax. The characters provide us with necessary exposition, the time frame of the play is significantly compressed (compared to episodic); scenes, locales, and characters are limited; and the plot is packaged neatly with no loose ends. *Gem*'s action spans five days, with the rising action taking place during Friday and Saturday, the climax on Sunday, and the falling action/denouement, Monday and Tuesday. However, Wilson uses what I refer to as an Ethnocultural Dramatic Structure (EDS) to arrange the sequence of events within the plot. EDS is a structural framework for transposing a given culture's philosophies of time within the dramatic structure of the play. *Gem*'s plot is mapped in accordance with the traditional Yoruba week calendar.

The Yoruba week calendar (Fig. 1) comprises a seven day cycle characterized by daily attributes that resulted from events which occurred in Yoruba creation stories and days on which to venerate specific Òrìsàs (Neimark 50–53). The Odù Oturapon-tura explains the purpose of the cycle stating, "Òrúnmìlá ... created [the days of the week] for the purpose of observing marriages and birthdays, for starting a business or moving into a new home, and so on. The days of the Òrìsà are also accounted for within these seven days for important observance of whatever may happen on the day of a particular divinity" (Epega 505–507). Thus, the week cycle is a way of organizing one's daily affairs so as to effect the most favorable outcomes. Philip Neimark's *The Way of the Orisa* sheds light on the mythology behind the characteristics of each day and its ruling divinity. The table below provides an overview of the week.

Gem begins on a Friday evening and two events confirm the energy that characterizes the tension of day. The first is Citizen's arrival. The play

> **Gem I.3-5**
> SUNDAY—Ojó Àikú
>   Day of long life and tranquility; ascension; immortality; and settling disputes—Obatala, Òrúnmìlá, Òrì
>
> **Gem II.1-4**
> MONDAY—Ojó Ajé
>   Day of commerce; initiating of educational, social programming; financial success—Yemọja/Olòkun
>
> **Gem II.5**
> TUESDAY—Ojó Ìségun
>   Day of victory—Ògún, Òsósì
>
> WEDNESDAY—Ojó Rú
>   Day of confusion; the day opens the door and goes out—Oyá
>
> THURSDAY—Ojó Bù
>   Day of fulfillment; creation; ancestral return; return of sun to its normal course—Sàngó
>
> **Gem Prologue**
> FRIDAY—Ojó Età
>   Day of trouble, prolonged struggle; fight; procrastination; postponement; impossibility; or quarrel—Òṣun
>
> **Gem I.1-2**
> SATURDAY—Ojó Àbáméta
>   Day of three suggestions; three evil resolutions; three negative incidents; or three wonders—Èṣù
>
> Figure 1. Yoruba Week Calendar

opens with his arrival at 1839 Wylie Ave looking to get his soul cleansed. He insistently queries Eli about an immediate audience with Aunt Ester. However, Eli informs him that she only works with clients on Tuesdays—the day of victory over enemies and challenges. Thus, his journey to the City of Bones is postponed. The second delayed event (which is not revealed until the following scene) is Garret Brown's funeral. Originally planned for Friday, it was interrupted by Caesar who informed the Reverend Flowers that providing funerary services for a man who committed suicide "was against the law. The Christian law" (Wilson, *Gem* 11).

Saturday (I.1-2) is devoted to exposition. The characters testify to the circumstances of the world that influences their lives. Interwoven in the fabric of this day are stories of three men who were all falsely accused—the Kentucky citizen turned outlaw after being indicted for horse stealing,

Jesus Christ, and Garret Brown, whose previously interrupted funeral takes place mid-afternoon. Each of these men, who themselves could be seen as three wonders or whose stories and the experiences contained therein seen as evil resolutions, walked to their deaths, "not, like the quarry-slave at night, scourged to his dungeon but, sustained and soothed by an unfaltering trust" (Bryant, *Gem* 59) in their innocence. Through these three examples, Wilson illustrates the notion of living and dying in truth resolutely. Furthermore, both Jesus Christ and Garret Brown were falsely accused of committing offences against the law; their lack of impartial hearings and subsequent deaths ignited varying levels of mayhem before new beginnings and peace ensued. The lore is that Christ's death saved the world. Garret Brown's suicide saved him but arguably was the catalyst for Citizen's spiritual renewal as well as the instigation the mill workers needed to contest their disenfranchisement. Reading them as both victims and saviors echoes sentiments surrounding the mythology of Oluorogbo, son of Moremi and Olujare of 14th century Ilé-Ifé. Oluorogbo, thought to be the Yorubanized Messiah, was sacrificed to a river goddess, Esinmirin, by his mother after she consulted with the goddess on the best strategy to appease unruly tensions between Ilé-Ifé and Igbo soldiers. In exchange for her services, Esinmirin requested the martyrdom of Moremi's only son. It is believed that his death restored order within Ilé-Ifé, but historical accounts differ as to whether Oluorogbo "was a victim of lawlessness" (and subsequently his mother's immortality and glorification) or "savior of his people" (Ogunyemi 87).

Sunday (I.3–5) is the day of settling disputes. Events that occur on this day build to the tipping point or are resolved. Thus far, mill workers have been on strike for three days in a row in defiance of management at the mill and have now begun rioting because their demands have gone unheard. Caesar and his ilk make over two hundred arrests before the riot is quelled. Subsequently, the Reverend Tolliver plans a strategy meeting.

Black Mary, who has been withstanding Aunt Ester's pressure to definitively answer one way or the other if she will accept the responsibilities of being a keeper of the memories, assuages her by stating that she does not reject the opportunity. However, Aunt Ester insists that her reticence is displayed in her actions. She says, "You act like it. Run from it all the time. I told myself Black Mary got to make up her mind. I don't know how much time I got left" (Wilson, *Gem*, 43). She presses her closer to a final answer by repeating her age, "going on three hundred years now ... two hundred eighty-five by my count" (Wilson, *Gem* 43) and reminding her that she can't figure out the mystery of life in advance but "trust the adventure" (Wilson, *Gem* 43).

After conferencing with Black Mary, Aunt Ester turns to Citizen asking, "Tell me about the man you killed. Tell me what you done, Mr. Citizen" (Wilson, *Gem* 44). He finally admits to stealing the bucket of nails and watching Garret Brown die instead of confessing to the crime in order that he might save his life. Citizen is then prepped for his journey to the City of Bones by being sent to Blawnox to collect items necessary for the ritual. I.5 ends with Solly, who believes that "making the people owe is worse than slavery" (Wilson, *Gem* 56) "[settling] the difference" (Wilson, *Gem* 61) and burning down the mill. Thus, three days after the death of Garret Brown, Act I ends with the symbolic fiery Phoenix rising at the hand of the black Christ bearer—Solly as Aganjú.

On Monday evening (II.1–4) three new adventures are initiated. Solly prepares to leave for Opelika. Less than twenty-four hours later Citizen returns from his journey to Blawnox with his two pennies and descends to the City of Bones. Black Mary finally declares that she will take up Aunt Ester's mantle and become the keeper of the ancestral memories.

Finally, Tuesday (II.5), the day of victory sees the fulfillment of goals. Solly ascends to Gatekeeper status upon death. In the opening of Act II he tells Citizen, "That's where I'm going when I die.... Got Twelve Gates and it's got Twelve Gatekeepers. That's what I always wanted to be. A Keeper of the Gate" (Wilson, *Gem* 56). A spiritually renewed Citizen returns to Alabama to retrieve Eliza and reconnect himself with his cultural roots in the South. The return South at the play's conclusion, seen here and in another Wilson play, *The Piano Lesson* (1987), harks back to one of Wilson's earlier arguments: "[black Americans] would have been better ... stronger if [they] had stayed in the south" (Bigsby 212). Coincidentally (or not), it is the south where all must return, "in order to rise to the highest level of [our] spiritual and cultural attainment," says Malidoma Some in his 1994 text, *Of Water and the Spirit* (279). The counterclockwise traverse and descent South on the African Cosmogram (regardless of the geo-ethnic population—Kemetic, Yoruba, Bakongo, etc.) leads to the attainment of spiritual wholeness. One has an understanding of the world of the living and the realm of the ancestors.

Wilson's usage of an Ethnocultural Dramatic Structure—a Yoruban temporal construct—allows for a discussion about the architectural formation of *Gem*'s plot without dependence on the dramatic constructs of Western classicists. The cyclical nature of the Yoruba week calendar inherently embodies Western dramaturgical nomenclature and sensibilities—

stasis, disturbance, rise of conflict, climax, and restoration. Wilson's employment of EDS as an expressive mode challenges the "hegemonic aesthetic priorities" Paul Carter Harrison writes about in "Toward a Critical Vocabulary for African Diaspora Expressivity" (2014) and expands the theoretical lexicon of critics who continue to evaluate plays like *Gem*, informed by Africanisms, through the white gaze.

Gem of the Ocean possesses a polyrhythmic dramaturgy that speaks on multiple levels. Although crafted with dramaturgical traditions and cultural references of the West, the black aesthetic—his sourcing of Yoruba cosmology and ritual in his character development, references to sacred objects, plot construction and spatial landscapes—is evident and perhaps predominates. Dramaturgical excavations which lift the veil and reveal such aesthetic markers can impact productions in striking ways. Actors can draw upon narratives and mythology of the Òrìṣà in creating riveting characters with clear, efficacious goals as it is the divine symbols upon which the characters are modeled that provide *Gem* with such gravitas. Reviews such as the one Ben Brantley wrote in the *New York Times* of the 2004 Broadway production of *Gem* miss the point of Wilson's employment of such majesty and otherworldliness. Writing on the difficulties of "playing a metaphor," Brantley writes, "[the characters] are more like pieces of parchment on which legends of the past and maps to the future have been drawn in swooping strokes of ink" (Brantley, "Sailing"). However, in a personal interview with the author Harrison stated, "it is the gods [who are] working through the actors ... characters for the salvation of the community" (Harrison). The fact that it was written after *King Hedley II* (1999) is key to understanding that *Gem* is about the rebirth of a people, their psyche, and their community. Thus, it is through the playwright and subsequently the actors that the gods are awakened and pulled down as their presence is necessary to the community's survival. It is important to privilege such cosmology and ritual within the text when producing and/or teaching *Gem*. Furthermore and despite Wilson's admitted Borgesian influence, conceptual frameworks rooted in "magical realism" should be problematized as the cultural narrative Wilson draws upon is sacred, functional, and *African*; not magical which implies fantasy and fiction. An application of Reggie Young's term "spiritual realism" (Young 134) should better illuminate the metaphysical world in *Gem* and achieve Wilson's goal of presenting "black art that feeds the spirit and celebrates the life of black America" (Wilson, "Ground"). The "strategies for [black America's] prosperity and survival" in *Gem of the Ocean* are the "opportunities [Wilson creates] for the characters, [readers, and viewers] to renew or redeem themselves" and "reconnect [with] their values and beliefs [and] sacred elements of the culture" (Young 135).

Notes

1. Research conducted for this essay was supported by a 2014 NEH Summer Institute grant. My findings do not necessarily reflect those of the National Endowment for the Humanities. A version of this essay titled "Their Song Is a Play: Mapping the Symbols in *Gem of the Ocean*" was presented at the 28th Annual Black Theatre Network Conference, "Our Play's the Thing." I would like to thank the following people who assisted in the intellectual and spiritual development of this essay—either through discussion, textual reference, and editing: Paul Carter Harrison, Joy King, Corey J. Roberts, and Julianna Sarr.

2. While Yoruban cosmological evidence is given primacy, I wish to acknowledge that there are indices in *Gem* of other Africanist spiritual traditions. What is recognized is labeled accordingly.

Works Cited

Abiodun, Rowland. "Hidden Power, Òṣun, the Seventeenth Odù." In *Òṣun Across the Waters: A Yoruba Goddess in Africa and the Americas*, edited by Joseph M. Murphy and Mei-Mei Sanford. Bloomington: Indiana University Press, 1998. 10–33. Print.
Barnes, Sandra T. *Africa's Ogun: Old World and New.* Bloomington: Indiana University Press, 1989. Print.
Bellegarde-Smith, Patrick. "Introduction: What if History Were Written by the Vanquished." In *Fragments of Bone: Neo-African Religions in a New World*, edited by Patrick Bellegarde-Smith. Champaign: University of Illinois, 2005. 1–12. *Google Book Search.* Web. 24 June 2014.
Bigsby, Christopher. "An Interview with August Wilson." In *The Cambridge Companion to August Wilson*, edited by Christophy Bigsby. Cambridge: Cambridge University Press, 2007. 202–213. Print.
Brantley, Ben. "Sailing into Collective Memory." *New York Times.* New York Times, 7 Dec. 2004. Web. 29 June 2014.
Bryant, W.C. (1811). "Thanatopsis." Quoted in *Gem of the Ocean.* New York: Theatre Communications Group, 2006. Print.
Canizares, Baba Raul. *Aganjú, Santeria and the Spirit of the Orishas of the Volcanoes and Wilderness.* Old Bethpage: Original, 2003. Print.
Dezell, Maureen. "A 10-Play Odyssey Continues with *Gem of the Ocean.*" In *Conversations with August Wilson*, edited by Jackson R. Bryer and Mary C. Hartig. Jackson: University Press of Mississippi, 2006. 253–256. Print.
Dumas, Henry. "The Ark of Bones." National Humanities Center Resource Toolbox. 1974. Web.
Elam, Harry, Jr. "*Gem of the Ocean* and the Redemptive Power of History." In *The Cambridge Companion to August Wilson*, edited by Christopher Bigsby. Cambridge: Cambridge University Press, 2007. 75–88. Print.

Epega, Afolabi A., and Philip John Neimark. *The Sacred Ifa Oracle*. New York: HarperCollins, 1995. Print.

Fatunmbi, Awo Fa'Lokun. *Ogun, Ifá and the Spirit of Iron*. Bronx: Original, 1992. Print.

———. *Ososi and the Spirit of the Tracker*. Bronx: Original, 1992. Print.

Fu-Kiau, Bunseki K.K. "Ntangu-Tandu-Kolo: The Bantu-Kongo Concept of Time." In *Time in the Black Experience*, edited by Joseph K. Adjaye. Westport: Greenwood Press, 1994. 22–23. Google Book Search. Web. 24 July 2014.

Harrison, Paul Carter. "Toward a Critical Vocabulary for African Diaspora Expressivity." *Continuum: The Journal of African Diaspora Drama, Theatre and Performance* 1.1 (2014).

———. Personal interview. 22 July 2014.

Herrington, Joan. *"i Ain't Sorry for Nothin' i Done:" August Wilson's Process of Playwriting*. New York: Limelight Editions, 1998. Print.

The Institute for Signifying Scriptures, a research center directed by Vincent L. Wimbush and housed at Claremont Graduate University in Claremont, California. 23 Jan. 2015. http://www.signifyingscriptures.org.

King, Martin Luther, Jr. "I have a dream." Lincoln Memorial, 28 August 1963.

Love, Velma E. *Divining the Self: A Study in Yoruba Myth and Human Consciousness*. University Park: Pennsylvania Press University, 2012. Print.

Lyons, Bonnie, and George Plimpton. *The Paris Review—August Wilson, The Art of Theatre No. 14*. Web. 30 July 2014.

Montgomery, Georgene Bess. *The Spirit and the Word, A Theory of Spirituality in Africana Literary Criticism*. Trenton: Africa World Press, 2008. Print.

Moyers, Bill. "August Wilson: Playwright." In *Conversations with August Wilson*, edited by Jackson R. Bryer and Mary C. Hartig. Jackson: University Press of Mississippi, 1988. Print.

Neimark, Philip John. *The Way of the Orisa: Empowering Your Life Through the Ancient African Religion of Ifa*. New York: HarperOne, 1993. Print.

Ogunyemi, Yemi D. *Introduction to Yoruba Philosophy, Religion and Literature*. Brooklyn: Athelia Henrietta Press, 1998. Print.

Okediji, Moyo. *The Shattered Gourd: Yoruba Forms in Twentieth-Century American Art*. Seattle: University of Washington Press, 2003. Print.

Rahming, Melvin B. "Reading Spirit: Cosmological Considerations in Garfield Linton's *Voodoomation: A Book of Foretelling*." In *Literary Expressions of African Spirituality*, edited by Carol P. Marsh-Lockett and Elizabeth J. West. Lanham: Lexington Books, 2013. 35–62. Print.

Rush, John A. *The Twelve Gates: A Spiritual Passage Through the Egyptian Books of the Dead*. Berkeley: Frog, 2007. Print.

Sarr, Julianna. Personal interview. 13 Feb. 2014.

Shaw, David T. "Columbia, The Gem of the Ocean." 1843. New York: Frederick A. Stokes, 1889. Google Book Search. Web. 24 July 2014.

Some, Malidoma. *Of Water and the Spirit: Ritual, Magic and Initiation in the Life of An African Shaman*. New York: Penguin, 1994.

Soyinka, Wole. *Myth, Literature and the African World*. New York: Cambridge University Press, 1990. Print.

Thompson, Robert Farris. *African Art in Motion: Icon and Act in the Collection of Katherine Coryton White*. Berkeley: University of California Press, 1974. *Google Book Search*. Web. 3 May 2014.

———. *Flash of the Spirit, African & Afro-American Art & Philosophy*. New York: Random House, Inc., 1983. Print.

Tishken, Joel E., Fálolá Tóyìn, and Akíntúndé Akínyẹmí. *Sango in the Africa and the African Diaspora*. Bloomington: Indiana University Press, 2009. Print.

Washington, Teresa N. In *Our Mother, Our Powers, Our Texts, Manifestations of Àjé in Africana Literature*. Bloomington: Indiana University Press, 2005. Print.

Wilson, August. *Gem of the Ocean*. New York: Theatre Communications Group, 2006. Print.

———. "The Ground on Which I Stand." *American Theatre* (Sept. 1996): 1–14. Print.

———. *King Hedley II*. New York: Theatre Communications Group, 2005. Print.

———. *Radio Golf*. New York: Theatre Communications Group, 2007. Print.

———. "Sailing the Stream of Black Culture." *New York Times* 23 Apr. 2000. Web. 29 June 2014.

———. *Two Trains Running*. New York: Plume, 1992. Print.

Young, Reggie. "Wilson's Joe Turner's and The Piano Lesson." *In August Wilson and Black Aesthetics*, edited by Dana A. Williams and Sandra G. Shannon. New York: Palgrave Macmillan, 2004. Print.

Epiphany and the "drama of souls"

Owen Seda

The late African American playwright August Wilson may well remain one of America's greatest playwrights of all time if the unprecedented critical and popular success of his ten-play cycle is his litmus test. August Wilson's dramatic *oeuvre* consists of a ten-play cycle which dramatizes post-emancipation African American experience in the 20th century. Wilson's plays explore the experience and the cultural heritage of African Americans, decade by decade, over the course of the last century.

This essay uses selected plays by August Wilson to argue that the playwright appropriates African belief systems rooted in ancestry and ancestor worship in order to present the reader with characters whose corporeal existence serve as no more than mere receptacles for the dramatization of mental processes or consciousnesses experiencing a crisis of identity. Following Marc Maufort, the essay argues that Wilson's "drama of souls" exposes the challenges of, and offers solutions to racial Otherness and marginality in epiphanic and significant ways.

The essay proceeds from the premise that because of his racial and historical location as an African American playwright, Wilson writes at the margins of history in order to challenge certain dominant paradigms in his society. His plays address a number of issues to do with African American identity at various times during the course of the last century. The essay adopts post-colonial theory as a theoretical frame of reference. The choice of post-colonial theory as a tool of analysis for Wilson's plays is informed by the oft-made observation that Eurocentric world views which valorize the white man have been the mainstay of traditional historiography. This has often been the case even in those instances when the history being written about is the history of the black man (Plum). Consequently, the cultural experience of marginalized groups (such as we encounter in the plays of August Wilson) has been written and interpreted by historians according to the values and ideals of a dominant white culture. Following this observation Jay Plum suggests that a significant feature of August Wilson's plays is the way in which the playwright explores some of the historical choices that have confronted African Americans during the course of the 20th century. As Plum rightly observes, the recovery and indeed the revaluation of African American history demands an alternative reading, which among other things, has to be distinctly African.

"Drama of souls" itself is a term that has been used in post-colonial theory to refer to the inner conflict of dramatic characters (Maufort). It is a dramatic technique which has the ability to physicalize human consciousness in crisis in such a way that at the end, protagonists encounter epiphanic revelations. These revelations often come as a solution to and an exposition of the meaninglessness of an Othered and marginalized existence.

Joe Turner's Come and Gone and *Gem of the Ocean* will be analyzed as two plays in which Wilson expropriates African belief systems rooted in ancestry and ancestor worship. The two plays are therefore presented as grand celebrations of African history, identity and indigenous knowledge systems. In line with William Du Bois, the playwright encourages fellow African Americans and other diasporic peoples of African descent to begin to adopt and to assimilate the African side of their "double consciousness."

It has been written that the determining condition of contemporary post-colonial discourse is the historical phenomenon of colonialism with its range of material practices and effects such as migration, displacement, slavery as well as racial and cultural discrimination (see Lawson & Tiffin, Bhabha, Ashcroft Griffiths & Tiffin, Gandhi, Huddleston). On the surface, August Wilson's plays obviously belong to what has often been referred to as First World literature. This is by dint of his citizenship of an advanced Western nation. However, this essay classifies his plays under the general rubric of post-colonial drama because of the United States' complex [internal as well as external] history of cultural and imperial domination. The essay also classifies Wilson's plays as post-colonial drama because of the playwright's obvious ancestral links with Africa as well as his thematic and stylistic concerns which are not only based on, but challenge racial Otherness and marginality. Wilson himself has alluded to the interconnectedness between his formal structure and style with that of other world cultures, particularly that of Africa when he observes, "I write about the black experience in America and try to explore in terms of the life I know best, those things which are common to all cultures" (quoted in Goldfarb & Wilson, 529). As Ashcroft, Griffiths and Tiffin also rightly observe in *The Empire Writes Back,* "The literature of the USA should also be placed in this category [i.e., the category of post-colonialism]. Perhaps because of its current position of power, and the neo-colonizing role it has played, its post-colonial nature has not been generally recognized" (2).

August Wilson's reference to the interconnectedness between his style and African discursive practices makes it relatively easy for the critic or the reader to subsume his writings within the larger rubric of alternative discourse. This is a discourse which challenges the hegemony of dominant Western representations. For this reason post-colonialism has been variously defined as a form of discourse which aims to recover knowledge systems previously marginalized or silenced by mainstream discourses emanating from the West (see Ashcroft Griffith & Tiffin, Gandhi, Lazarus). As Benita Parry rightly observes, post-colonial texts (such as we observe in Wilson's *Joe Turner's Come and Gone* and *Gem of the Ocean*) not only incorporate and transgress the forms and cognitive resources of Western traditions, but they also draw upon and foreground traditional narrative forms and idioms.

Because it is, by nature, a discourse of resistance, post-colonial drama engages with issues to do with the historical experience of displacement, transportation and racial discrimination. As a result post-colonial drama often presents the reader with a world that is distorted and generally fragmented. The two plays analyzed here present the reader with a set of characters who are in search of personal fulfillment, identity and self-worth in a destabilized universe following forced uprooting from their ancestral homes. In both plays the reader comes across a group of characters that faces a range of personal crises. These crises are underpinned by a sense of loss and alienation from the characters' material circumstances, leading to racial marginality. As the playwright observes in the opening stage directions of *Joe Turner's Come and Gone,*

> From the deep and near South the sons of newly freed African slaves wander into the city. Isolated, cut off from memory, having forgotten the names of the gods and only guessing at their faces, they arrive dazed and stunned, their heart kicking in their chest with a song worth singing. They arrive carrying Bibles and guitars, their pockets lined with dust and fresh hope, marked men and women seeking to scrape from the narrow crooked cobbles and the

fiery blasts of the coke furnace a way of bludgeoning and shaping the malleable parts of themselves into a new identity as free men of definite and sincere worth [Wilson i].

The above is not dissimilar to *Gem of the Ocean* where the reader is also presented with Citizen Barlow who is introduced as "a young man from Alabama who is in spiritual turmoil." That mutual sense of loss and lack of direction which is encountered in both plays only begins to go away after the principal characters experience their ancestral epiphanies. This is the "drama of souls" in August Wilson's plays to which the postcolonial critic Marc Maufort refers as the dramatization of the inner conflict of dramatic characters. According to Maufort, "drama of souls" has the capacity to make apparent consciousness in crisis. It is usually accompanied by epiphanic revelations. These revelations come across as an exposition of the meaninglessness of life. In this post-colonial "drama of souls" the self is shown to be in a state of mental turmoil as it lacks a sense of belonging. In the case of Wilson's two plays, the self only assumes a sense of fulfillment, identity and self-worth after experiencing these ancestral epiphanies. The "drama of souls" in *Joe Turner's Come and Gone* and *Gem of the Ocean* therefore presents the reader with marginalized characters whose corporeal existence is in essence a dramatization of consciousness in search of identity. Through the lens of post-colonialism, the playwright seems to be suggesting that these marginalized and alienated characters can only emerge from slavery to find a meaningful identity if they integrate with their African past of ancestor worship. Through these two plays, Wilson suggests that unless such integration occurs, these characters will continue to go round in circles, stuck in some form of "fixed action."

Joe Turner and *Gem* revolve around the mythical powers of the characters of Aunt Ester in *Gem of the Ocean* and Bynum in *Joe Turner's Come and Gone*, both of whom are able to invoke visions of a mythical African past in order to redeem the present and foretell the future. The essay argues that the mythical powers of Aunt Ester and Bynum are reposed in forms of traditional African ancestor worship which August Wilson implores contemporary African Americans to embrace if they are to forge a meaningful identity for themselves going forward.

In *Joe Turner* and *Gem*, August Wilson suggests that African Americans will not be able to find a viable identity or economic prosperity unless they establish a link with their African ancestry. The sense of characters whose lives and destinies is stuck without any real sense of direction comes across through the playwright's manipulation of plot. On the surface, the two plays seem to follow the linear pattern of traditional realism where Seth's Holly's boarding house and Aunt Ester's home are occupied by a cross-section of individual African Americans in search of identity and a sense of post-emancipation self-fulfillment. In practice, however, these apparently realistic linear plot structures do not necessarily "move." In both plays Wilson demonstrates that freedom for the blacks may well be nothing more than just an illusion and an elixir. Wilson demonstrates this lack of movement by transgressing the "motion" of the linear plot structure as generally found in traditional realism. He presents the reader with extended narratives of the past which come as conversational previous action that is based on past events in the lives of the different characters. This transgression of realist narrative linearity of motion is further complemented by the incorporation of trance-like visions of the past and epiphanic revelations of a future which is to come. All this happens as part of Wilson's attempt to dramatize an alternative cultural vision linking African Americans to their African past if they are to realize true freedom and move forward into a more viable racial identity.

The alternative cultural vision which will enable African Americans to find true freedom is realized through two epiphanies that are conjured by Aunt Ester and Bynum in the lives of Citizen Barlow and Herald Loomis, respectively. Before these ancestral epiphanies occur, the reader is presented with a group of individualized characters who, as part of their ceaseless search for identity and a sense of self-fulfillment, are all caught up in repetitive and seamless daily routines of existence on the margins of race and class. For instance in *Joe Turner's Come and Gone*, Jeremy Furlow has to contend with highly exploitative (slave wage) labor relations on white-controlled road construction gangs as he is also forced to resort to an aimless life of playing the guitar, womanizing and gambling as he marks time in Seth Holly's boarding house. Two other residents of the boarding house namely Mattie Campbell and Molly Cunningham are also presented as drifters who are on the road in search of love and an elusive sense of human companionship. Meanwhile, although Bynum appears to be the only stable individual among the characters found in Seth's boarding house, before the ancestral epiphany, he too is engaged in a seemingly endless wait for his encounter with destiny and his much anticipated epiphanic "shiny man." It is only with the arrival of Herald Loomis that the static routines for all these different characters are jolted into some form of motion. This occurs when Herald goes into an epiphanic trance that is replete with metaphorical and symbolic elements which are rooted in African rituals of ancestry and ancestor worship. While in this trance-like encounter, Herald Loomis speaks in tongues as he recounts a vision in which he encounters the bones of his long departed ancestors rising out of the Atlantic as he re-unites with them, giving him (Herald Loomis) a new sense of direction and identity that will provide a fresh start in life.

The theme of ancestral epiphanies which serves as a point of departure for progress and a sense of identity for post-emancipation African Americans is also carried forward in *Gem of the Ocean*. Here the reader is also confronted with a seemingly static plot wherein another set of characters assembled in Aunt Ester's household is equally caught up in seamless routines of life in search of progress and a sense of personal fulfillment having escaped from the racial injustices of the south. Like the characters in *Joe Turner's Come and Gone*, they too can only find a useable identity and a sense of fulfillment through the epiphanies conjured by the mythical Aunt Ester who, at 285 years of age, is something of a mythical character. Aunt Ester is part of a long line of African American matriarchs who have been carrying the collective memory of their people right from the time of slavery. Similar to what happens in *Joe Turner's Come and Gone*, the characters in *Gem of the Ocean* as typified by Citizen Barlow and Solly Two Kings are only able to muster their sense of identity and self-fulfillment after Aunt Ester "washes" their souls by having them undertake a symbolic trip to the City of Bones where they are re-united with ancestors who perished during the Middle Passage.

In both plays, therefore, Wilson deploys ancestral trance-like visions of the past and a future which is to come. These ancestral visions serve as epiphanic revelations of a desirable destiny for the black man that is rooted in continuity between the present and the African past. Until these epiphanic encounters are realized, all the characters are caught up in a seemingly static existence. More significantly, these epiphanies display strong link with elements of African ancestor worship in which the chief characters (Herald Loomis in *Joe Turner's Come and Gone* and Citizen Barlow in *Gem of the Ocean*) see visions of bones of long departed ancestors before they can start afresh as free men. What Wilson suggests through these epiphanies is that the freed former slave and his or her descendants can only find a proper footing by re-connecting with their African ancestry and cultural traditions. Wilson's presentation of "fixed characters" who are caught up in what Rust Hills has referred to as "fixed action" before they encounter these epiphanies constitutes Marc Maufort's "Drama of Souls" in *Joe Turner's Come and Gone* and *Gem of the Ocean*.

The above is clearly evident in *Joe Turner's Come and Gone* where all the characters assembled in Seth Holly's boarding house are drifters in search of a sense of place and identity having recently arrived from the south. It is of significance therefore that all these characters are on the road with each one of them on some form of quest. For instance Seth Holly has striven in vain to define his freedom and success on the basis of a borrowed yardstick established by white America in the north. His yardstick for success certainly has no place for anything that is remotely African. This is evidenced by his aversion towards Bynum's root-working and Herald Loomis's vision of African ancestors. While he barely tolerates Bynum, Seth is firmly prepared to turn out Herald Loomis from his so-called "respectable" lodgings. Other inhabitants of the boarding house such as Jeremy Furlow, Mattie Campbell and Molly Cunningham are equally caught up in this fixed action as they too are engaged on a ceaseless quest for true freedom and a meaningful identity as free men and women in the north. Until the collective juba dance during which Herald Loomis and Bynum experience their epiphanic encounters with ancestral bones and the "shiny man" respectively, Wilson seems to be suggesting that his African American protagonists can only remain lost and adrift in the ostensibly free north. It is for this reason that the playwright presents the reader with the character of Bynum who serves as a foil against which the extent of loss for all the other characters may be assessed. Bynum leads a life which is rooted in the observance of African rituals and ancestor worship. Notwithstanding Bynum's own search for his "shiny man" or godlike figure (strikingly comparable to the biblical Christ), Bynum certainly comes across as the most stable and sure-footed of all the characters encountered in *Joe Turner's Come and Gone.*

Wilson uses Bynum's ancestral beliefs and his (i.e., Bynum's) ceaseless search for the "shiny man" who will bring him his "own song" as a metaphor for the search for true freedom and identity. This search can only find closure through the ancestral epiphanies encountered in the play. In this way Bynum functions as an African traditionalist who is able to provide a viable link between the past and the present. He, therefore, advises the "lost" characters that unless they find their "own song"—which in this case comes about through an ancestral epiphany—they may never establish a viable identity within the context of an Othered and marginalized existence in post-emancipation America. The juba dance which is regularly coordinated by Bynum every Sunday evening, culminating in Herald Loomis's epiphany has its roots in West African ancestor worship. Richards refers to Sterling Stuckey's belief that in its original context, the juba was performed in honor of West African gods and ancestors. So central is the juba dance enacted in *Joe Turner's Come and Gone* to the central argument advanced in this paper about the link between epiphany, the "drama of souls" and African belief systems that its presentation in *Joe Turner's Come and Gone* is quoted at length as follows:

> [The juba] is ... a call and response dance. Bynum sits at the table and drums. He calls the dance as others clap hands, shuffle and stomp around the table. It should be as African as possible, with the performers working themselves up into a near frenzy [Wilson 52].

Significantly, it is at the very moment when Bynum's juba dance reaches a crescendo that Herald Loomis steps back into Seth's boarding house and falls into a trance in which he begins to speak in tongues, describing a vision where he encounters the bones of his long departed ancestors rising from the ocean as he re-unites with them.

Bynum's juba dance thus becomes a significant moment of epiphany in terms of the provenance of African belief systems in *Joe Turner's Come and Gone*. Not only does it allow Herald Loomis's troubled consciousness to come to terms with itself, it also allows the rest of the cast to realize that in order for emancipated blacks to find a viable identity, they have to reconnect with their African past. This significant sense of self-discovery is further sustained in a similar moment of epiphany which comes right at the end of the play as Herald Loomis slashes himself across the chest with a knife in an act of self-flagellation or self-sacrifice as he shouts at all around him saying, "I'm standing! I'm standing! My legs stood up! I'm standing now!" (Wilson 94). This significant moment of epiphany is reinforced by the playwright's stage directions which follow immediately after as follows:

> Having found his song, the song of self-sufficiency, fully resurrected, cleansed and given breath, free from any encumbrance other than the workings of his own heart and the bonds of the flesh, having accepted the responsibility for his own presence in the world, he is free to soar above the environs that weighed and pushed his spirit into terrifying contractions [Wilson 94].

Herald Loomis's moment of epiphany as described above also becomes a moment of revelation for Bynum, who is the play's most sure-footed and grounded representative of African belief systems as he responds with the triumphant shout, "Herald Loomis, you shining! You shining like new money!" (Wilson 94).

In *Gem of the Ocean*, August Wilson presents the reader with yet another dramatic scenario which bears a striking resemblance to the ancestral epiphany encountered in *Joe Turner's Come and Gone*. Like Seth Holly's boarding house in *Joe Turner's Come and Gone*, Aunt Ester's home in *Gem of the Ocean* is inhabited by a motley crowd of post-emancipation African Americans who are similarly caught-up in a web of fixed action, having recently arrived from the south in search of identity and a sense of self-worth. However, in so far as *Gem of the Ocean* addresses the second decade of the Twentieth Century in Wilson's historical project, the characters encountered in this play are relatively more far removed from the direct experience of slavery than those found in *Joe Turner's Come and Gone*. As Constance Zaytoun rightly observes, "At its heart it [i.e., *Gem of the Ocean*] tells the story about the need for a new kind of black Everyman ... representing black generations who never experienced slavery, to integrate himself into his people's collective history" (715). Citizen Barlow comes to represent this "black Everyman" who will continue to wallow in a rootless and aimless existence of crime that is also marked by "spiritual turmoil" until he finds that historical integration.

For this crucial historical integration to take place, the playwright indicates that the "black Everyman" has to experience an epiphanic encounter (such as the one encountered by Citizen Barlow) that will bring him in direct communion with his ancestral bonds. Citizen Barlow thus becomes an embodiment of the post-colonial "drama of souls" which is also represented by Herald Loomis and the other characters in *Joe Turner's Come and Gone*. In as much as Herald Loomis and the rest of the characters in *Joe Turner's Come and Gone* are navigated to their epiphanic encounter via the ancestral mysticism of Bynum the root worker, Citizen Barlow and the characters in *Gem of the Ocean* have to rely on the mythical powers of Aunt Ester's extraordinary ability to conjure epiphanic encounters with African ancestry. Aunt Ester's ability to "wash people's souls" echoes directly, the "drama of souls" which constitutes the central argument in this essay.

It is in this context that the play's most significant moment comes in Act Two when Aunt Ester agrees to transport Citizen Barlow to the City of Bones where he will encounter an epiphanic vision of his ancestors. In a way that is strikingly similar to the juba dance in *Joe Turner's Come and Gone*, Citizen Barlow's trip to the City of Bones in *Gem of the Ocean* is also framed in the form of ancestor worship rooted in African belief systems. Like Bynum's juba dance, Citizen Barlow's trip to the City of Bones is also a communal call-and-response sequence that is highly reminiscent of traditional rituals of ancestor worship. The communal nature of the redemptive ancestral epiphanies encountered by the characters in both plays (including those who do not directly experience these epiphanies) means that Wilson's characters are able to learn significant lessons of African American history and identity vicariously.

August Wilson is an African American playwright whose ten-year cycle of plays operates on the margins of race, class and culture in order to challenge hegemonic discourses emanating from America's traumatic history of slavery. *Joe Turner's Come and Gone* and *Gem of the Ocean* have been analyzed using the theoretical framework of post-colonial theory, which has enabled an alternative reading of August Wilson's two plays as examples of the provenance of epiphany and the "drama of souls." August Wilson's *Joe Turner's Come and Gone* and *Gem of the Ocean* present the reader with a set of African American characters who are caught up in "fixed action" and a post-emancipation crisis of consciousness. These various characters' search for identity and a sense of personal fulfillment only finds resolution when Wilson's protagonists encounter certain epiphanic revelations rooted in traditions of ancestry and African ancestor worship. Epiphany and the "drama of souls" is a technique of post-colonial drama which enables Wilson's protagonists to realize and find viable solutions to the meaninglessness of an Othered existence on the margins of race and class in post-emancipation America. This is a reading which suggests alternative perspectives for the total emancipation of diasporic black races.

Works Cited

Ashcroft, Bill, Griffith Gareth, et al. *The Empire Writes Back: Theory & Practice in Postcolonial Literatures*. London: Routledge, 1989. Print.

_____. *The Post-Colonial Studies Reader*. London: Routledge, 1995. Print.

Bhabha, Homi. *The Location of Culture*. London: Routledge, 1994.

Du Bois, William. *The Souls of Black Folks*. 1903. Boston: Bedford, 1997. Print.

Gandhi, Leela. *Post-Colonial Studies: A Critical Introduction*. New South Wales: Allen and Unwin, 1998. Print.

Goldfarb, Alvin, and Edwin Wilson. *The Living Theatre: An Anthology of Great Plays*, 2d ed. New York: McGraw-Hill, 2001. Print.

Hiddleston, Jane. *Understanding Postcolonialism*. London: Acumen Books, 2009. Print.

Hills, Rust. *Writing in General and the Short Story in Particular*. Boston: Mariner, 2000. Print.

Lawson, Alan, and Chris Tiffin, eds. *De-scribing Empire: Post-Colonialism and Textuality*. London: Routledge, 1994. Print.

Lazarus, Neil, ed. *The Cambridge Introduction to Post-Colonial Literatures in English*. Cambridge: Cambridge University Press, 2004. Print.

Maufort, Marc. *Transgressive Itineraries: Post-Colonial Hybridizations of Dramatic Realism*. New York: Peter Lang, 2006. Print.

Parry, Benita. "The Institutionalization of Postcolonial Studies." In *Postcolonial Literary Studies*, ed. Neil Lazarus. Cambridge: Cambridge University Press, 2004. 66–80. Print.

Plum, Jay. "Blues, History and the Dramaturgy of August Wilson." *African American Review* 27, no. 4 (Winter 1993): 561–567. Print.

Richards, Sandra. "Yoruba Gods on the American Stage: August Wilson's *Joe Turner's Come and Gone*." *Research in African Literatures* 30, no. 4 (Winter 1999): 92–105. Print.

Wilson, August. *Gem of the Ocean*. New York: Theatre Communications Group, 2006. Print.

_____. *Joe Turner's Come and Gone*. New York: New American Library, 1988. Print.

Zaytoun, Constance. "*Gem of the Ocean*: A Review." *Theatre Journal* 57, no. 4 (Dec. 2005): 715–717. Print.

Conjuring Africa in August Wilson's Plays

CONNIE RAPOO

Consider the following four scenarios: first, the stepping traditions in African American fraternities and sororities as shown in the motion picture *Stomp the Yard* (Sylvain White, 2007); second, the "krump" dance form in the documentary movie *Rize* (David La Chapelle, 2005); third, singer Beyonce Knowles' choreographic designs in the video of her track *Run the World (Girls)*; and fourth, the nightmarish dream sequences, African dance steps, and ritualized sacrifice of Saartjie Baartman (the so-called Hottentot Venus) in playwright Lydia Diamond's production *Voyeurs de Venus* (2006). These are a few examples of how African American performances borrow from traditional African dance and movement styles, as well as enactments of African ritual. The film *Stomp the Yard* is a dance and drama cinematic representation of black youth culture which does not only bring to the screen stepping competitions but also portrays African American collective cultural memory. It elaborates forms of black cultural production that combine "ritual soundscape"[1] (Gilbert and Tompkins 63) with enactments of racial memory and identity (Hugley) and exuberant bodily movements.

More pointedly, the step dance routines of African American fraternities and sororities are reminiscent of African dance forms and initiation processes such as the South African *gumboot* dance, the Bakgatla ethnic group's initiatory dances in Botswana, and warrior dances and representations of mock battles from various parts of Africa. These dance forms, performed by gender-based initiatory organizations and regiments, make use of step dance, song, chants, and particularly in the case of initiation rituals, symbolic rituals to which only the initiates are privy. *Rize*, as critic William Booth observes, draws inspiration from African ritual dances.

The Krump dance in *Rize* exhibits aspects of the footwork and body movements of South African Zulu war dances and, as Ryan Parker notes, the film evokes voodoo religious ritual dances from Cuba and Haiti. Beyonce's *Run the World (Girls)* video similarly borrows from Africa through its deployment of the South African *pantsula* dance. The sacrificial event in *Voyeurs de Venus* during which the playwright stages the historical dismemberment of Baartman is a poignant articulation of African acts of blood sacrifice, and how blood-letting rituals are connected to the search for identity by African American characters.[2]

This essay draws attention to these four scenarios as examples of contemporary African American popular cultural forms that re-memorialize Africa. More examples—sacred, secular, secular-sacred, cinematic, literary, globalized and mainstream representational forms—exist that elaborate how Africa is conjured in African America. This article focuses primarily on how playwright August Wilson remembers and re-members African ritualized dance forms, ritual observances, and other representations of African ancestral culture in his plays. The protagonists in these plays bring Africa and African America into a network of relations and significations. Enactments of cultural memory in these plays reinforce Wilson's scripting of the significance and relevance of cultural resilience to African American acts of self-determination. Writing in *The Past as Present in the Drama of August Wilson*, performance critic Harry J. Elam, Jr. (167) observes,

> In Wilson's twentieth-century cycle, the spiritual has evolved as a significant force enabling the resurrection of the African in African American experiences.... The plays' crises create a context for spiritual acts that conjoin politics and culture, past and present, history and memory, individual and community. The embrace of the spiritual, the engagement in what one would call "faith-based" cultural practices—in that they foreground spiritual commitment—serve Wilson's Africans in America as critical survival strategies.

This essay examines acts of spiritual commitment, ritualized summons of the living dead, and embodied acts of self-assertion in Wilson's plays. The essay reads these plays through the notion of conjuring—understood as the performance of calling forth the power of African ancestral memory in order to instill a sense of assertiveness.

Conjuring African Rites of Sacrifice in African America

Ways of remembering and imaging Africa in the transnational imaginary manifest in a number of ways, particularly through constructions of the mysterious, the fantastical, and the occult. One is reminded of Joseph Conrad's *Heart of Darkness*, Karen Blixen's *Out of Africa*, and Edward Zwick's *Blood Diamond*, among the many literary and cinematic representations of Africa. While the plays examined in this article might indeed echo these globalized imaginings, what is of particular interest is how August Wilson's plays articulate notions of ancestral memory and the continuum of African ritual observances in African America. In Wilson's plays, the staging of the mysterious and the occult elaborates the seemingly inextricable link between the violent and the sacred (Rene Girard) and highlights the values and meanings behind ritualized acts of self-determination. This is demonstrated through performative acts of conjuring and revisionist practices of "sacrifice." In this essay, the notion of conjuring is read as the performance strategy of recalling, calling forth, remembering, invoking, or summoning Africa into existence in order to reinforce acts of self-assertion. This idea echoes critics Marjorie Pryse and Hortense Spillers' articulation of "conjuring" as the ancient power of deploying the literary tradition in order to reassert pride (Pryse and Spillers). The essay uses the notion of "sacrifice" to denote sacred acts of spiritual appeasement ritualistically expressed through either bloodletting acts or sacred observances, which are geared towards a healing collective identification. Thus, sacrifice is commensurate with cosmic and metaphysical capital. The economy of sacrifice appears to be anchored more on agency and harmony rather than the exchange of belligerence and propitiation, suggested by Rene Girard. Based on this reading, "acts of sacrifice" denotes practices that reinforce the spiritual capital of social harmony and cosmic balance; that is, religious observances that are redeployed to remember the spiritual African past in order to restore cosmic order. "Acts of sacrifice" also refer to spiritual practices that function as critical survival strategies for individuals, to echo theorist Harry J. Elam, Jr. (167).

    Revisionist practices of rites of sacrifice and ancestral retentions figure prominently in August Wilson's plays, particularly *Joe Turners' Come and Gone* and *Gem of the Ocean*. These plays cast various figures that dramatize the notion of sacrifice and call forth traditional African epistemologies surrounding notions of sacrifice, death, burial, and the need to appease the dead. These figures operate as sites of black cultural production and reassemble memories of what defines blackness and Africa for African Americans. These plays conjure dead and sacrificial figures to underscore the idea that the experiences of identity crisis and cultural rupture are not tied to the past, but instead permeate current moments of everyday American history. The thematic explorations of these plays corroborate Samuel Allen's observation that "the African heritage may serve as a fertile source of inspiration and of renewal for the Afro-American" (625).

African cultural practices of sacrifice in August Wilson's selected plays could be illuminated through Paul Carter Harrison's notion of *Nommo*. According to Harrison, *Nommo* is the physical-spiritual life force that rejuvenates "sleeping" forces through conjuring images (Harrison 2). It is the power of the Word; it animates the dramatic mode by demonstrating "the intersection between spiritual invocation and theatrical practice throughout the African Diaspora" (Harrison 9). *Nommo* could be expanded to incorporate song, drum, dance, incarnations, oral narrative, re-membering rituals, and their conjoining with African American theatre aesthetics and rites. The practice of *Nommo* sheds light on acts of re-traditionalized sacrifice and moments of "symbolic reversal of sacred and social codes" (Harrison 4) for the transformation of black consciousness. *Symbolic reversal*, the strategy of contextualizing African-inspired values in the African Diaspora, functions to reinvest negative stereotypes of blackness and to overcome the trauma of dislocation and subjugation. The plays of August Wilson offer such a theatre—a ritualized collective ethos which "binds, cleanses, and heals" (Harrison 4).

Enlivening Blood Memories

Ritual observances and cultural recollections of Africa are prevalent in August Wilson's *Joe Turner's Come and Gone*. Set against the backdrop of slavery and its aftermath, this play makes use of visual and sonic metaphors that resonate with how Africa is remembered by African Americans. As Stephanie Arnold observes in *The Creative Spirit* (Arnold 66), the play is "about the damage done to the spirit, which must be healed before people can take their rightful place in the world." It incorporates narratives that resonate with ritual observances, including the sacrificing of pigeons by the "root-worker" named Bynum, the search for the "Shiny Man," encounters with ghosts, mysterious visions of the dead, and acts of self-scarification. The protagonist of the drama is Herald Loomis, a victim of forced labor by Joe Turner. Herald Loomis is looking for his estranged wife Martha whom he believes will give him "a starting place in the world." He returns from serving in Joe Turner's "chain gang" and joins other residents in the boardinghouse managed by Seth and Bertha Holly.

August Wilson's *Joe Turner's Come and Gone* is a poignant articulation of the characters' search for a sense of identity. Most of the characters are either in search of something, or have experienced loss and are in search of healing. Bynum, aptly called "a conjure man" (78), is searching for the "Shiny Man" who figures as a spiritual force that will anchor his existence. As critic Sandra L. Richards observes, the "shiny man" evokes Yoruba cosmology in memorializing the Yoruba gods Ogun and Esu (92). Mattie Campbell is searching for her husband Jack. She is also mourning the loss of her two babies. Herald Loomis embodies physical and spiritual enslavement. For seven years he was physically enslaved by Joe Turner. Spiritually, he is oppressed by memories of the haunting vision of seeing bones "rise up and begin to walk" on top of the waters of the Atlantic Ocean. The vision of the bones of African slaves—a vision that suggests his memory and spiritual heritage—cripples him to a point where he is unable to walk. He collapses and cries out, "My legs won't stand up! My legs won't stand up!" (98). Loomis only gains his freedom once he embraces his African spiritual heritage and cuts ties with Christian beliefs. The play scripts a poignant scene in which Loomis cuts his chest with a knife, and rubs the blood over his face. This ritualistic act marks Loomis's point of epiphany. When Martha reminds him of the Christian doctrine of Jesus bleeding to save the world, he declares, "I don't need nobody to bleed for me! I can bleed for myself" (93). Only after this act of self-scarification and blood-letting does he gain a sense of "self-sufficiency" and begin to shine "like new money" (114). At the end of the play, Loomis ritualistically transforms into the Shiny Man invoked in Bynum's spiritual experiences. The blood functions to revitalize his bodily and spiritual energy. As Harry J. Elam, Jr. (209) correctly points out, this ritualistic act of slashing himself across the chest and rubbing blood over his face "expresses self-determination and agency. It is a resolute act of will. As he cuts and marks himself physically, he liberates himself from his previous debilitating psychological marking as one of Joe Turner's niggers." Loomis's ritual act of blood-letting is a corporeal marking that re-members African spiritual knowledge, freedom, and agency into African American cultural memory and heritage. This performance of memory asserts African American agency.

"Blood memory"—read as the embodied knowledge that binds people and reinforces their collective experience and identification—figures predominantly in *Joe Turner's Come and Gone*. In this play, blood memory manifests through two processes of remembrance and (un)binding. For Seth, blood memory takes shapes in the heritage that he gained from his father. On several occasions he remembers the skills of metal production that he learnt from his father. Seth's heritage has enabled him to establish his boardinghouse business. Blood memory in the case of Seth has empowered him to provide a place where estranged blacks can find refuge and a sense of community and harmony. Blood memory for Bynum takes shape in his ceremonies and memories as they serve a bonding function. He has inherited the wisdom of "binding souls" and the skills of helping people find their "binding song" from his father. His act of sacrificing pigeons is in keeping with the African occult practices and metaphysical epistemologies of cosmic balance.

According to African scholar Wole Soyinka (1976), in Yoruba cosmology, acts of sacrifice are necessary to maintain the link between the gods and humans, and to restore cosmic order. In *Myth, Literature, and the African World*, Soyinka (144) offers that

> this gulf [created through cosmic conflict, through the abyss of dissolution and the tragic experience of the separation between gods and humans] is what must be constantly diminished by the sacrifices, the rituals, the ceremonies of appeasement to those cosmic powers which lie guardian to the gulf. Spiritually, the primordial disquiet of the Yoruba psyche may be expressed as the existence in collective memory of a primal severance in transitional ether, whose first effective defiance is symbolized in the myth of the gods' descent to earth and the battle with immense chaotic growth which had sealed off reunion with man.

Rites of transition, such as birth, death, and the tragic actor's movement across the three spheres of the living, the dead, and the yet-unborn, according to Soyinka are part of the "fourth stage" that manifests as chaos. Ritualistic practices thus symbolically diminish the chasm of tragic experience and reinforce unity and bonding. Bynum's ritualized acts, for example, contribute towards the harmony and stability of the boardinghouse, so much that even Seth who initially vehemently dismissed them as "heebie-jeebie nonsense" comes to appreciate their effect. "If it wasn't for Bynum," declares Seth, "ain't no telling what would have happened [when Loomis was 'possessed' by his vision of the 'bones people']" (100). In conformity with the African *Setlhabelo* sacrifice and propitiation ritual, Bynum sacrifices the pigeons and offers them as propitiatory gifts to bind, cleanse, and heal the atmosphere at the boardinghouse. A common ritualistic practice among the Tswana people, the *Setlhabelo* offers worshippers an opportunity to spill the blood of either a rooster, a goat, or a cow, in order to appease the ancestors or deity (Schapera & Comaroff). The blood of the sacrificial object is poured on the earth to "cleanse" it, while the flesh is eaten during a sacrificial feast, with some selected organs being buried on the ground as an offering for the ancestors. Bynum's act thus reinforces belief in cosmic balance as per African traditional epistemologies. Through the character of Bynum and his enactments of African spirituality and blood memory, August Wilson stages African cultural memory and agency.

Other characters' behaviors are similarly symbolic of the essence of "blood memory" and individual agency. Mattie Campbell's will and power is nourished by the memory and blood-ties to her mother. Loomis' blood memory is particularly poignant in its re-memorialization of links with African religious esthetics and acts of liberation. Considering that he is a former Christian priest, it is ironic that his redemption comes through African-inspired acts of bloodletting and re-memory as opposed to Christian forms of worship. "Terror-stricken by his vision" (98), Loomis vicariously experiences the terror that framed the Middle Passage. As Harry J. Elam, Jr., would have it, Loomis' enactment is a "blood memory of earlier blood sacrifice" experienced by the African slaves (202). His remembrance of blood bond with Africa, his embracing of African ancestral memory and spiritual heritage, and his insurgent act of bleeding for himself anchors his agency and freedom.

Harry J. Elam, Jr. writes that "blood memory in Wilson's theatrical construction operates as a metaphor for his central reimagining history and for appreciating how the African and African American past is implicated in the present" (xviii). Further, blood memory, according to Elam operates symbolically to represent the ways in which collective memory and race are the products of historical, cultural and social construction (xviii). While I agree with the constructed-ness of the notion of "blood memory," I argue that "blood memory" in African American plays evokes the spiritual imaginings and cultural equivocations of an African sacred past. This ritualized past resists erasure through embodied acts of transmission, or as theatre scholar and critic Sandra G. Shannon ("Framing" 28) would have it, embodied "recollections of a shared past that emerges unexplained from the irrepressible ancestral ties with Africa." Blood memory operates symbolically to remember and re-member Africa in African America.

The metaphor of blood memory is also symbolically echoed through the Juba religious observance. Every Sunday after dinner, residents of the Holly boardinghouse gather together and perform the Juba celebratory and sacred ring shout dance. The stage directions elaborate,

> The Juba is reminiscent of the Ring Shouts of the African slaves. It is a call and response dance.... It should be as African as possible, with the performers working themselves up into a near frenzy [Arnold 98].

The Juba dance reinforces the "acoustic community" of *Joe Turner's Come and Gone*. Acoustic community, as sound theorist Barry Truax (66) has it, refers to a community that is bound by sonic experiences and collective acts of memory. The residents of the Holly boardinghouse energize the stage with stomping, shuffling, and hand clapping. Coupled with "near-hysterical laughter" that celebrates life's pain and blessing enacted by Bertha, Mattie and Bynum in Scene 4, the Juba is the rite that reinforces a sense of collective healing and identification in this play. The celebration of the Juba and the ritualized laughter in the play recall century-old African magical remedies that connect the characters to their blood's memory (Arnold 111). These sonic acts perform unity, healing, and cultural recuperation. Bound by memories of slavery and the African past, the boardinghouse residents trade on the spiritual capital of the Juba dance in its economy of unity and bonding. A sacred ritual among the Yoruba of Nigeria, the Juba is conjured by the denizens of *Joe Turner's Come and Gone* to create a sense of harmony and social cohesion.

Soul Washing, Propitiation and the Recuperation of Blood Economies

August Wilson continues the staging of ritualistic concepts—bloodletting, propitiation, appeasement, cosmic retribution, and cosmic order—as part of conjuring and re-membering Africa in his play, *Gem of the Ocean*. Set in 1904 in Pittsburg, this play casts the protagonist Citizen Barlow who "is in spiritual turmoil" and seeks to "get his soul washed" by Aunt Ester Tyler, whom we are told is a 285-year-old "vital spiritual advisor for the community" (Wilson 6). Citizen comes to seek the services of Aunt Ester after committing a crime that led to the death of a man named Garret Brown. Citizen stole a bucket of nails at his previous workplace, a crime for which he did not confess, and for which Garret was framed. When Garret adamantly maintains his innocence to the point of jumping into the river, and dying in the process, Citizen, overwhelmed with guilt, resolves to "get his soul washed" by Aunt Ester. The "soul washing," a metaphor for absolution, manifests as Aunt Ester takes Citizen to the mythical City of Bones, the graveyard for victims of the Middle Passage. We learn from one of the major characters named Solly Two Kings that the City of Bones is "something like you ain't never seen. A whole city a half mile by a half mile made of bones. All kinds of bones. Leg bones. Arm bones. Head bones. It's a beautiful city" (Wilson 56). On visiting the City of Bones, Citizen discovers, much to his horror, that the Gate Keeper is Garret Brown, the man who was framed for his theft. It is here that Citizen learns that he must get reconciled with Garret before he can get the redemption or "soul washing" that he yearns for.

Solly Two Kings, a friend to Aunt Ester who is a former slave and Underground Conductor, is also at the center of the drama. Solly plays the critical role of leading people from Alabama to their freedom in the north. The play also stages Black Mary, Aunt Ester's protégé; Ceasar Wilks, Black Mary's brother and local constable; Solly's friend Eli, who is also Aunt Ester's gate-keeper; and Rutherford Selig the white traveling peddler. As the play develops, the African American community is rioting and staging a protest for Garret's death. The riots lead to arson, which was apparently started by Solly. As the constable, Caesar arrests and shoots Solly to death. The play concludes with preparations for Solly's burial, led by Aunt Ester, Black Mary, and Eli. The final action of the play is a symbolic act of expiation embodied by Citizen who determines to go to Alabama to continue Solly's cause of rescuing African Americans in the South, including Solly's sister. Citizen "puts on Solly's coat and hat and takes his stick" (85), objects that are reminiscent of Solly's political activities as a "man of the people" who carried "sixty-two people to Freedom" (57). This act of *surrogation*[3] (Roach) is performed as compensation for the wrong Citizen committed. For this, he receives his desired "soul washing" experience.

Enactments of collective cultural memory and recollections of African cultural identity take center stage in *Gem of the Ocean*. In this play, Wilson stages Aunt Ester as the granary of spiritual sustenance, and, according to Harry J. Elam, Jr., a "critical figure mediating between the African past and the African American present, between the practice of Christianity and an Africanist-based spirituality" (Wilson 184). Aunt Ester thus embodies inscriptions of African cultural memory and identification. Through the character of Aunt Ester, August Wilson brings to the stage African rituals symbols, acts of collective memory and identification, and acts that transact on violence and sacrifice. Wilson's "aesthetic of excavation and his figurative and spiritual return to Africa" (Shannon "Framing" 27) reinforce the playwright's purpose to make relevant African spirituality to African American identity and cultural consciousness. It is through the character of Aunt Ester that Wilson implicates the ways that the "troubled transplant" can "take" (Shannon "Framing"); otherwise, all the African American characters will perpetually remain in turmoil, alienated, and un-rooted. In other words, the roots of cultural memory must remain nourished for the transplant to take.

We see a dramatization of Wilson's aesthetic through Aunt Ester's acts as the spiritual advisor to Citizen and the choreographer of Solly's burial. Aunt Ester performs the conjure role, like Bynum in *Joe Turner's Come and Gone*, as she invokes the visions of African American ancestry when she transports Citizen to the City of Bones. She leads the trance dance aboard the slave ship, the *Gem of the Ocean*, until Citizen sees visions of the denizens of the City of Bones. He hears people who "got some powerful gods," and "sees people chained to the boat," and "begins to sing an African lullaby to himself, a song his mother taught him." This ritualized act of partaking in the collective re-memorialization of the tragic drama of the Middle Passage enables Citizen to learn and embrace his cultural history, to reconnect with his ancestors, among them the newly membered Garret Brown, and to gain a sense of self-assertion. The stage directions state, "Overwhelmed by the sheer beauty of the city and the people with their tongues on fire, Citizen Barlow, now reborn as a man of the people, sits down and begins to cry" (69). It is this moment of epiphany that empowers Citizen to surrogate Solly as a "man of the people." This reading is enhanced by Citizen's appropriation of Solly's "stick" of liberation at the end of the play.

Through the characters of Aunt Ester, Solly, Garret, and Citizen, playwright August Wilson also recuperates the values of African acts of bloodletting. As the community's spiritual advisor, Aunt Ester is at the center of the characters' spiritual and sacrificial imaginings. The deaths of Solly and Garret conform to Rene Girard's reading of the violence of sacred religious observances. Girard theorizes in *Violence and the Sacred* about "sacrificial substitutions" (3) that religious communities perform by identifying a surrogate victim, or monstrous double. "The surrogate victim," argues Girard, "dies so that the entire community, threatened by the same fate, can be reborn in a new or renewed cultural order" (255). To Girard, therefore, sacrifice is "primarily an act of violence without risk of vengeance (13). This is elaborated in *Gem of the Ocean* by the Solly and Garret, whose deaths are interpreted in religious terms by the African American the community. Aunt Ester likens Garret to Jesus Christ who was similarly falsely accused (Wilson 21). In a similar vein, Garret's immolation offers Citizen Barlow's redemption. Solly is arguably the "victim of sacrificial expenditure" (Roach 182) because the spilling of his blood is offered in exchange for Citizen's spiritual empowerment. To borrow from Harry J. Elam, Jr., these scenarios of sacrifice and blood-letting evoke African spirituality and elaborate "ritualized cultural practices that negotiate the dynamics of power to create new liberatory possibilities" (Elam

Jr. 169). The trade in blood in this play translates the spiritual, the violent, and the sacred profitable by transacting African cultural heritage for African American self-determination.

In addition to the metaphysical re-presentations of the City of Bones and blood-letting acts, Wilson also reclaims Africa by scripting African oral and performance traditions. This is evident in scripting of singing and story-telling. At the beginning of the play, we meet Solly singing, "I belong to the band," and later to Aunt Ester singing a lullaby "Go sleep, my child" for Citizen. The play, however, stages two symbolic sonic events: first when the characters are singing during the ritualized visit to the City of Bones, and secondly when they prepare for Solly's burial. The African call-and-response aesthetic is enacted during the trance-like City of Bones enactment. Aunt Ester whose body is inscribed with the cultural memory of these African traditions leads these performances. As in *Joe Turner's Come and Gone*, the musical tradition in *Gem of the Ocean* serves a boding function. Like the contemporary popular performances cited at the beginning of this essay, these sonic enactments function to underscore the Africa–African America affiliations.

August Wilson's two plays *Joe Turner's Come and Gone* and *Gem of the Ocean* are significant theatrical offerings of African recuperation. These plays bring to the stage African spiritual and sacred imaginings that reinforce African American cultural history, identity, and agency. Throughout these plays, Wilson reconstructs and circulates tropes of recuperating lost connections, histories, and identities. Wilson's scripting of these tropes serves to reassemble memories of Africa that are particularly significant for African American acts of self-determination. It is quite significant that these cultural portrayals are recurrent in August Wilson's other plays, particularly *Ma Rainey's Black Bottom* and *The Piano Lesson*. In *Ma Rainey's Black Bottom* Wilson restages the significance of sacrificial acts through the killing of Toledo, among other acts of memory. *The Piano Lesson,* is similar to the two plays examined here through the staging of ancestors, ancestral ghosts, ritualized songs, and the inscription of memory onto the piano. These plays are critical articulations of how August Wilson conjures Africa in African America.

NOTES

1. Critics Helen Gilbert and Joanne Tompkins use this term to refer to the "ritualistic representations" comprising music, chants, incantations, choral effects, the rhythm of the drum, verse, and other affective forms of communication. See Gilbert and Tompkins, 63–64.

2. See Rapoo for a detailed discussion of Lydia Diamond's play *Voyeurs de Venus* and the resonances of rituals of blood-letting acts.

3. I use the notion of *surrogation* in the sense that Joseph Roach does to refer to the way that society, through acts of memory, performance, and substitution, reproduces itself. Acts of surrogation, according to Roach partake in social continuity and culture preservation.

Works Cited

Arnold, Stephanie. *The Creative Spirit*. New York: McGraw-Hill, 2008. Print.
Booth, William. "The Exuberant Warrior Kings of Krumping." *Washington Post* June 25, 2005. Accessed July 12, 2013. Print.
Effiong, Philip U. "History, Myth, and Revolt in Lorraine Hansberry's 'Les Blancs.'" *African American Review* 32.2 (1998): 273–283. Print.
Elam, H. J., Jr. *The Past as Present in the Drama of August Wilson*. Ann Arbor: University of Michigan Press, 2006. Print.
Gilbert, H., and J. Tompkins. *Post-colonial Drama: Theory, Practice, Politics*. London: Routledge, 1996. Print.
Girard, Rene. *Violence and the Sacred*. Trans. Patrick Gregory. Baltimore: John Hopkins University Press, 1972. Print.
Harrison, Paul Carter. "Praise/Word." *Black Theatre: Ritual Performance in the African Diaspora*. Ed. P.C. Harrison, Victor Leo Walker II and Gus Edwards. Philadelphia: Temple University Press, 2002. Print.
Hughey, Matthew W. "Re-membering Black Greeks: Racial Memory and Identity in Stomp the Yard." *Critical Sociology* 37. 1 (2011): 103–123. Print.
Parker, Ryan. "Krump Theology: Street Kingdom, Faith, and America's Best Dance Crew." *Pop Theology*, May 23, 2011. Accessed July 12, 2013. Print.
Pryse, Marjorie, and H. Spillers. *Conjuring: Black Women, Fiction, and the Literary Tradition*. Bloomington: Indiana University Press, 1985. Print.
Rapoo, C. *Figures of Sacrifice: Africa in the Transnational Imaginary*. Ph.D. thesis, 2008. Print.
Richards, Sandra L. "Yoruba Gods on the American Stage: August Wilson's Joe Turner's Come and Gone." *Research in African Literatures* 30.4 (1999): 92–105. Print.
Roach, J. *Cities of the Dead: Circum-Atlantic Performance*. New York: Columbia University Press, 1996. Print.
Schapera, I., and J.L. Comaroff. *The Tswana*. London: Kegan Paul International, 1991.
Shannon, Sandra G. *The Dramatic Vision of August Wilson*. Washington, D.C.: Howard University Press, 1995. Print.
_____. "Framing African American Cultural Identity: The Bookends Plays in August Wilson's 10-Play Cycle." *College Literature* 36.2 (2009): 26–39. Print.
_____. "A Transplant That Did Not Take: August Wilson's Views on the Great Migration." *African American Review* 31.4 (1997): 659–67. Print.
Truax, B. *Acoustic Communication*. Westport: Ablex, 2001. Print.
Wilson, August. *Gem of the Ocean*. New York: Theatre Communications Group, 2006. Print.
_____. *Joe Turner's Come and Gone*. New York: New America Library, 1998. Print.

Re-Evaluating the Legacy of the Ten-Play Cycle

Susan C.W. Abbotson

> [Theater] has provided us with a mirror that forces us to face personal truths and enables us to discover within ourselves an indomitable spirit that recognizes, sometimes across wide social barriers, those common concerns that make possible genuine cultural fusion.
> —August Wilson ("Preface," *King Hedley II*, x)
>
> What good is freedom if you can't do something with it?
> —Solly Two Kings, *Gem of the Ocean*, 25

Wilson enjoyed much success over his sadly truncated career, winning two Pulitzer prizes and much praise from critics and scholars. Shortly after his death in October of 2005, Broadway's Virginia Theatre was renamed the August Wilson Theatre to make him the first and only African American with a Broadway theater to bear his name. However, the question of his legacy arises, and for what he will be best remembered? Might his portrayals of the African American experience of the past century relegate him, also, to the past, or can his work be viewed as holding important directives for the future? Is he an old-fashioned realist, or might his plays be offering a new form of drama that reflects our increasingly hybrid world?[1] Does his work hold universal implications, or has it only particular significance for the black community?[2] These are all issues over which scholarship is currently in debate, providing currents through which this essay will attempt to navigate.

In the early 1990s, Wilson asserted his belief that African Americans could provide the whole of American society with solid lessons as to how to survive the tribulations of "America" ("Preface to *Three Plays*" xiv). In an interview with Vera Sheppard, he explained: "I don't write for black people or white people. I write about the black experience in America. And contained within that experience, because it is a human experience, are all universalities" (Jackson and Hartig 109). A noble endeavor, but how are we to judge if this is something his plays have achieved?

In response to Wilson's call to establish aesthetic criteria that can recognize the worth of his plays, this essay does not fashion something entirely new, but in Wilsonian fashion, brings forward an aesthetic already articulated, but not yet connected to Wilson's work. By approaching his plays through a critical lens foregrounded by the positive humanism of postmodern critics such as Alan Wilde, John McGowan, and Linda Hutcheon, we can draw out an underlying moral pattern that weaves through Wilson's cycle, to discover a persuasive mode that insists on maintaining a humanistic, and ultimately, optimistic outlook through social commitment and irony, while also acknowledging the contingencies and uncertainties of modern existence. It is a mode that is timely, innovative and wide in its implications. Wilson questions the increasingly problematic nature of freedom and autonomy, and resolves the issue in new ways that allow individuals and society as a whole to achieve their fullest potential. It is essential that we recognize the importance of this humanistic democratic vision, in relation to our contemporary society and the problems it continues to face, as that, after all, is the central point behind Wilson's whole cycle. These are plays that hold profound relevance for the future of humanity, and do so in a unique style that transcends race.

Wilson was deeply concerned with establishing personal morality and value in a world he saw as increasingly devoid of both. The turn of the millennium was marked by a wide spread insistence on the evaporation of meaning in people's lives. Wilson insisted that meaning still exists and, through his dramas, illustrated how it could be reinstated. His plays insist on the presence of a moral and humanistic impulse to counter the dehumanizing forces of early postmodern visions.[3] Wilson's characters struggle and even, at times, fail to embrace this impulse, but they serve to validate its existence. By reinforcing our connection to both the good and bad about our pasts, Wilson envisions a future culture that centers on a humanistic concept of selfhood in a supportive, democratic community. As Harry J. Elam, Jr., explains, "Only through the collective communion of men and women can Wilson's characters achieve levels of liberating self-definition and collective healing" (19). The greater value of community is much evidenced in Wilson's plays by the way in which we can see that while individuals might die—from Solly or Toledo, to Floyd Barton or King Hedley—there remain others to whom they are connected who continue to live. Writing about how Wilson portrays these communities in his plays, Keith Clark suggests, "Wilson depicts how the performative, in addition to being an organic process, requires a psychic and spiritual intermingling of self and others" (Bloom 52). He connects this to the multi-rhythmic concepts within blues and jazz, as each instrument joins in to become part of a whole. Wilson's characters, in more than just the obviously titled *Seven Guitars*, can be equated to such instruments; while some may offer a wonderful solo, they are at their best when they perform together. While we may not see these democratic communities fully accomplished in his plays, we see their possibility. There must be rules, however, to ensure we do not simple produce a discordant cacophony of sound (or social chaos). These rules are articulated in the theories of John McGowan.

McGowan rejects what he refers to as the "negative freedom" put forward by postmodern critics who refuse to allow value judgments, and, thus, negate the concept of value itself, and calls postmodernists to embrace a "model of engagement" rather than one of "alienation" (25), thus guiding us towards connection rather than negative freedom, a direction he terms "positive freedom." The jazz musician, Wynton Marsalis, connects a similar notion of "positive freedom" to both democracy and the form of African American music in particular: "The principle of American democracy is that you have freedom. The question is 'How will you use it?' which is also the central question in jazz. In democracy, as in jazz, you have freedom with restraint. It's not absolute freedom, it's freedom within a structure" (35). So as Clark suggests, Wilson's use of music and song to represent strength and cohesion on both metaphoric and literal levels clearly illustrates Marsalis' description of "freedom with restraint," just as his emphasis on the choices his characters constantly face allows for the "positive freedom" described by McGowan.

In the fragmented and suspicious world in which we currently live, plays and performance can create an alternative world in which a lost sense of community is momentarily restored among both actors and audience: it is toward this end that much of Wilson's drama strives. His theatrical scenes of connection help combat the threat of outside chaos. Craig Werner sees the polyrhythmic language of Wilson's plays that combine both African American and Euro-American expressive traditions, as an indication of his commitment to heal both individuals and communities: "The point of polyrhythmic discourse is not to destroy or replace binary discourses but to understand them as part of a larger chaotic context in which other voices sound freely ... Wilson's jazz call envisions the transformation of 'vague' and 'paradoxical' regularities into the foundation for a healthy and healing community," which welcomes the presence of multitudinous (polyrhythmic) resonances in all our lives rather than reject them (Nadel *Fences* 38–39). In this way Wilson can be said to have been responding "to the call of a desperately fragmented world" (Nadel *Fences* 46), and asking his audiences to understand that what they make of that world would be truly up to them. Werner concludes, "Reconciling but not resolving, Wilson offers us his vision: a binding song for desperate times" (47).

Wilson is centrally concerned with the idea of connection, as he told Christopher Bigsby: "The theme I keep coming back to is the need to reconnect yourself" (*Companion* 297). Wilson traced his concern to the propensity for disconnection from which African Americans have historically suffered, beginning with a disconnection from their African homeland, continuing through the harsh institution of slavery, and reoccurring on a national scale as so many African Americans allowed themselves to be driven North looking for opportunity, and, thereby, disconnecting themselves from their Southern roots. By retelling these events, Wilson hoped to reforge connections which would give all African Americans a stronger sense of identity, showing them to be a people with a common past that, one would hope, could become a common present and lead to a common future. Wilson illustrated this through the many characters in his plays who learn, during the course of their experiences, how to renew connections they had believed to be unnecessary—from Citizen Barlow (*Gem*) to Harmond Wilkes (*Golf*) (the latter being a descendant of Black Mary and Caesar Wilkes from *Gem*).

Naturally, the most important connection of all that Wilson's plays promote is that between individuals and their society. This is conveyed most directly through the ensemble construction of most plays in the cycle that presents us with a group dynamic, rather than a solo protagonist.[4] We should also note how each play presents us with characters from several generations, and includes stories that draw in even more characters and experiences. Thus, the entire cycle collectively creates one giant community as connections between the plays span the century and earlier characters reappear, or are referenced in later decades.

The critical stance of McGowan insists that "significant individual differences are possible and can be preserved only within a social whole that recognizes such differences and contains norms and institutions empowered to protect them. Freedom, then, is only possible within the terms of membership in a society" (15); thus, McGowan and Wilson turn postmodernism towards a dynamic of inclusion rather than exclusion.

Wilson best portrays this complex balance between individual and social needs and interests through his central warrior spirits who illustrate the need to embrace a moral responsibility towards both self and others.

The issue of moral responsibility is clearly integral to the creation of an effective self and an effective society. Morality is not innate but a matter of *choice*, and so, though in one sense confining, moral responsibility is a matter of freedom so long as we believe in the existence of free will and in man as an essentially responsible and progressive being. This issue of choice is central to all of Wilson's plays. Described by Sandra Shannon as "apocalyptic" in its depiction of "the chaotic homicide-ridden urban landscape of mid 1980s America" (Nadel *Cycle* 126), *King Hedley II* is Wilson's darkest play, filled with arson, theft, drive-by shootings, broken relationships, a string of assaults, and the death of Ester. As King says: "It used to be you get killed over something. Now you get killed over nothing" (34). But *Hedley* is also a play filled with choices: to keep a child, to allow an insult to pass, to select a twenty-pound bag of potatoes. Each choice has its repercussions, but it is a choice nonetheless. As Ruby explains, "Life's got its own rhythm. It don't always go along with your rhythm. It don't always be what you think it's gonna be" but life is all about "trying to match up them two rhythms" (42). The challenge is to find the right balance.

While Donald E. Pease acknowledges the "vertiginous cycle of violence that threatens to swallow the entire community" (Nadel *Cycle* 71) in *Hedley*, he sees King being able to resist retributive violence and bring "two cycles of violence to a close in a single act of rejection" (91). King's decision not to shoot Elmore when he has the chance causes Elmore's killing of Leroy Slater and Hedley's killing of Floyd Barton to be laid to rest, and we see the cycle's disruption as Elmore resultingly cannot fire on King. Though King then dies, he has illustrated the "key" lesson of forgiveness, becoming a Messiah figure for the community who, as Stool Pigeon had earlier explained, would "by the remission of blood make whole that which is torn assunder" (*Hedley* 21). As Elam suggests, "King's sacrifice serves as a beacon of hope, promising a new tomorrow against the bleak backdrop of tragic loss and unfulfilled promise" (87). Pease draws attention to Ruby rediscovering her song at this point, suggesting that although Ruby was instrumental in her son's sacrifice, her "song delivers King to Aunt Ester, who has returned to the community to bear witness to the figure who had transformed it" (Nadel *Cycle* 93). It is through King's choices that the world continues.

Since good and evil exist in everything, we must choose to look for the good. Wilson ensures that we do not fall into the trap of forgetting we have the important and self-affirming capacity to choose. His protagonists may at times make the wrong choices, but they are always offered a choice of some kind. Sometimes these choices are psychological—creating one's own identity against accepting one created by others, as in the case of Herald Loomis in *Joe Turner*.[5] At other times these choices are more physical—as in selling or keeping a piano. In the final play of the cycle, *Radio Golf*, Wilson looks back to the last and forward to the new millennium, assessing how far his characters have come by their choices, and just how far they have not.[6] The possibilities of hope and despair are twinned, as Booker suggests in her assessment of the play's two main characters who are faced with distinct choices: "Harmond discovers the value of history and memory contained within the community whereas Roosevelt threatens its very existence" (Bloom 158). Roosevelt assimilates and sells out to the white investors and so lessens the advance of his community, while Harmon stays loyal to the African American community to reinforce its value. When Wilson wrote this play he knew he was dying, and Elam points out how it "directly reaches back to *Gem*, connecting the characters past and present and providing more threads to the genealogy uniting the cycle as a whole" (Nadel *Cycle* 187). This final play, Elam rightly insists, "clarifies meanings within this cycle as a whole and reaffirms the power of Wilson's intertextuality" (187).

Wilson's plays insist that whatever the state of the world, we still have free will and it is our responsibility to create the society in which we would live. He recognized that aspects of our lives, such as capitalism, patriarchy, and liberal humanism, are in fact cultural creations that did not exist until we made them; therefore, it is in our power to change them if necessary. In several plays, we hear both on and off stage characters complain about the existing system, but those who just complain achieve nothing. Those, however, who, despite a prevailing feeling it will be useless to complain, stand up for their rights, are surprised when they actually win their demands—such as Memphis in *Two Trains* or the offstage character Hop in *Hedley*. Then there are also those, such as Ma Rainey, or Troy Maxson, who may make some compromises and bad choices at times, but have the strength to make progress through sheer will—as when Ma forces the white producers to employ her nephew, Sylvester, or when Troy gets himself promoted to driver without even having a driving license!

But it is a moral responsibility toward the self *and* others that lies at the core of Wilson's plays: to neglect either personal or social responsibility is tantamount to self-destruction. A moral responsibility can only be fully recognized by those who have an understanding of their own identities:

as individuals *and* members of a society. As Elam points out, in Wilson's plays, "Freedom by itself is not enough" (Bloom 173), and the playwright clearly felt that total freedom is not good for people, and some restraints are necessary to produce an effective society. What Wilson strives for is more of a *democratic* freedom, the maintenance of which demands a form, which is, necessarily, restrictive.

Our guides toward a better way of living are numerous and—be it Troy's maxim regarding the acceptance of crookeds and straights, Bynum's insistence that everyone must find their own song, Boy Willie or Youngblood reminding us of the importance of owning property, Becker insisting his gypsy cab station provides a "service to the community" (*Jitney* 86), or Aunt Ester's insistence that people need to fight to take control of their lives—their messages combine to offer a meaningful way forward. Just as Sterling, in Wilson's play for the 1960s, *Two Trains*, takes on a social responsibility alongside asserting his own individuality as he claims Hambone's ham for him, and inspires everyone at that diner to strive for more, Wilson saw himself as having been fired in the kiln of the Black Power movement of the 1960s: "The ideas of self-determination, self-respect and self-defense that governed my life in the '60s I find just as valid and self-urging in 1996. The need to alter our relationship to the society and to alter the shared expectations of ourselves as a racial group I find of greater urgency now than it was then" ("The Ground" 15).

This contemporary strain of humanism that we can see within Wilson's plays is reflected in the theories of Alan Wilde, who views such humanism as situating people "in a world to which their acts bring value and meaning but not ... definitive truth" (*Middle* 108). Matters are not always resolved in a Wilson play, but there is always a sense of growth by the close, rather than dissolution or despair. While characters like Solly (*Gem*), Toledo (*Ma Rainey*), Floyd (*Seven Guitars*), Troy (*Fences*), Hambone (*Two Trains*), Becker (*Jitney*), King and Aunt Ester (*Hedley*) all die, their deaths do not betoken an end, as the community around them lives on, and becomes a community somewhat enlightened and in some respects, emboldened, by the death they have witnessed. Solly's bravery and insistence on the truth inspire Eli and Barlow to keep fighting, just as Hambone's certainty inspires Sterling; while Toledo lies bleeding, Levee's trumpet, though muted, continues to struggle "*for the highest possibilities*" as he transmutes his pain into music (*Ma Rainey* 111); and Floyd and Troy are both envisioned rising to heaven as their friends and family continue their lives (and in the case of Troy, both sons reach a new understanding of their own potential through the example of their father, as does Booster after Becker's death). Even Hedley's death allows for the resurrection of the guiding spirit of Aunt Ester.

We only meet Ester in *Gem*, but her presence recurs throughout the cycle, for as Wilson tells us, she "represents the entire 349 years that blacks have been in America. She represents our tradition, our philosophy, our folk wisdom, our hobbies, our culture, whatever you care to call it" (Elkins 212–213). For Wilson, Ester's importance to us and his characters grew along with the cycle: "The wisdom and tradition she embodies are valuable tools for the reconstruction of their personality and for dealing with a society in which the contradictions, over the decades, have grown more fierce, and for exposing all the places it is lacking in virtue" (*Hedley* x). His characters, Wilson explains, "still place their faith in America's willingness to live up to the meaning of her creed so as not to make a mockery of her ideals. It is this belief in America's honor that allows them to pursue the American Dream even as it remains elusive" (ix). While Wilson allows her a physical death in *Hedley*, her spirit is not subdued. At the close of *Hedley*, she is symbolically resurrected through a blood sacrifice, and while Aunt Ester, again reported dead in *Golf*, we are told that Barlow's "daughter," Black Mary, will be returning to Ester's old house at 1839 Wylie Avenue, which may be taken as a different form of resurrection. We glean from *Gem* and *Golf* that Aunt Ester's supernatural powers can be passed along, and the name of her apprentice is Black Mary.

In the 1980s, Wilde made a call for a revitalized and flexible "contemporary humanism," as opposed to the confident and imperialistic humanism of the past, "which can claim not that man is the measure of the world's meaning but that he is its agent or partner in the task of bringing meaning into being" (*Middle* 128). Wilson's work answers that call, for, in his plays, his protagonists do not work alone, but within communities. The play that Wilson felt best represented his vision was *Joe Turner*, as he explained "most of the ideas of the other plays are contained in that one play" (Jackson and Hartig 251). Set in a boarding house filled with a variety of transients, we witness how this disparate group finally coalesces into a sustaining community. The issue of identity is key, as the play's characters grope towards the necessary balance between self-awareness (individual identity) and a sense of security through connection to others (social identity), which will allow everyone to live with dignity and direction. Herald Loomis represents an ideal here as he ultimately achieves this balance, quite literally, rising to his feet by the close of the play. Seth Holly seems to represent the dangers of those who largely fail, though he is partially saved by the slender connection to others that he maintains through his wife.

To achieve true cohesion, Wilde advocates for a revitalized humanism for a postmodern age that does not elitistically defend individualism, although it recognizes the worth of individuals and such individuals' need and capacity to realize their own potential for being, but it also acknowledges "the variousness of human beings and the messy unclassifiability of their experiences" (*Middle* 10). If we connect this idea to John McGowan's suggestion that the individualistic concept of autonomy of the past should be replaced by a "semiautonomy" that will allow for a "significant differentiation within the totality, while also insisting on the interconnectedness of the whole" (154), we should recognize the dilemma faced by so many of Wilson's protagonists to find the right balance between the needs of the individual and those of the larger community. In many ways, to be unacknowledged is tantamount to not existing; therefore, just as society needs to acknowledge the individual, so too must the individual acknowledge society. This is depicted by Sterling embracing Hambone's cause, or Booster in *Jitney* recognizing the importance of his father's business to the community, or Loomis "shining like new money" as he embraces "*responsibility for his presence in the world*" (*Joe Turner* 94), and steps forward with a new sense of direction at the close of the play. Each acknowledgment validates the importance of the Other alongside the Self, and it is in this way that semiautonomy is achieved. The double ideal toward which we should strive is a society of individuals *and* a collective unity. As McGowan insists, "Semiautonomy can yield a participatory democracy" (271). McGowan links his view of postmodernism to democracy on a conceptual level, seeing both as containing "concomitant values of egalitarianism and pluralism" (15).

The potential self-contradiction of McGowan's "semiautonomy," which asks us to privilege both Self and Other simultaneously, can be explained by Linda Hutcheon's description of postmodernism as simultaneous complicity and critique. In such a world nothing can be entirely one thing or the other—thus the troubling and unresolvable concept of binary opposition is being replaced with one of duality in which two contradictory impulses can be simultaneously true. Wilson's plays, which present characters striving to understand this complex balance between individual versus social needs and interests, clearly fulfill the demands of both Wilde and McGowan. Returning to *The Piano Lesson*, as I previously suggested in response to the way critics try to decide who best deserves to get the piano, "Wilson does not want us to take sides; in fact, he feels it is important that we do not" (*Piano* 84). Both Berniece and Boy Willy have excellent claims, and Wilson has created a perfect postmodern situation in which we cannot privilege one's claim over the other, but must accept both simultaneously. What this allows us to do is to better balance "the pros and cons of each character's behavior, to ascertain what is the best combination of responses to the dilemmas these people face" (*Piano* 84). For when postmodernism exhibits a tension between apparent opposites, Linda Hutcheon insists that a compromise must be reached (2)—a new "middle ground," as it were; the place to which Wilde is guiding his reader.

This whole postmodern notion of duality also may be linked, usefully, to what W. E. B. DuBois called "double-consciousness;" a term he coined in order to comment on the way in which African Americans were made to feel a "twoness,—an American, a Negro; two souls, two thoughts, two unreconcilable strivings; two warring ideals in one dark body, whose dogged strength alone keeps it from being torn asunder" (5). Bernard Bell translates DuBois' concepts of "double-consciousness" into the "biracial and bicultural identities of Afro-Americans," which he sees as a "socialized ambivalence" allowing both "integration and separation" in a society that has almost institutionalized racism (xvi).

Wilson recognized that the African American identity contains a duality which is a strange mix of African and European aspects: "To say that I am an African, and I can participate in this society as an African, is to say that I don't have to adopt European values, European aesthetics and European ways of doing things in order to live in the world. We would not be here had we not learned to adapt to American culture. Blacks know more about whites in white culture and white life than whites know about blacks" (Moyers 17). Such knowledge has been a necessity for African American survival. Bakhtinian dialogism, which suggests that all experience contains both self and other, exposes the contradictions of humanism while simultaneously making humanist premises available for reconsideration. For Wilson, life (and all we term positive) becomes a continuous balancing act against the very death (and all we term negative) that helps to define it. It is the very indeterminacy of such a world that enables it to operate. Thus, his plays are filled with illustrations of the positive effects of this balance (as we see communities form stronger bonds)—and warnings of what happens when that balance is missing (manifest in acts of violence). Murder in Wilson's plays is often shown to be through a mistake of judgment—Levee killing Toledo, Hedley killing Floyd, Ruby killing King—and they each mark a loss, but they are not depicted as ends, as the remainder of these characters' communities continue.

Wilson's cycle is filled with the messy, dark-side of life, and offers no easy utopian visions. All the plays but *Ma Rainey* are set in the troubled

Hill District of Pittsburgh, and we see this neighborhood constantly under threat of demolition as well as facing countless situations of not just white privilege and racism, but also problems within the African American community. The plays set in the later decades more clearly tackle contemporary African American concerns, such as teen pregnancy and abortion, post-traumatic stress syndrome, the problems inherent in the increasing gentrification of traditionally black neighborhoods, and growing class division and violence within the African American community. The last of these, however, has been in the background of all of his plays, which constantly warn against the dangers of black-on-black violence, such as Levee's needless killing of Toledo, Hedley's slaughter of Floyd, up to Ruby's unfortunate killing of her son. But even while fragmentation and the presence of evil are acknowledged in Wilson's work, spiritual, moral, and even patriotic values also exist, guided by the playwright's unfailing humanistic and life-affirming beliefs.

Wilson once declared, "I find a lot of humor in life, though there's also a lot of pain. As one of my characters says, 'Life's hard, but it's not impossible'" (DiGaetani 282). Wilson's characters tend to "make-do;" they repair their property, and keep on trying to improve their standard of living. In this, Alice Mills suggests, "Wilson's theater bears witness to a will to be happy in spite of everything" (34). As Wilson suggested, "There's always new life. There's always the next generation in my plays" (Nadel *Fences* 130). He is referring to such youthful characters as Zonia (*Joe Turner*), Maretha (*Piano Lesson*) and Raynell (*Fences*).[7]

Texts that hold such contradictory dynamics must be viewed as ironic in nature, for only irony, with its self-contradictory undercurrents, is suited to displaying this dynamic by what Hutcheon calls, its "commitment to doubleness, or duplicity" (1). Thus, Wilson's plays can be said to contain ironic cores in that they constantly offer up contradictions that we must accept. Situations and characters are simultaneously comic and tragic—such as those problematic "idiot savant" characters. Things are also real and imaginary, like the City of Bones, Troy's tales of resistance, or Aunt Ester. Characters are right and wrong, such as Troy in his treatment of Cory, King and Floyd's dreams and resultant burglaries, or Youngblood's house purchase without Tonya's inclusion. Actions can be both generous and selfish, such as the way Rose takes over Troy's life, Selig Rutherford's simultaneous aid and exploitation, or how Ruby treats Hedley in *Seven Guitars*. People are African and American—nearly every character we meet.

Postmodern irony is described by Wilde as "suspensive," in which "an indecision about the meanings or relations of things is matched by a willingness to live with uncertainty, to tolerate and, in some cases, to welcome a world seen as random and multiple, even, at times, absurd" (*Horizons* 44). Wilde asks that we react to the world with a "suspensive irony" which may indicate disorder and chaos, but also contains its own irony of order and form. He goes on to insist that we attempt to create "ironic enclaves of values in the face of—but not in place of—a meaningless universe" (*Horizons* 148). We all need to strive towards an "affirmation of life," that is, an inculcation of values which affirm notions of "effort and concern, of caring and trying, and even of goodness," for these are the "human possibilities of a senseless universe" (*Horizons* 160).

However, as Wilde explains, suspensive irony contains the danger of becoming "reductive" if we simply replace the real world with an imaginary one. We need to accept the world as it is and embrace its very ordinariness in order to make the irony "generative" (*Horizons* 149). Wilde advocates the existence of a "middle ground" most critics ignore, a stance which rejects equally the extremes of realism and experimentalism and "invites us to perceive the moral as well as the epistemological perplexities of inhabiting and coming to terms with a world that is itself ontologically contingent and problematic," and such writing offers "the best hope of American fiction" (*Middle* 4). He associates the idea of "possibility" with the best "midfiction," which can be described as "moral studies of how to deal with a world it is impossible either to dismiss or to understand," and which attempt to "re-create value and meaning in the felt absence of either" (*Middle* 35). Wilde does not consider dramatic works, but Wilson's cycle offers clear examples of what could be termed "midplays." They offer us effective visions of the world we live in and the world we would like to live in (if we only knew how). And such is the legacy that Wilson has left for us all, whatever the color of our skin.

Wilson wrote about the black experience in America, in order to explain in terms of the life he knew best those things which are common to all cultures. This is a concept he learned from the painter Romare Bearden, a great influence on his development. But Wilson also cites another major influence: "I see myself as answering James Baldwin's call for a profound articulation of the black experience, which he defined as 'that field of manners and ritual of intercourse that can sustain a man once he has left this father's house.' I try to concretize the values of the black American and place them on stage in loud action to demonstrate the existence of the above 'field of manners' and point to some avenues of sustenance" (Anderson 571).

In order to face the difficulties of life in a postmodern age and survive, it is important that a person have a sense of values and Wilson insists we can learn these values through watching his plays. Ralph Ellison has long seen the African American heritage as something positive for all Americans to consider because it offers lessons in stability, adaptability, and the recognition of reality. These qualities may help all Americans to live in a world "which has taken on much of the insecurity and blues-like absurdity known to those who brought it into being" (58–59). Wilson often talked of the first time he listened to a recording of Bessie Smith and the profound effect this had on him: "I began to look at people in the rooming house differently. I had seen them as beaten. I was twenty, and these were old people. I didn't see the value to their lives. You could never have told me there was a richness and a fullness to their lives. I began to see it" (Brown 122). Building on this lesson he gained from the blues, Wilson extends it to us through the extended metaphor of characters who seek their songs that runs throughout the cycle from Loomis to Ruby. Through this, we witness an array of people searching for the best way to live in a fractured world. When each finds their song, as both Loomis and Ruby do, whatever the rubble around them, new hope is born.

What Wilson insists upon is the persistence of human ideals that will help the human spirit to triumph, and create a moral order in the world to combat the surrounding chaos. Bigsby's description of Wilson as a writer who moved "towards a concern for spiritualism" in a world of failed ideologies, failed psychologies, materialism, and incompetent social rituals (*Modern* 204), leads us to embrace Wilson's iconic Aunt Ester as the best guide toward self-discovery. Shannon points to Ester as a figure of "African cosmology" (Bloom 37), but Wilson balances this with connections to European Christianity that allows Ester to be all things to all people. As Lloyd Richards explains to Richard Pettengill: "Anybody who comes back from Aunt Ester doesn't have a prescription, or an answer, but they all come back with faith and their ability to act. Aunt Ester's is a place of personal, spiritual revival of oneself" (Elkins 206). In other words, Aunt Ester's greatest ability is to show people their own potential, she acts as a kind of mirror in which they can discover this for themselves. But she also observes the divine gift of allowing people free will by which they can decide for themselves how to behave.

Philip D. Beidler suggests that Wilson might be "the greatest writer of our generation" as he wrote "about the entire cultural sweep of American life in the twentieth century" (Bloom 133). In this Wilson achieved the epic sweep of which Eugene O'Neill only dreamed: a self-defining American chronicle for the ages. Albeit through a lens of black experience in America, Wilson's cycle speaks to all human beings, though especially to Americans with their dream of democracy, as it explores solutions to the problems of identity, responsibility, and hope, in the formation of a democratic society that truly offers everyone the opportunity to be all that they can be.

What Wilson is modeling through this cycle are lessons of responsibility, connection, history and identity, which combine to create a final vision of what contemporary society most needs: active democracy. On different levels, from the family to the larger community, he conveys how this democratic spirit might be embraced, as his characters suggest ways in which individual and social responsibilities may be connected to provide a more positive outlook for the future. Elam views Eli's final "So live" in *Gem* as "a noble petition of hope for the future of the gathered community and a powerful plea for African Americans to live a life founded on personal integrity and committed to the collected struggle for truth" (Bloom 161), and in certain ways this is repeated at each play's end, though the call is not just to African Americans, but to all humanity.

Notes

1. Douglas Watt praises Wilson for his "intention on showing the realities behind the stereotypical facade of the black lower class" (*Fences* 316), and encouragingly defines his style as "slice-of-life" (*Ma Rainey* 197). Clive Barnes describes Wilson's characters as "sharply representative of their race, time, and profession ... drawn with the observation of life" (*Ma Rainey* 198), and praises Wilson's ability to "break away from the confines of art into a dense, complex realization of reality" ("Fiery" 316). Sandra Shannon, on the other hand, insists that Wilson is "in the forefront of playwrights who are experimenting with performance techniques to usher in a new activist-artistic era" (Bloom 39–40).

2. Some critics, such as Robert Brustein, suggest that Wilson's work only deals with "narrow aspects of the black experience" to highlight "white culpability and black martyrdom" (100). Barnes even asserted that *Two Trains Running* is not relevant to a white audience seeking "edification" but only to an African American one seeking "identification" ("*Trains*" 138). Actor Brian Stokes Mitchell, who starred as King Hedley in 2001, offers the other side, comparing Wilson to Shakespeare: "He takes these gigantic, grand themes about humanity and the human experience and puts them in a small setting with character and people that we all know and we all live with and we all can relate to" (Ifill). In Wilson's own words, the role of black theater is no different from that of white, "to create art that responds to or illuminates the human condition" (Jackson and Hartig 247).

3. Such as those depicted in works by Frederic Jameson and Jacques Derrida.

4. The play Wilson has often said least represents his work is *Fences*, with its more dominant single protagonist. However, it depicts an extended Maxson family that also displays close roots to the local community, so it is hardly a one-man show.

5. As Elam suggests, "For Wilson the key to defining a new liberatory vision lies in the steps his black figures take towards self-determination" (Bloom 173).

6. Wilson confessed to Shannon and Dana Williams, "It's a summation, if you will. It tells where we are at the end of the century as we prepare to go on to the next century" (Jackson and Hartig 244).

7. Mills, also, sees Wilson's work abounding with "images of healthy children, abundant fruit and fertile seeds" (34). Consider, for example, the significance of Bynum's oranges (*Joe Turner*), Gabriel's plums (*Fences*), or Boy Willie's watermelons (*Lesson*). There are also the sprouting seeds of Raynell (*Fences*) and King Hedley (*Hedley*); although King's plants get torn out, there remains the "seed" he has planted in Tonya, which it seems likely that Ruby has persuaded her to keep, as "you never know what God have planned" (42).

WORKS CITED

Abbotson, Susan C. W. "What Does August Wilson Teach in *The Piano Lesson*? The Place of the Past and Why Boy Willie Knows More Than Berniece." *Journal of American Drama and Theater* 12.1 (Winter 2000): 83–101. Print.

Anderson, Adell. "August Wilson." *Contemporary American Dramatists*. Ed. Ed Burney. 571–573. London: St. James Press, 1994. Print.

Barnes, Clive. "Fiery Fences." *New York Post* 27 Mar. 1987. *New York Theatre Critics' Review* 49 (1987): 316–317. Print.

_____. "*Ma Rainey*—The Black Experience." *New York Post* 12 Oct. 1984. *New York Theatre Critics' Review* 45 (1984): 197–198. Print.

_____. "*Trains* Doesn't Run." *New York Post* 14 Apr. 1992. *New York Theatre Critics' Review* 53 (1992): 138. Print.

Bell, Bernard W. *The Afro-American Novel and Its Tradition*. Amherst: University of Massachusetts Press, 1987. Print.

Bigsby, Christopher. *Cambridge Companion to August Wilson*. Cambridge: Cambridge University Press, 2007. Print.

_____. *Modern American Drama 1945–1990*. Cambridge: Cambridge University Press, 1992. Print.

Bloom, Harold, ed. *August Wilson*. New York: Infobase, 2009. Print.

Brown, Chip. "The Light in August." *Esquire* 111 (Apr. 1989): 116–27. Print.

Brustein, Robert. *Reimagining American Theatre*. New York: Hill, 1991. Print.

Bryer, Jackson R., and Mary C. Hartig. *Conversations with August Wilson*. Jackson: University Press of Mississippi, 2006. Print.

Derrida, Jacques. *Writing and Difference*. Trans. Alan Bass. Chicago: Chicago University Press, 1978. Print.

DiGaetani, John. "August Wilson." In *A Search for a Postmodern Theater: Interviews with Contemporary Playwrights*, 275–284. New York: Greenwood, 1991. Print.

DuBois, W. E. B. *The Souls of Black Folk*. New York: Random House, 1994. Print.

Elam, Harry J., Jr. *Past as Present in the Drama of August Wilson*. Ann Arbor: University of Michigan Press, 2006. Print.

Elkins, Marilyn, ed. *August Wilson: A Casebook*. New York: Garland, 1994. Print.

Ellison, Ralph. *Shadow and Act*. New York: Random House, 1972. Print.

Hutcheon, Linda. *The Politics of Postmodernism*. New York: Routledge, 1989. Print.
Ifill, Gwen. *PBS Newshour*. 6 Apr. 2001. *PBS*. Web. 12 Feb. 2013.
Jameson, Frederic. *Postmodernism, or The Cultural Logic of Late Capitalism*. Durham: Duke University Press, 1991. Print.
Marsalis, Wynton. Interview with Tony Scherman. "The Music of Democracy." *American Heritage* (October 1995). *Utne Reader* (March/April 1996): 29–36. Print.
McGowan, John. *Postmodernism and Its Critics*. Ithaca: Cornell University Press, 1991. Print.
Mills, Alice. "The Walking Blues." *Black Scholar* 25.2 (Spring 1995): 30–35. Print.
Moyers, Bill. "August Wilson's America: A Conversation with Bill Moyers." *American Theatre* 6 (June 1989–1990): 12–17, 54–56. Print.
Nadel, Alan, ed. *August Wilson: Completing the Twentieth Century Cycle*. Iowa City: University of Iowa Press, 2010. Print.
———. *May All Your Fences Have Gates*. Iowa City: University of Iowa Press, 1994. Print.
Watt, Douglas. "*Fences* Is All Over the Lot." *Daily News* 3 Apr. 1987. In *New York Theatre Critics' Review* 48 (1987): 316. Print.
Wilde, Alan. *Horizons of Assent: Modernism, Postmodernism and the Ironic Imagination*. Baltimore: Johns Hopkins University Press, 1981. Print.
———. *Middle Grounds: Studies in Contemporary American Fiction*. Philadelphia: University of Pennsylvania Press, 1987. Print.
Wilson, August. *Fences*. New York: Plume, 1986. Print.
———. *Gem of the Ocean*. New York: Theatre Communications Group, 2006. Print.
———. "The Ground on Which I Stand." *American Theatre* (Sept. 1996): 14–16, 71–74. Print.
———. *Jitney*. New York: Overlook, 2003. Print.
———. *Joe Turner's Come and Gone*. New York: Plume, 1988. Print.
———. *King Hedley II*. New York: Theatre Communications Group, 2005. Print.
———. *Ma Rainey's Black Bottom*. New York: Plume, 1985. Print.
———. *The Piano Lesson*. New York: Plume, 1990. Print.
———. Preface to *August Wilson Three Plays* by August Wilson, vii–xiv. Pittsburgh: University of Pittsburgh Press, 1991. Print.
———. *Radio Golf*. New York: Theatre Communications Group, 2007. Print.
———. *Seven Guitars*. New York: Dutton, 1996. Print.
———. *Two Trains Running*. New York: Plume, 1993. Print.

About the Contributors

Susan C.W. **Abbotson** is a professor of modern and contemporary drama at Rhode Island College and author of several books, including *Masterpieces of 20th-century American Drama*, *Thematic Guide to Modern Drama* and *Critical Companion to Arthur Miller*.

Christopher B. **Bell** is an associate professor of English at the University of North Georgia, where he specializes in American drama.

Ellen **Bonds** has taught in the English Department at Villanova University since 1987. In addition to teaching courses in her specialty (20th century American literature), she teaches courses in women's literature and African American literature.

Paul **Bryant-Jackson** is a professor and director of Graduate Studies at Miami University, Ohio. His teaching, directing and research interests rest at the intersections of race, class, gender and sexuality.

Jesslyn **Collins-Frohlich** teaches in the Department of English at the College of Charleston.

Michael **Downing** is an associate professor of English at Kutztown University of Pennsylvania. He is also the webmaster of AugustWilson.net, manager of the August Wilson Blog, and coordinator of the August Wilson Society through the American Literature Association.

Artisia **Green** is an associate professor of theatre and Africana studies at the College of William and Mary, director and dramaturge. Her research interests include decoding traditional African systems of thought in creative expression with a particular interest in Yorùbá philosophical systems.

Joyce **Hope Scott** is an associate professor of American studies and humanities at Wheelock College where she teaches African American literature, theatre, American popular culture, literature and history of the Caribbean, and African spirituality in the literature and culture of America.

Connie **Rapoo** is a lecturer in theatre and performance studies at the University of Botswana. Her areas of research interest include African and African American theatre, African popular culture, African indigenous performance traditions, and constructions of Africa in the transnational imaginary.

Sarah **Saddler** is a PhD candidate studying theatre historiography at the University of Minnesota. Her research examines the application of drama-based training methodologies within rapidly globalizing spheres of the South Asian economy.

Owen **Seda** is the head of the department of Performing Arts Technology at Tshwane University of Technology in Pretoria, RSA. A former Fulbright Scholar and recipient of a Fulbright Alumni Initiatives Awards Grant, he has also taught at the universities of Zimbabwe, Botswana, Africa University and California State Polytechnic University, Pomona.

Psyche **Williams-Forson** is an associate professor of American studies at the University of Maryland, College Park. Her research and teaching interests include cultural studies, material culture, food, women's studies, social and cultural history of the United States in the late 19th and 20th centuries.

Isaiah Matthew **Wooden** is a writer, performer and doctoral candidate in theater and performance studies at Stanford University. His critical writing on contemporary art, theater, and performance has appeared in *Callaloo, PAJ: Performing Arts Journal, Southern Studies, Theatre Journal*, and Yale's *Theater*.

Jacqueline **Zeff** is a professor emerita of English at the University of Michigan, Flint, where she served as director of the Masters in Liberal Studies program. She has special teaching and research interests in women's and ethnic studies with a current focus on Latina/o literature in the United States.

Index

Abbotson, Susan 11
Abiodun, Rowland 150, 151
Adé 34*n*3
Adell, Sandra 102
Africa: African Babalawos 20; African diaspora 178; African gods 20; African memory 3; African spirituality 20, 21; Africanisms 21; Africanity 21; Africans in America 2, 4, 5, 7, 10
African American Southerners in Slavery, Civil War, and Reconstruction (Nolen) 99*n*5
Aganju Santeria and the Spirit of the Orishas of the Volcanoes and Wilderness (Canizares) 151
Akpoli, Togbe Kaley 34–35*n*3
Alaga Syrup 124
Alexander, Newby 16
All Stories Are True: History, Myth, and Trauma in the Works of John Wideman (Guzzio) 5
Allison, Robert 20
The America Play (Parks) 52
American Dream 56
Anderson, Telia 138
The Archive and the Repertoire: Performing Cultural Memory in the Americas (Taylor) 49, 52, 53
Aristotelian tragic figure 4
Aristotle 41, 143
Armstrong, Neil 52
Arnold, Stephanie 178
Ashcraft, Bill 166
Ashé 31, 32
Atlantic Ocean 123
August Wilson: Completing the Twentieth Century Cycle (Nadel) 68, 73
August Wilson: The Ground on Which I Stand 12
August Wilson Theatre 187
Augustus, Caesar 92
Aunt Ester (*GO, TTR, KH, RG*) 7, 9, 56,
81, 90–98, 102–114*n*1, 118–126, 136, 142, 144, 147, 148–150, 153–159, 167–169, 172, 182–184, 193, 194, 197, 199
autoethnographic impulse 5–6

Baartman, Saartjie 175, 176
Bakgatla (Botswanan ethnic dance) 175
Bakhtin, Mikhail 18; Bakhtin dialogism 196
Baldwin, James 198
Ballantyne, Darcy 19
Baraka, Amiri 5
Barlow, Citizen (*KH, RG*) 3, 90–98, 104, 105, 119, 122, 123, 142, 145–149, 153–156, 158, 159, 167, 168, 169, 182–184, 190, 193, 194; as black Everyman 172
Barnes, Clive 200*n*1, 200*n*2
Barton, Floyd (*SG*) 61, 63, 65, 67, 71, 72, 124, 188, 191, 193, 196, 197
Baskerfield, John D. 26, 28
Bearden, Romare 22, 77, 143, 198
Beavers, Herman 73*n*5
Becker, James (*JTY*) 193, 194
Bedford Avenue 117
Beidler, Philip D. 199
Bell, Bernard 196
Bell, Christopher 9
Bellegard-Smith, Patrick 154
Beloved (Morrison) 24, 54
"Berta, Berta" (*F*) 25
Best, Stephen 88–90, 99*n*2, 99*n*4
Between Memory and History: Les Lieux de Memoire (Nora) 23
Bible 44
Bigsby, Christopher 76, 118, 190, 199
Bissiri, Amadou 10
Bitler, Marianne 139
Black Arts movement 6
Black Caesar 92
Black Codes 18
Black Mary (*GO*) 90, 92, 96–98, 103,

205

104, 110, 111, 120–123, 142, 144, 148–150, 153, 158, 159, 183, 190, 194
Black Nationalism 46
Black Power movement 6, 54
Black Power/Black Arts aesthetic 46
The Black Public Sphere Collective 133
Black Reconstruction 15, 16
Blixen, Karen 177
Blood Diamond (Zwick) 177
Blood memory 179, 181, 182
Blues 5, 85
Bly, Robert 81
Bokonons of Ifa 20
Bolden, Buddy 71, 73
Bonds, Ellen 8
Booker, Margaret 192
Booster (*JTY*) 193, 195
Booth, William 175
Brantley, Ben 160
Brown, Garrett (GO) 92, 93, 98, 103, 119, 123, 146, 148, 157–159, 183, 184
Brown, Judge Homer S. 111
Brustein, Robert 118, 200n2
Bryant, W. C. 122
Bryant-Jackson, Paul 8
Butler, George (*SG*) 63

Caesar, Julius 92
Camp Sibert Alabama 70
Campbell, Joseph 78, 81
Campbell, Mattie (*JT*) 168, 170, 179, 181
Canewell (*SG*) 66, 67, 71, 72, 73, 124
Canizares, Baba Raul 151
Capeci, Dominic J. 69, 70
Carl Jung: The Wounded Healer of the Soul (Dunn) 11–12n1
Carmichael, Stokely 54
Carpenteir, Alejo , 29, 32
Carter, President Jimmy 69
Carter, Red (*SG*) 63, 66, 72
Castigan-Wagner, Bill 64
Catholicism 151
Century Project 50, 85 (See also Century Cycle, and Pittsburgh Cycle)
Chambers, Yvonne 122
Chang, Heewon 6
Charles, Berniece (*PL*) 24, 30, 32, 196
Charles, Boy Willie (*PL*) 26, 30, 31, 32, 78, 83, 193, 196, 201n7
Charles, Doaker (*PL*) 24, 25, 30
Charles, Papa Boy Willie (*PL*) 27, 28, 34n3
Check It While I Wreck It: Black Womanhood, Hip-Hop Culture, and the Public Sphere 133
Chekhovian gun 147
Chicago 5, 63, 67, 105

A Chronology of African American Military Service 66, 70
City of Bones (*GO*) 97, 98, 104, 105, 122, 123, 147, 154, 155, 157, 159, 169, 172, 182, 184, 185, 197
Civil Rights Act of 1968 56
Civil Rights movement 6, 50, 52, 55, 62
Civil War 16
Clark, Keith 189
Cohen, Larry 92
Collins, Patricia Hill 79, 134
Collins-Frohlich, Jesslyn 9
Columbia, the Gem of the Ocean 154
Columbia University Butler Library 58n2
Columbus, Christopher 52
Commonwealth of Pennsylvania penal code 111
Compagna, Adam 19
"Condition of the Mother" 113, 114n2
Conjuring 177
Conn, Billy 62, 70
Conrad, Joseph 177
Cory (*F*) 197
Counihan, Carole 128
Counterinsurgent literacy 113
The Creative Spirit (Arnold) 178
Crisis magazine 24
Cunningham, Mollie (*JT*) 168, 170, 182
Cutler (*MR*) 108, 112, 113

David, King 150
Davis, Doris 81
Derrida, Jacques 200n3
Detroit 66, 68
DeVault, Marjorie 136
Dezell, Maureen 47, 142, 143
Diamond, Lydia 175, 186n2
Diner Magazine 131
Djouba 34n2
Dobard, Raymond G. 27
Down on Parchman Farm: The Great Prison in the Mississippi Delta (Taylor) 25
Downing, Michael 8
Dozens 132; culinary dozens 134
drama of souls 165, 167, 172, 173
The Dramatic Vision of August Wilson (Shannon) 7, 61
Du Bois, W.E.B. 15–17, 22, 24, 29, 30, 165, 196
Dumas, Henry 154; Dumasian ark 154
Dunn, Clair 12
Dussie Mae (*MR*) 81, 115n5
Dust Tracks on the Road (Hurston) 131
Dyer, Bill 64

Ebony 54
1839 Wylie Avenue 119, 120, 144, 145, 157, 194
Elam, Harry Justin 7, 28, 60, 62, 71, 72, 73n6, 74n12, 92, 95, 97, 99, 101, 106, 107, 114n4, 119, 123–125, 129, 134, 154, 176, 177, 179, 181, 183, 188, 191, 192, 193, 200, 201n5
Eli (*GO*) 90, 92, 93, 95, 96, 98, 142, 144, 145, 152, 153, 157, 183, 193, 200
Eliza (*G0*) 144, 151, 159
Ellison, Ralph 199
Elmore (*KH*) 126, 191
Emancipation Proclamation 94
Epega, Afolabi 148, 156
Erikson, Erik 43
Ernest, John 16
Esau 45
Evers, Medgar 50, 52
Executive Order 8802 66
Executive Order 9981 66

Fair Employment Practices Commission 66
Fair Housing Act of 1968, 56
Faseyan, Awotunde Yao 34n3
Fatunmbi, Awo Fa Lokun 153
Feingold, Michael 77
Fences 2, 4, 6, 62, 77, 85, 200n4
Food deserts 139n2
Foucault, Michael 73
4 B's 41
400-year-old autobiography 2, 6, 41
Fourteenth Amendment 122
Francois, Irline 32
Freedomland 94
Fu-kiau, Bunsel 147
Furlow, Jeremy (*JT*) 168, 170

Gabriel (*F*) 201n7
Galeano, Eduardo 29, 32
Gantt, Patricia 130
Gates, Henry Louis 30, 31
Gayle, Addison 33
Gem of the Ocean 3, 9, 10, 88, 90, 91, 93, 94, 95, 96, 98, 99n1, 99n8, 101, 102, 105, 118–121, 123, 124, 135, 126, 142, 149, 156, 159, 160, 161n2, 165–167, 169, 173, 177, 182–185, 192, 194, 200; Judaeo-Christian tones 143; Yoruban cosmology in 143, 144
Ghandi, Leela 166
Ghost of the Yellow Dog (*PI*) 25, 26, 28, 30, 34n3
Gilbert, Helen 185n1
Gioube 34
Girard, Renee 177, 184

Glasco, Laurence 117, 118
Goffman, Erving 44
Goodwyn, Doris 64, 65
Gordon, Milton 31
Gorovodu 35n3
Grant, Jilson (*GO*) 148
Grant, Nathan 129, 134
Grant, General Ulysses 94
Great Depression 64
Great Migration 16, 17, 20, 22–24, 30, 60, 63, 68, 73n6
Green, Artisia 10
Griffiths, Gareth 166
Grimes, William 49
The Ground on Which I Stand (1996 Speech at Theatre Communications Group Convention) 1, 130
The Ground on Which I Stand (Wilson) 1, 7, 114n4, 115n5, 130
Guzzio, Tracie 5

Haider, Steven 139
Hambone (*TTR*) 56, 57, 128, 136, 137, 138, 139, 139n4, 193, 195
Harlem Renaissance 12n2
Harris, Trudier 77
Harris, Wilson 29, 32
Harrison, Paul Carter 3, 22, 160, 161n1, 178
Hartman, Sadiya 88, 89, 90, 99n2, 99n4
Heart of Darkness (Conrad) 177
Hedley (*SG*) 71, 73, 73n6
Heffner, Hubert 41, 42
Hemengway, Robert 30
Henderson, Mae G. 24
Herrington, Joan Fishman 77, 143
Hill District 6, 56, 58, 91, 102, 103, 117, 118, 121
Hills, Rust 169
Hindu Krishna 83
Hitler, Adolf 68
Holloway (*TTR*) 134, 147
Holly, Bertha (*JT*) 136, 178, 182
Holly, Seth (*JT*) 18, 20, 23, 168–170, 178–180, 194
Hop (*KH*) 125
Hottentot Venus 175
House, Callie 89
Hughes, Langston 3, 12n2
Hurley, Andrew 130, 131
Hurston, Zora Neale 30, 131–132
Hutcheon, Linda 11, 188, 195–197

I-Chin Tu, Janet 64
Institute for Signifying Scriptures 155
Irvin (*MR*) 81, 84, 106, 107, 108, 112, 115n5

Jacob 45
James, C.L.R. 50
James, William 61
Jameson, Frederic 200n3
The Janitor 7, 39, 41, 42, 44, 46, 47
Jerome L. Greene Performance Space 11
Jesus Christ 158
Jewish Passover 40
Jim Crow 17, 18, 21, 24, 30, 70, 131, 143
Joe Louis: America's Hero Betrayed (Video) 68, 69
Joe Louis Day 69
"Joe Turner Blues" 18
Joe Turner's Come and Gone 2, 3, 4, 7, 9, 10, 16, 17, 18, 20, 25, 26, 28, 32, 33, 85, 123, 155, 165, 166, 167, 168, 169, 170, 172, 173, 177, 178, 179, 182, 184, 185, 192, 192; significance of food in 128, 136
Johansen, Bruce 131
Johnson, Jack 69, 73n9
Johnson, Robert 19
Juba 21, 34n2, 170, 172, 181, 182
Jump back dance 71
June Bug (*GO*) 147; *see also* Scarabaeus Sacer
Juneteenth Celebration 40
Jung, Carl 2, 6, 11–12n1

Katzman, David 17
Kennedy, Robert F. 55
Khepri 147
King (*KHII*) 191, 196, 197, 200n2
King, Joy 161n1
King, Martin Luther, Jr. 50, 52, 55, 142
King Hedley II 2, 3, 4, 9, 72, 73, 96, 114n1, 117, 118, 122–126
King Hedley II (*KHII*) 2, 3, 4, 125, 126, 155, 156, 160, 188, 191, 194
Kirshenblatt-Gimblett, Barbara 139
Kittel, Frederick 1, 86
Knowles, Beyonce 175, 176
Kongolese spiritual medicine 146
Krump (dance) 175–176
Kubitschek, Missy Dehn 111
Kushner, Tony 62, 66, 68, 72, 73n2

Lafargue Clinic 74n12
Lahr, John 64, 65
Lassane, Patricia 30
Levee (*MR*) 2, 3, 81, 82, 83, 108, 112, 193, 196
Levy, Paul 6
Lewis, Barbara 19, 120
Lieux de memoire 23
Lincoln, President Abraham 94
Literacy 114n4

Litwack, Leon E. 34n1
Living Black History: How Reimagining the African American Past Can Remake America's Racial Future (Marable) 49, 50, 51, 53
Livingston, Dinah 40, 42, 46, 47
Loomis, Herald (*JT*) 2, 3, 4, 19, 21, 123, 168, 169, 170, 178, 179, 181, 191, 194, 195, 199
Loomis, Martha (*JT*) 178, 179
Louis, Joe 60–62, 68–70, 71, 73, 74n11
Louis-Conn fight 68, 70, 71
Louis-Walcott fight 71
Louise (*SG*) 66, 68, 135
Louverture, Toussaint 71, 73n6
Lutz Meat Market (*TTR*) 136, 138
Lymon (*PL*) 26
Lyons, Bonnie 143

Ma Rainey (blues singer) 9, 76–87, 102, 106, 108, 109, 112, 113, 114, 115n5, 192; "Mother of the Blues" 101, 106, 108
Ma Rainey's Black Bottom 2, 6, 9, 41, 78, 79, 83, 85, 101, 102, 105, 113, 159, 185, 197—significance of food in 128
"Ma Rainey's Black Bottom" (song title) 107
Madison Square Garden 69
Major, Clarence 131
Malcolm X 55, 56, 57
Mama Tchamba 34n3
Marable, Manning 8, 49–55, 58n2
Maretha (*PL*) 197
Marra, Kim 139n1
Marsalis, Wynton 189
Marshall, Paule 31
Martin, Trayvon 89, 90
Maufort, Marc 164, 167, 169
Maxson, Rose (*F*) 197
Maxson, Troy (*F*) 2, 3, 4, 83, 85, 192, 193, 197
Maxwell, Justin 18
May All Your Fences Have Gates: Essays on the Drama of August Wilson (Nadel) 73n2, 129
Mays, Willie 124
McGowan, John 11, 188–190, 194, 195
McHale, Brian 29
Mead, Chris 69, 73n9
Mears, James 131
Memory 21; remembering 22, 24
Memphis (*TTR*) 56, 57; Memphis Lee's Home Style Restaurant 131–133, 136–139
Middle Passage 6, 60, 97, 169, 179, 181, 182, 184
"Midnight Special" 25

Mills, Alice 197, 201*n*7
Miss Ophelia (*PL*) 27
Mississippi, John Hurt 18
Mitchell, Brian Stokes 200*n*2
Monaco, Pamela Jean 77
Morales, Michael 23
Morrison, Toni 18, 24, 29, 31, 54
Moten, Fred 90
Moyers, Bill 2, 40, 117, 154
Murrell, Peter C., Jr. 42–44, 46
Myth, Literature, and the African World (Soyinka) 180

NAACP (National Association for the Advancement of Colored People) 55
Nadel, Alan 4, 61, 62, 64, 67, 73, 73*n*2, 102, 106
The Nation 12*n*2
Nation of Islam 55
National Ex-Slave Mutual Relief, Bounty and Pension Association 89
National Urban League 69
Navy Relief Society Benefit 69
Neimark, Philip John 145, 156
New Deal program 64
New Dramatists 39, 42
New Negro Renaissance 24
New South 34*n*1
New York Post 68
New York Times 55, 65, 74*n*11
New Yorker 64
Newby-Alexander, Cassandra 16
Nkondi (minkisi phenomenology) 146, 147
Nolen, Claude 99*n*5
Nommo 178
Nora, Pierre 23; *lieu de memoire* 23, 71; "memorial consciousness" 23

Obama, Barack 62
Of Water and the Spirit (Some) 159
Ogunyemi, Yemi 155
Okediji, Moyo 143
Old Testament Kings 150
O'Mara, Mark 99*n*3
O'Neill, Eugene 199
Onyewueni, Innocent 31
Orisa archetypes 10
Oshinsky, David 25
Out of Africa (Blixen) 177

Palmer, Don 2, 6
Parchman Farm 25–27
The Paris Review 7, 39, 41, 48*n*1, 76, 77, 78
Park-Fuller, Linda 6
Parker, Ryan 176

Parks, Suzan-Lori 52, 53
Parry, Benita 166
Passover 154
The Past as Present in the Drama of August Wilson (Elam) 7, 60, 73*n*6, 99, 124, 125
Pathways to Bliss: Mythology and Personal Transformation (Campbell) 81
Pease, Donald e. 72, 191
Pennsylvania 1, 146
A People's History of the American Revolution: How Common People Shaped the Fight for Independence (Raphael) 15, 16, 176
Pereira, Kim 77, 83
Perkins, Kathy 58*n*4
Pernell (*KH*) 125, 126
Pettengil, Richard 39, 199
The Piano Lesson: significance of food in 128, 130, 131, 134, 136, 147, 193
Pittsburgh 1, 5, 117, 119; Civic Arena 117, 118; Hill District 102, 103, 117, 118; Homewood and Hill District 6; Lower Hill 117; Middle Hill 117; Pittsburgh Penguins 117
Pittsburgh Cycle 7, 8, 58, 90, 95–96, 98; *see also* Century Cycle and Century Project
Plum, Jay 165
Poetics (Aristotle) 41, 143
The Politics of Performance (Phelan) 58*n*4
Postmodernist Fiction (McHale) 29
Pough, Gwendolyn 133, 139*n*3
The Power of Myth (Campbell) 78
Powers, Kim 4, 6, 47, 115*n*7
The Presentation of Self in Everyday Life (Goffman) 44
Promised Land 17
Prophet Samuel (*TTR*) 57
Pryse, Marjorie 177

Radio Golf 144, 145, 192, 194
Rahming, Melvin B. 143
Randolph, A. Philip 65, 66, 73*n*8
Raphael, Ray 15, 17
Rapoo, Connie 10, 186*n*2
Rawson, Christopher 117
Raynelle (*F*) 196, 201*n*7
Reagon, Bernice Johnson 136, 138
Reconstruction 15, 17, 93
Redding, Saunders 30
Redress Project 88, 99*n*2
Representations 88
Republic of Benin 34*n*3
Reverend Flowers (*GO*) 157
Richards, Lloyd 199

Richards, Sandra L. 10, 179
Risa (*TTR*) 55, 56, 130–138, 139, 139*n*3; connections with the Divine 138
Rize 175, 176
Roach, Joseph 186*n*3
Roberts, Brian Henry 128
Roberts, Corey 160*n*1
Robinson, Sugar Ray 70
Rockefeller, Nelson 67
Roosevelt (*RG*) 192
Roosevelt, Eleanor 65, 73*n*7
Roosevelt, Franklin Delano 61, 64, 66
Rosen, Carol 41
Rosenthal, Judy 35*n*3
Ruby (*SG*) 72, 124, 125, 126, 191, 196, 197, 199
Run the World (Girls) 175, 176

Saddler, Sarah 8
Saint Christopher 150, 151
Sarr, Julianna 161*n*1
Savran, David 42, 128
Scarabaeus Sacer 147; *see also* June Bug
Schmeling, Max 68, 69, 70
Scott, David 23
Scott, Joyce Hope 7
Seattle Times 64
Seda, Owen 9, 10
Selig, Rutherford (*JT*, *GO*) 144, 183, 197
Senate Bill No. 1718, 89
Setlhabelo ritual 180
Seven Guitars 7, 9, 60, 70, 72, 124; significance of food 128, 135, 189, 197
Shakespeare, William 200*n*2
Shango 151
Shannon, Sandra G. 7, 39, 41, 54, 63, 73*n*3, 76, 77, 80, 101, 107, 115*n*5, 129, 136, 181, 191, 199, 200*n*1, 201*n*6
Shaw, David T. 154
Sheppard, Vera 41, 187
Shiny Man 20, 21, 170, 178, 179
Signifying Monkey: A Theory of African American Literary Criticism (Gates) 31; Signifying 131
Sklaroff, Lauren Rebecca 69
Slater, Leroy (*KH*) 191
Slavery 6
Slow Drag (*MR*) 80, 112, 113
Smith, Bessie 199
Smitherman, Geneva 30, 132
Sokol, Justin 43
Solly Two Kings (*GO*) 90, 92–95, 98, 99, 99*n*8, 104, 109, 110, 119, 120, 122, 123, 142, 149, 150–152, 154, 159, 169, 182–184, 188, 193
Solomon, King 150

Some, Malidome 159
Soul washing 183
Souls of Black Folks (Du Bois) 29, 30
South African Zulu (war dances) 176
Soyinka, Wole 77, 147, 180
Spencer, Vivian 122
Spiller, Hortense 177
Spry, Tami 6
Sterling (*TTR*) 56, 132, 135, 138, 193, 195
Stevens, Judith 58*n*4
Stomp the Yard 175
Stool Pigeon (*KH*) 73, 124, 125, 126, 155
Stovall (*TTR*) 26
Sturdyvant (*MR*) 78, 80, 81, 83–85, 106–108, 112
Sunflower County, Mississippi 25
Surrogation 183, 186*n*3
Sutter, Robert (*PL*) 28
Sutter's Ghost (*PL*) 24, 28, 30, 32
Sylvester (*MR*) 78–79, 81, 111–112, 115*n*5, 192

Taylor, Diana 8, 49, 50, 52, 53, 54, 58, 58*n*1, 58*n*4
Taylor, William Banks 25
Tchamba Ade 28, 34–35*n*3
Thompson, Robert Farris 145
Timpane, John 73, 73*n*2, 73*n*4
Tobin, Jacqueline 27
Toledo (*MR*) 41, 83, 112, 113, 114, 185, 188, 193, 196
Tolliver, Reverend 21, 151
Tompkins, Joanne 185*n*1
Tonya (*KH*) 126, 197, 201*n*7
Tracy, Steven C. 73*n*1
Traux, Barry 182
Truman, Harry S. 66, 71
Tswana people 180
Turner, Joe 19, 21, 178, 179
Turner, Victor 53
Turney, Joe 19, 34*n*1
Two Trains Running 3, 9, 39, 50, 54, 55, 56, 58, 96; significance of food 128, 130, 131, 134, 136, 147, 193
Tyler, Aunt Ester (*GO*, *TTR*, *RG*) 3, 150, 182; *see also* Aunt Ester

Underground Railroad 95

Van Cleave, Rachel F. 27
Vardaman, James K. 26
Vega-Gonzalez, Susana 29
Vera (*SG*) 65, 66, 67, 71, 72, 73
Violence and the Sacred (Girard) 184
Virginia Theater 187

Vodou 34*n*3
Voyeurs de Venus (Diamond) 175, 176, 186*n*2
Vultee Air 65

Wagner, Bryan 99
Walcott, Joe 68, 69, 71
Walker, Alice 131
Walker, Bynum 3, 18–19, 20, 21, 32, 85, 155, 168, 170, 178, 180, 181, 182, 184, 193, 201*n*7
Wall, Cheryl 16
Warner, Craig Hansen 99*n*7
Washington, Teresa 144
Wata, Mami 34*n*3
Watt, Douglass 200*n*1
The Way of the Orisa (Neimark) 156
Webster, Milton 65
Werner, Craig 189, 190
West (*TTR*) 57, 134, 147; West's Funeral Home 137, 138
West African Ancestor worship 170
White, John Valery 46–47
White, Walter 64
White privilege 92
Wideman, John 5, 6
Wilde, Alan 11, 188, 193, 194, 195, 198, 198
Wilkerson, Martha 69, 70
Wilks, Caesar (*GO*) 91–95, 98, 99*n*8, 104, 109–111, 113, 115*n*6, 119, 121, 123, 142, 144, 153, 154, 157, 158, 183, 190, 198; Christian reference 99*n*6
Wilks, Harmond (*RG*) 3, 144, 190, 192
Williams, Dana 41, 46
Williams-Forson, Psyche 9, 133
Williamson, Fred "The Hammer" 92
Wimbush, Vincent 155
Wining Boy (*PL*) 24, 26
Wolf (*TTR*) 55, 57, 133

The Woman Question (Collins) 134
Wooden, Isiah 8–9
World War I 17
World War II 60–73, 130
Worse than Slavery: Parchman Farm and the Ordeal of Jim Crow Justice (Oshinsky) 25
Wounded healer 6–8, 11, 12*n*1

Yeveh/Gorovodu 34–35*n*3
Yoruba cosmology 10, 29, 143–145, 151, 160, 161*n*1, 179, 180, 182; Aganju 150, 151; Aganju/Sango 144, 150, 151, 159; Ase 144, 152; Egungun 145; Esinmirin 156; Esu 179; Ethnocultural Dramatic Structure 156, 158; Ifa/Orisa tradition 144, 154, 155; Ile Ife 144, 158; Igbo 156; Irunmole 150; Moremi 156; Odu 148, 150; Odu Oturapon-tura 156; Ogun 144, 145, 146, 148, 153, 179; Ogundameji 148, 150; Okuta 144; Olarosa 144, 145; Olodumare 152; Olokun 154, 155; Olujare 156; Oluorogbo (mythology of) 158; Orisa archetypes 143, 144, 150, 152, 156, 160; Orunmila 152, 156; Ososi 144, 145, 153; Osun 144, 145, 148, 149, 150; Oyo kingdom 151; Sango archetype 151–152; Sixteen Truths Ifa 155; Yorubanized Messiah 156
Young, Harvey 58*n*3
Young, Reggie 160
Youngblood (*JTY*) 193, 197

Zaytoun, Constance 172
Zeff, Jacqueline 7
Zimmerman, George 89, 90, 99*n*3
Zonia (*JT*) 197
Zwick, Edward 177

www.ingramcontent.com/pod-product-compliance
Lightning Source LLC
Chambersburg PA
CBHW020828230426
43666CB00007B/1150